BRITAIN'S
FORGOTTEN
FILM FACTORY

BRITAIN'S FORGOTTEN FILM FACTORY

The Story of Isleworth Studios

ED HARRIS

AMBERLEY

First published 2012

Amberley Publishing
The Hill, Stroud
Gloucestershire, GL5 4EP

www.amberley-books.com

British Library Cataloguing in Publication Data.
A catalogue record for this book is available from the British Library.

ISBN 978 1 4456 0489 3
ISBN (EBOOK) 978 1 4456 1187 7

Typeset in 10pt on 12pt Sabon.
Typesetting and Origination by Amberley Publishing.
Printed in the UK.

Contents

Preface

It was over lunch at Shepperton Studios that I caused something of a stir. The River Ash (that once formed part of the backlot) doubled for the lethal Congolese waters in *The African Queen*, I was told. Everyone knows that. But I had to disagree. The flocks of rose-ringed parakeets that infest the Shepperton skies and beyond are descendants of the exotic birds recruited to dress the jungle settings, legend has it. Wrong. When I made it plain that UK filming for *The African Queen* was done entirely at Worton Hall Studios in Isleworth a sense of alarm filled the recently refurbished restaurant. A small crowd gathered. The sumptuous *Visual Celebration* of Shepperton Studios was removed from its lectern on the bar where it rests like some holy relic. The glossy pages were turned for the full extent of my heresy to be revealed. Undeterred, I outlined the facts of the matter and more. The studio managers especially were devastated. The story of Shepperton Studios as handed down is flawed. To exclude its long-forgotten sibling at Isleworth is to imagine Laurel without Hardy, Bonnie without Clyde, Bogart without Bacall. *The African Queen* is but one example where I can no longer allow a good story to get in the way of the facts.

Ed Harris, January 2012

Acknowledgements

Sincere thanks to William Cooke, Southall Studios History Project; Christine Diwell, The Isleworth Society; James Marshall and Guy Bedminster, Local Studies Collection, London Borough of Hounslow; Janice Turner, Editor of *Stage, Screen and Radio* magazine, and those who responded to my plea in that tome for information: Bill Lewthwaite, John Rosetti, Ron Goodwin, Lillian Haynes, Joe Marks and Fiona Kelly, with special thanks to Les McCallum for his enthusiastic assistance. To Mrs Sheila Gould RGN, Matron, Entertainment Artistes' Benevolent Fund, Brinsworth House; Theodore Bikel; Faye Thompson, Photographic Archive Coordinator, Academy of Motion Picture Arts and Sciences; Heather Heckman and Dorinda Hartmann, Wisconsin Center for Film & Theater Research; Desmond Davis; Angela Allen; Guy Hamilton; Nick Pollard, Sunbury and Shepperton Local History Society; Kristine Krueger, National Film Information Service, Margaret Herrick Library; Rachael Keene, Special Collections and all staff at the British Film Institute; Jeff Woodbridge, Shepperton Studios, Emma Slade and Dean Horne, Assistant Studio Managers, Shepperton Studios; and to Martin Humphries and volunteers at the excellent Cinema Museum. Special thanks to David and Sir Sydney Samuelson (and Debbie Nyman) for their generous help and assistance, and to the Samuelson family biographer, the late Harold Dunham for producing the 'Bertie' years; likewise David Blake for generous access to his archive and extensive collection of images.

Introduction

Matthew Sweet's hilarious and haunting book *Shepperton Babylon* is a unique exploration into the lost worlds of British cinema. Out of hundreds of conversations with former British film stars and creative types from the silent days to the exploitation era, he has created an archive of lost souls more than a history of the industry of which they were once part. Most of the studios that acted as backdrops to the sometimes harrowing, often uproarious, but more occasionally desperately sad personal accounts of those interviewed, have been demolished or, like Worton Hall studios (which is not mentioned), depleted. 'Don't mourn them,' says Sweet, for 'the story of the British studio system is not legible in its architectural remains'. Despite the rich nostalgic power that attends the names of these places, he suggests that visiting them is no more evocative than 'touring a shabby biscuit factory on an idle Sunday'. Walking around even the most evocative names in British film history, Sweet comes away with nothing more to contemplate than clusters of anonymous hangars, steel girders and corrugated iron.

In the summer of 1999, the British Film Institute celebrated the centenary of Alfred Hitchcock's birth with a reception at the old Gainsborough Studios in Hoxton in north-east London. Billed as the 'Ultimate Hitchcock Exhibition', entrance to the shell was free from June to December and people flocked in to amble around the carcass, soaking up the atmosphere. At a special party thrown by the British Film Institute to celebrate the birth of the legendary director, various elderly actors and directors were bussed in to fraternise with journalists, including Matthew Sweet. There was talk of movie-making returning to this gentrified former heartland of Cockney London. Developers were poised to give the old building a thorough make-over, including the predictable restaurant, smart apartments and trendy work units. Since the Rank Organisation sold the studio in 1949, the building has accommodated a carpet warehouse and been used as a whisky depot.

Despite his cool approach to what he and the other guests were doing there, Sweet could not resist exploring the space beyond the designated hospitality area, passing the colossal bank that once supplied electricity to the studio stage, and running a finger over the huge switches and dials. A sign pointing towards the dressing rooms had survived all the changes, leaving him and his companion no option but to follow it. 'The building told no tales. There was nothing of Novello here,' he states, peering down into the courtyard onto 'the real guardians of British studio history', the veterans of the day and their stories of when this shell was used to manufacture film. 'Nostalgia hung heavy in the air as the old-timers reminisced over the tea and buck's fizz,' wrote *The Independent*'s Geoffrey MacNab, also a guest. 'At least now it has achieved a little belated dignity,' he adds in defence of the battered old building, as though it too was a former player imbued with the same charisma as the film-makers and actors milling about it.

What survives at Isleworth is no different. As it was when a working studio, people scurry about the place from one building to another; carts and lorries deliver stuff, the sounds of power tools mix with the everyday noises of individuals making odd sorts of livings, getting by, creating, making, saving, or putting all manner of things into storage. The place is still dominated by the huge sheds that give a film studio its special look. The height and girth of these great structures accommodate oversize doors made to shift vast painted flats of scenery into and out of use, their low-pitched roof spaces specifically designed for the carrying of banks of lighting used to recreate nature's moods and her natural cycle at the flick of a switch. Then there are the old dressing rooms, edit suites, the processing plant, the stores and myriad workshops where carpenters, plasterers, wardrobe and other craftspeople plied their skills in bringing to life the dreams transferred from paper onto film. The faded and jaded complex at Isleworth retains all of this, albeit in feel and atmosphere only, but it remains as though in a coma waiting almost to be revived, for the bell to ring out again as the great barn doors are slid shut and where the enclosed assembly awaits that immortal command: 'Action!'

Much of the trappings of film-making in the built form have managed to survive at Isleworth long after the last wrap was sounded. Only now, as these words appear before me on this small screen, is more of its essence eking away, year by year. The current recession sees the number of vacant units multiplying as new housing starts to fill tempting lots. Even at its very heart, on the venerable mansion's rear lawn, where a photographer stood in the summer of 1914 to capture a shot of the film pioneers posing proudly on the steps, a row of houses has sprung up; a precursor perhaps to the fate of the waning industrial activity. This domestic occupancy has come complete with the ubiquitous gate that means it is no longer possible for the casual observer to enter the estate, to soak up the atmosphere on an idle Sunday afternoon, to recreate in the mind the days when this was a dream factory, and to imagine all of the people who made it happen. Perhaps observers such as Matthew Sweet are right. Paper can indeed outlive flesh and celluloid, but what a sorry world this would be if nothing of the built landscape was celebrated except for castles, great houses and gardens.

Aside from churches and perhaps great factories, only those who have worked in a theatre or a cinema know the tingle of that special atmosphere when these buildings become 'dark'; that is dormant for whatever reason. There is a tangible feeling about the place, almost like a haunting, where it's impossible to tune out of all the noise and excitement both sides of the stage and where the passions of past performances, whether recorded or live, pervade. Now an industrial estate, business park, call it what you will, it is still very possible to hone in on Worton Hall as a working studio in all its guises; directions barked through a megaphone to make-up-caked actors captured for posterity on a hand-cranked camera rolling on the first-ever Sherlock Holmes film shot in Britain by G. B. Samuelson, Britain's first movie mogul; the age of sound and Alexander Korda looking to rival Hollywood, followed by Douglas Fairbanks Jr looking to rival Korda. And Buster Keaton, struggling to make his swan song through an alcoholic haze; Richard Burton making his screen debut; Bogart, Hepburn and Huston on the Oscar trail out of Africa, and Emeric Pressburger directing his first and only film. Little by little the old studio's physical shape is crumbling or is altered, or is disappearing altogether. Soon it may be gone altogether. Peripheral it may have been in the greater scheme of things, but Worton Hall has a history worthy of much more than just an addendum in the annals of the British film industry.

1
Establishing a Dream

Worton is a long-defunct former Middlesex hamlet situated 10 miles west of London, not large enough to be a village and never a parish. Few people outside of a mile radius of its modest epicentre have ever heard of it and those who live there generally accept Hounslow or Isleworth as their address. William Eystons of Isleworth was granted the Manor of Worton by Edward III in 1375 when it comprised 93 acres, a moated house and a chapel. In 1417, Henry V granted the manor to the Abbess of Syon and thereafter it passed from tenant to tenant along with all the lands belonging to the Abbey. In 1604, Henry Percy, the 9th Earl of Northumberland, was gifted the freehold of Syon by King James I and it has remained in the ownership of the Percy family for the last 400 years.

Before 1935 Worton slumbered amid lush meadows and picturesque farms, a mile to the north of the Rugby Football Union's ever-expanding stadium, tucked into the border of Twickenham. Before the tsunami of bricks and mortar spewed out from the capital to cover West Middlesex, Worton boasted a village street with two inns, a farm and a pair of fine country mansions: Worton Court and Worton Hall, the latter built in 1783 by a rich merchant and extended during the Regency period to present the fine white stuccoed mansion we see today sat beside Worton Road. The front lawn is now bared of its fine trees and its carriage drive welcomes hosts of learner drivers to the test centre based there. An application to convert the building into eight flats was approved in 2006 and only now nears completion. The brutal intrusion of five two-storey dwellings built on the rear lawn is a precursor perhaps to the eventual redevelopment of the entire estate flanked to the north, east and west by predictable inter-war housing and to the south by the malodorous Mogden sewage works. Such is the present condition of this once beautiful country estate that close to a century ago was rented out to one George Berthold (Bertie) Samuelson, a successful film renter who harboured ambitions to make films of his own.

Bertie Samuelson was born on 6 July 1889 at 41 Nevill Street in Southport, the youngest of five children. His parents were Prussian Jews who came to Ireland in the 1840s and adopted the family name Samuelson. His father, Henschel, eventually opened a tobacconist in Southport where he died seven weeks after Bertie's birth. Educated at the University School in Southport, Bertie left school at fourteen, and looking around for something to do his eye fell upon an advertisement for a film for sale of King Edward VII opening Parliament. Thinking it would be great fun to own his own film, he raided his money box to find exactly the fifteen shillings asked for the 45-foot strip of celluloid, which ran for 45 seconds at the standard 16 frames per second silent speed. This he took to the manager of a local music hall (there being no local picture house in Southport) and got him to hire the film for a week at fifteen shillings. With his capital and his property returned, the young entrepreneur then took the film to a neighbouring town where he rented it to the owner of the local cinematograph theatre for ten shillings a week, reducing thereafter. Realising altogether two pounds fifteen shillings, he rented an office, which set him on the road to earning a fortune in the region of six figures. At least that's how he told the story.

G. B. Samuelson's Royal Film Agency (RFA) was first advertised in *The Bioscope* on 17 February 1910, and such was his success as a film renter and cinema proprietor three years later that he was asked why he didn't make a film of his own. 'There's nothing I would like more,' he replied. 'I think I could make a successful picture, but I'd need a good, strong story – something with a broad canvas as a background.' After pondering the proposition for a while, he came up with the idea of the life of Queen Victoria. It had everything; adventure, historical incidents, drama, wars and romance. Duly establishing the Samuelson Film Manufacturing Company, he set about a screen adaptation of Herbert Maxwell's book, *Sixty Years A Queen*, the story of Queen Victoria's reign and life from 1837 to 1901. That Samuelson decided to co-write the script for the ambitious 6,000-foot epic, with seasoned scribblers Arthur Shirley and Harry Engholm, offers a clear indication of his confidence and attitude towards how his contribution to British film-making would evolve.

Scenarios were then the precursors to screenplays. In the beginning they were simple documents written for short silent films, brief descriptions of action with little or nothing in the way of dialogue. Before 1913 most scenarios were vague directions committed to memory. Today, the script is the bedrock of any film production and so, as silent films developed, it became clear to forward-thinking businessmen such as Samuelson that direction and the disciplining of cast and crew to the storyline drove the business of budgeting across all departments from start to finish. With two 'scenarists' on the payroll (excluding himself), Samuelson was setting out to play the game within the context of effective film manufacturing.

Bertie Samuelson was at the same time what we today refer to as a 'suit' as much as he was a craftsman and even an artist. He knew his limitations but he was out to learn. In this he teamed up with larger-than-life impresario Will Barker, who had the vision to outstrip the small, intimate and very British productions of his rivals, attracting the best people around him to work his magic.

Barker was prone to exaggeration, on one occasion declaring that he invented the trade show and on another that he was the first man in the world to manufacture films. He began in film production in 1904 at Stamford Bridge in North London, typically shooting out-of-doors on a wooden platform with a scaffolding frame and painted back-cloth, but he soon realised that this was not the way forward and so in 1907 he shifted his business to Ealing, west of London, where he purchased two properties on Ealing Common and built his film studio under the auspices of Barker Motion Picture Photography Ltd. When Samuelson was considering setting up his own film manufacturing company, Will Barker was already established as a major player in the industry, enjoying huge success with an adaptation of Mary Wood's sensational novel, *East Lynne*, Britain's first six-reeler and considered to be one of the best and most technically proficient British films produced to date. Its director, Bert Haldane, had joined Barker in 1912 and already had a string of notable crime and social dramas to his credit.

It's not difficult to understand why Samuelson was attracted by Haldane's talent and the business acumen of his boss, whom he asked to join him in the making of his own epic film covering the life of Queen Victoria. From receiving news of her accession as a young princess through to the siege of Ladysmith during the Boer War, the production was budgeted at £12,000, an unprecedented sum for a British feature at the time. *Sixty Years A Queen* epitomised everything Barker was about as a film-maker. It was a bold, patriotic pageant on the grand scale, but subtle when necessary, exactly the subject matter for his studio and the talent he was able to attract. Samuelson was therefore confident in using his own capital to finance the film in which he would play a major part in the production. He came away from this collaboration with Will Barker a much richer and far wiser man; so successful, in fact, that he decided to acquire his own studios and to establish himself in the film manufacturing business proper.

Despite any misgivings he might have had about Samuelson entering the business as a serious rival, Barker publicly wished 'the new recruit' the best of luck, a commodity that never entered the Samuelson equation as he scouted around for the finest talent and support that his frugality would allow. In Harry Engholm, as company director and secretary, Samuelson would find a strong lieutenant. A journalist by profession, Engholm had joined Barker as a writer and in all wrote some forty scenarios for him, including the critically acclaimed *East Lynne*. He had got to know the ebullient Samuelson when working as co-scenarist with him and Arthur Shirley on *Sixty Years A Queen*. He openly acknowledged that he owed all he knew about cinematography to Will Barker and his 'wonderful cinema school' at Ealing, but had no qualms about accepting Samuelson's invitation. Bertie's gaze had also fallen on cameraman Walter (Wally) Buckstone, who had also begun his career at Barker's studio before moving to Pathé Frères where he met George Pearson, a former headmaster turned film director who had begun his cinematography career writing scenarios for Pathé before moving on to become a producer in charge of its London studio. Through Buckstone, Samuelson heard that Pearson was frustrated in failing to persuade Pathé to open a new studio at Alexandra Palace in North London and so armed with this information he treated Pearson to lunch at the Waldorf Hotel, where he persuaded him to join him in his new enterprise.

In his autobiography, *Flashback*, Pearson recalls his mounting respect for a man who was genuinely in love with the cinema and not simply a spectator looking to make a quick fortune. Ideas of production and possible subjects poured out of Samuelson, fuelling the ambition shared by both men to make worthy films. Samuelson asked Pearson directly if he would direct films for him. 'Well, have you got a company?' asked Pearson. 'No,' replied Samuelson, declaring that he would have one the following day. 'Have you got a studio?' Pearson asked. 'No,' replied Samuelson, 'but I'll buy a studio if you agree to work with me.'

It was March 1914 and the Worton Hall estate in Isleworth was vacated by one Colonel Cecil Paget and put up for sale. In his memoirs, Pearson recalls Samuelson first renting the property with an option of purchasing it for £200, which he later did. Wasting no time, Samuelson opened up negotiations with the Urban District Council of Heston & Isleworth's electrical engineer for a connection to his proposed cinematograph studio with a demand for about 50–60 kilowatts. At a cost of around £150, the request was granted in principal provided the company agreed to consume electric current to the value of £200 per year. The same council official reported a recent connection to another studio in St Margarets (now Twickenham Studios) with half this demand. Also under consideration was an application for yet another studio to be built roughly equidistant between the two at Whitton Dean, which, if realised, would have represented a string of film studios eight miles from the centre of London that might one day have become the Hollywood in England.

Negotiations between the local council and the Samuelson Film Manufacturing Company were completed on 13 May 1914. Originally the estate comprised some thirteen acres, but by 1913 had been reduced to about nine, comprising terraces, lawns, paddocks, orchards, vineries, a farm and woodland, offering a wide variety of outdoor filming options. The old trade entrance was down a narrow lane running south of the drive and between two associated buildings south of the Hall, probably former estate offices. The plans for the new cinematograph studio submitted by a Mr Gilbert W. Booth offer the only substantial impact on the landscape at this time in the form of a 50-foot by 40-foot glass studio set about 120 feet to the south-east of the mansion. Suggestive of a sense of impermanence surrounding this new industry, these plans were agreed on condition that the structure stood for no more than five years, a feature of the planning application process that would follow the progress of the studio throughout most of its active life.

The partnership of Cricks and Martin was another talent pool that Bertie Samuelson set about plundering. By the end of 1911 George Cricks and John Martin boasted the largest production staff of any British film company, producing their first feature-length film, *Pirates of 1920*, that same year. It was, however, to be their undoing. Martin quit the partnership in 1913 to set up Merton Park studios, leaving Cricks to continue producing features at Croydon, growing more disillusioned until in 1918 he retired from film production. Fred Paul, who had started his cinema career with Cricks and Martin as a bit-part actor, joined the Samuelson Film Manufacturing Company as a lead actor. Experienced in both the theatrical and the moving picture worlds as an actor, *The Cinema* described Paul as one who brought 'a very high intelligence to bear on his art. Handsome and debonair, he is indeed an ideal leading man, and bids fair to become known as an English Kerrigan and Costello rolled into one.'

Jack Clair was another actor who began his film career with Cricks and Martin, switching from the music hall in 1904. Latterly with Union Films as their stage manager, *The Cinema* magazine was confident that Samuelson had secured the right man in that same capacity. '*Experientia docet*', the publication gaily declared in his defence, minus the translation ('experience teaches even fools') and looked forward to hearing of Mr Clair's promotion in the firm.

The same magazine quoted George Pearson describing his new boss, G. B. Samuelson, as 'a young man with amazing enthusiasm and boundless energy; his excitement regarding his adventures was infectious'. *The Cinema* knew that Samuelson's chief producer at Worton Hall was not a man bound by hard-and-fast conventions and would strive to turn out the most artistic productions possible. 'After talking to Mr Pearson, and actually seeing him at work,' the periodical explained, 'we have no doubt that he will do quite his fair share in placing the firm under which he now serves, in the first rank of English manufacturers.' On 30 May, the Samuelson Film Manufacturing Company Ltd was incorporated with a nominal capital of £2,000 in £1 shares. The original subscribers were George Berthold Samuelson and Harry William Engholm, who was also secretary of the company. The trademark was singularly appropriate, namely a picture of Samson pulling down a house, under which was written, 'Samson Films bring down the house'.

With his key players in place, Samuelson led Buckstone and Pearson through the grounds of the late-eighteenth-century estate which had been cleared of excess shrubs and undergrowth and made ready for a clean start. Having selected the site, they stuck pegs in the soil to mark the position of the 50-foot by 40-foot glass studio. Not for Bertie Samuelson a disused basement, an old schoolroom, converted skating rink or even an abandoned gasometer; this was a studio built specifically for the purpose of cinematography. Clad in Muranese, or Morocco-type glass, which was good for diffusing the sunlight and reducing shadows, it blended into the landscape alongside the acres of market garden hothouses dotted around Worton Hall, such as those belonging to W. J. Lobjoit & Sons who worked the neighbouring Worton Farm. Jessie Lobjoit Collins recalls in her memoirs, *Key of the Fields*, the purchase of Worton Hall by Samuelson; 'his high studio, all glass, resembling a vast greenhouse … was placed in the grounds of the Hall in a direct line with our greenhouses, making them look squat'.

Built to the standard pattern established by Georges Méliès in the 1890s, Samuelson's structure consisted of a glass roof and three glass walls, similar to the large studios used for still photography to maximise daylight. Thin cotton cloth, or calico, was stretched below the roof to diffuse the sunlight, producing a soft overall light without harsh shadows. Enjoying the same dimensions as that of a theatrical stage, West End sets could be slid into the same large sliding side-doors comprising one side of the studio, which also allowed the cameraman to set up outside for long shots, sometimes with additional sections of the set erected in the open air. The real world could be viewed through a set window by shooting from inside the studio with the sliding doors open.

Colin N. Bennett, F.C.S held a regular surgery on the business of film-making in the *Kinematograph and Lantern Weekly*. The 'knotty point' tackled in the August 1914 edition was that of Daylight Studios. 'After a bit one gets to know the production of the newcomer in staged photo-play filming by looking at the lighting of the indoor studio scenes,' he begins. Everyone was likely to make the odd howler with studio lighting effects; even old hands finding themselves inside a strange glass room for the first time. Odd glaring white patches and unlit nooks and crannies were bound to appear in the maiden productions of each newly erected or newly occupied studio, according to Mr Bennett. 'It is a failing in technique for which the camera man and stage director may be at least partially excused the first time or two,' noting a number of 'terrible examples of these blunders' made by some 'great American studios'.

While the portrait photographer set out to light static individual sitters, the cinematograph studio photographer required a cross between the same intimate lighting and the general floodlight of a theatrical stage, managed by means of multiple roof and side blinds of varying degrees of transparency, ranging from thin white chiffon to black twill to portable highlight screens for the head and body as well as adjustable white reflectors. The glass itself cladding the studio was also of paramount importance. It was required to break up the rays of direct sunlight as much as possible while not seriously reducing light on dull days. Ground glass was considered too light-absorbent, so the sort to go for was a rough or fluted variety, the rougher the surface the better.

The aspect of the studio and its elevation above ground level was also important in its command of a good expanse of clear sky. A studio having a fairly north and south aspect with a roof at least 20 feet high above the stage at all points, and with the glazing carried down to a distance of 3 feet off the floor on either side, was considered suitable for most purposes.

And then there was the temperature of such a studio, with actors and staff suffering terribly from the effects of excessive heat on a sultry day unless generously ventilated by means of large electric fans of ample power and capacity.

Thus, it was according to these standards that Bertie Samuelson's studio not only met the requirements of the day but exceeded them, with its generous backlot and sprawling mansion complete with ballroom and dining hall, initially left intact for filming, although later converted into property stores. The ground floor was turned over to offices, property and wardrobe rooms, a projection theatre, a cutting-and-joining room and a canteen. The eleven bedrooms comprising the first and top floors were converted into flats to accommodate overnight stays. One wing was used as dressing rooms for the actresses and the other for the actors. 'The old time mansion of Worton Hall,' so the *Middlesex Chronicle* reported, 'naturally lends itself to pictures. The front and back of the house provides no fewer than twenty different views, and there is even a wood, which, with its giant trees and undergrowth, successfully poses for the cinema as a dense forest'.

With what producer George Pearson described as 'a small but capable staff', filming for the Samuelson Film Manufacturing Company began on 8 June 1914, not at Worton Hall but on location while the equipping of the studio neared completion. With his cameraman, Walter Buckstone, Pearson set out for Cheddar Gorge in Somerset to begin work on the ambitious six-reel production of Arthur Conan Doyle's Sherlock Holmes mystery, *A Study in Scarlet*, the first British screen outing for what would one day become the nation's favourite detective. Sometimes erroneously cited as the first ever Sherlock Holmes film adaptation, that credit goes to American Biograph for its 1903 production, *Sherlock Holmes Baffled*. Nine other productions followed from various companies around the globe until Samuelson brought to screen the thrilling tale of murder, love, revenge and detection that takes place among the Mormon pioneers of Utah in 1850.

Some ambitious locations were called upon to create the Salt Lake plains and the Rockies and so with the use of suggested camera-angles to hide geographical inaccuracies, Cheddar Gorge was selected and Southport Sands as the Utah Salt Plains. While Pearson took on Cheddar Gorge, Jack Clair covered Southport with Samuelson preparing the plans for the great Mormon trek across the desert where the scene called for a score or more covered wagons complete with their huge white tilts, drivers, numerous cowboys on horseback, cattle, women and children, all in exact accordance with the famous 1,500-mile caravan pilgrimage across the hostile Utah wilderness. Having undertaken the task that a modern production manager would find daunting even with all of today's sophisticated communication tools, no sooner was the exposed negative 'in the box' than the cast and crew were on the afternoon train to London, the footage shot at Cheddar Gorge and Southport Sands processed the following day.

The Worton Hall Cinematograph Studio officially opened on Wednesday 1 July 1914, with *The Cinema* magazine vibrantly declaring that it would require a poet 'to adequately describe the beauties of the place, which had been acquired by the Samuelson Film Manufacturing Company Ltd'. It was an old English mansion complete with terraces, lawns, wooded glades, orchards and fields, 'affording opportunities for some of the finest exterior pictures which it is possible to conceive'. The *Middlesex Chronicle* similarly waxed lyrical but went on to make plain that the new enterprise on the block was an all-British organisation formed to challenge the American supremacy in 'spectacular film producing', specialising in the film dramatisation of popular novels, and indeed had already started with Sir Conan Doyle's *A Study in Scarlet*. 'The up-to-date studios have been erected,' it declared, 'and machinery installed capable of taking pictures at the rate of a thousand per minute.'

The guest of honour for the grand opening was Miss Vesta Tilley, one of the most famous and highly paid musical hall artistes of the day and a leading proponent in the art of male impersonation. She and her fellow guests were met that morning by a retinue of motor cars at the Queen's Hotel, Leicester Square, and driven to Worton Hall; the procession photographed by 'cinema operators' along the route to be 'thrown onto the screen' later with other news items of the day. Miss Tilley and her husband Mr Walter de Freece (or Frece), a top agent and music hall owner, were joined by a number of high-profile people from the entertainment business, many representatives of the cinema industry and the London and provincial press. Will Barker was there as was Mr Crome, a well-known literary agent; Julian Wylie, the music hall agent (and Bertie Samuelson's brother), W. Bernisconi, the chief scenic artist, Harry Engholm and Miss Agnes Glynne (the leading lady) and Mr Fred Paul (the leading man).

After presenting Miss Tilley with a bouquet at the main entrance, the crumbling remains of which today guard the new housing, the guests were directed by megaphone to halt under the stretch of flags as the darling of the music hall was requested to cut the ribbon barring entry with a pair of golden scissors. She refused to do so until she had handed over a penny for them 'lest she should sever friendship', and with her theatrical superstitions abated, declared the studio open; expressing a sincere wish that it would prove in every way successful and profitable to the company. After she and the other guests were conducted around the picturesque grounds, the inspection of the 'appliances' was kept brief with the sun shining fiercely through the glass of 'the great studio'. Lunch was then announced, served in a large open marquee by Messrs Lyons, accompanied by Partan's Blue Hungarian Band.

'Everything was of the best,' declared one press representative, 'and even more important, the tent proved as cool as the iced edibles and drinks.' Mr de Freece presided, 'supported on his right hand' by George Samuelson and on his left by his celebrated wife, and Samuelson's proud mother sat to the right of her son. By all accounts, Walter de Freece made an excellent chairman, and after the loyal toast had been duly honoured, he asked the company to drink to the success of the Samuelson Film Manufacturing Company. They had only to look around, he said, to see what could be accomplished by an energetic man in the short space of four months since the company was formed. It was an extraordinary thing to him, and the only solution must be that Mr Samuelson had surrounded himself with willing and loyal assistants. And this was just the start of a very promising career.

Personally, de Freece had to admit that he felt himself in an odd position with all his capital invested in live theatre and here he was proposing the success of a competitor. Three or four years ago, he admitted, he would have felt some qualms, but this was now a point in history where the marketplace positively located these alternative places of entertainment and he was convinced that Mr Samuelson was actually doing the theatre good. 'The cinema theatres were educating the public for other forms of amusement,' he opined.

It was initially feared that the cinema would provide entertainment at a very low cost (something like £22 per week) and was therefore viewed as a very serious competitor to the music hall. But now, witnessing the heavy investment required by film-makers such as Samuelson, de Freece took satisfaction in the knowledge that their product didn't come cheap and on that basis did not for a moment quarrel with such competition. For De Freece, like Samuelson, was a businessman, the leading figure in music hall in fact. The two strands of the same business had managed to exist side by side for a number of years and were enjoyed by the same audience in much the same programme format and in the same theatres.

Film had grown as a music hall turn itself, shown as part of the same bill, but where it differed was in its versatility. Films contained a broad mixture of the topical to the comic, the dramatic to low comedy. By 1914, film as an entertainment medium had developed as an autonomous industry with its own purpose-built cinema venues while at the same time maintaining an important relationship with the music hall. Even with the rise of the feature-length film, theatre and music hall men like de Freece clearly saw little threat to live entertainment. He graciously welcomed Mr Samuelson's enterprise because he was convinced 'that the picture patrons were attending a school which would eventually bring them to the door of the theatre'.

Bertie Samuelson, in reply to the enthusiastic reception accorded the toast, rose above the ill-disguised condescension and said it gave him great pleasure to see so many visitors that day, and he hoped to see them many times in the future. In erecting a studio it was his great ambition to produce films that would compare favourably with those produced by the American market, and to show that British enterprise could successfully compete with their cousins over the water. When he had read of the dreadful things that were happening abroad, such as the assassination of the Archduke of Austria the previous Sunday, he was glad to feel English, and that his monarch could walk fearlessly among his loyal subjects. And he meant to put up a fight in the direction of the film business. 'In directing this studio,' he declared, 'I shall produce films which will compare favourably with those on the American market. I want the English to be on top. There is a big fight ahead in the film business. We mean to win. But one thing I promise you, Ladies and Gentlemen, it is this; if we fail we'll give in like sportsmen!'

Bertie's passionate outpouring, whipping up a hearty round of 'For He's a Jolly Good Fellow', appears to have been met with a resounding silence from Will Barker, making plain instead that he was 'the father of the cinema trade', reminding the congregation that he was present at 'the first inauguration of the manufactory'. Barker possibly felt the sting of de Freece's superciliousness more than Bertie Samuelson, reminding the assembly of how he had persuaded the great Sir Herbert Tree to play Henry VIII in his studio in the interests of Art 'with a big A'. In cocking a snoop at de Freece's comments, Barker said that he had secured the services of the celebrated actor by claiming that the cinema was a preparatory school for the legitimate stage.

The toast was heartily accorded to the strains of 'Jolly Good Luck to the Girl Who Loves a Sailor', Vesta Tilley's most successful song. Called upon for a speech, she rose and said, 'I thank you very much for all the nice things that you have said about me, but I am anything but a good speaker. My husband is the one for that. Walter, get up!' she duly commanded, much to the amusement of the assembly. Having obeyed, de Freece paid tribute to Samuelson's entrepreneurial spirit in offering a peek inside his studio and a prize of £50 to those picture-goers who correctly guessed what the heroine said in a particular scene. Business manager Harry Engholm was confident that the 'What did she say?' idea would prove very popular in the picture palaces where 'Samuelson films' were shown. They had only been in the old world mansion but a few weeks, he went on, but already the company was halfway through *A Study in Scarlet*, which was expected to run to about 6,000 feet and was therefore a big undertaking for such a young a company. Without the press, he schmoozed, the company was 'helpless and hopeless'. In reply, Mr Hibbert of the *Sunday Chronicle* and *New York Herald* bizarrely responded with the admission that he didn't know how long he had been making love to Vesta Tilley in print, at which point tea was served in the marquee.

The guests were later taken to the projection theatre, which was situated on the first floor of the mansion. Here was shown the procession of cars leaving London that morning; their arrival at Worton Hall and the opening of the studio, all of which had been processed, perforated and assembled as the honoured guests enjoyed the hospitality. The equipment at this time was crude, with rack frames trawling film through developing tanks, carried out on huge revolving wooden drums hand-turned by principal cast members usefully occupying their paid hours spooling up film as it came off the drying machine. The cutting-and-joining room was where the unwanted sequences of film would be physically cut out and the 'keeper' sequences glued together; the days of films made as one continuous shot with cuts made in the camera long gone. After some scenes were shown from *A Study in Scarlet*, the visitors were driven back to town and the business of Britain's newest cinematograph studio resumed in earnest on Monday 6 July, when members of the press were invited back to watch filming in progress.

Readers were informed that, contrary to general opinion, no dialogue was used during the shooting process. The focus having been adjusted, the natural lighting arranged and the stage limit chalked out, George Pearson simply explained what he wanted the actors to do, maintaining a 'running fire of instruction' while they did it. Walter Buckstone, a former Pathé man, used their latest camera, imported from France in 1914. Costing £70 (without accessories) it was considered to be quite revolutionary. Mounted on a heavy wooden tripod, the camera angle was a constant dead-centre of the set, with its two-inch German manufactured lens equally permanent. A tape or chalk line across the floor marked the down-stage limit of the actors. If they moved across it, their feet would be cut off. The close-up was achieved either by removing the camera off its capstan or bringing the actors over the chalk-line. The film negative was moved through the camera at a steady speed of 1 foot per second, maintained by the turning of a handle. If the camera had to swing laterally to follow a moving character, a second handle had to be turned simultaneously to ensure smoothness, a knack requiring much dexterity. Innovations in camera mobility were mostly being developed in Germany at this time; the 'dolly' being some way off and born of a travelling platform carrying the cameraman and later some additional lamps, which allowed for changing distances and angles obtained in smooth continuity as the camera moved in and around the scene.

As well as all the interruptions and hold-ups that were part of the filming process, perhaps the most daunting experience from an actor's point of view was that for the first time in the history of their art the dramatic flow of what they were called upon to produce was fragmented. Up until the advent of moving pictures an actor played out a scene as it flowed in a production, interrupted only by an intermission. Now they were required to stop and start while maintaining that flow and whatever emotion the scene called for. It very quickly became second nature but initially this method of working was entirely foreign. As the silent years moved on, so acting in the medium became easier and an art form of its own. Principles developed, although by no means adopted by all. The better screen actor would subtly externalise his or her thoughts in gesture and facial expression reduced to a minimum to avoid the melodramatic. Pauses were, as ever, the arbiter of a good performance. According to the American film pioneer, D. W. Griffith, it was the light within the actor's soul that put characterisation and emotion across, without which the actor might represent things, but would be incapable of interpreting them.

The performance given at Worton Hall for the edification of the newspaper reporters was that of a murder by strangling, which was achieved over the three set phases; an explanation of the scene for the benefit of cast and crew, a rehearsal, and then the finished article, or what would become known as 'the take'. In actuality, George Pearson explained, the process might take six or seven attempts before he was satisfied. The actor was simply told what to do and kept on doing it until he or she got it right. Apart from anything else, a close watch had to be kept on the shooting time, as the footage had always to be taken at the same speed. This required the producer holding his watch in his hand at the same time as the scene was being played. 'Of course', Pearson added, the little show he had put on was all bluff. The handle was turned but there was no film in the camera. There was no point in wasting £4 or £5 for nothing, he said.

No record of the filming schedule for *A Study in Scarlet* exists; indeed the very film itself has gone the way of the millions of feet of silent nitrate stock long since lost to history. What have survived are the publicity campaign sheets, which contain a number of production stills where the ambitious exterior footage of the Salt Lake plains, the Rockies and the great Mormon trek offer the distinct impression of a quality picture. Most of the interiors, too, such as the log cabin of John Ferrier and the Great Church in Salt Lake City, are reasonably convincing, whereas the 'empty house' where Holmes eventually appears quite late on in the film is more end of the pier.

The Bioscope magazine believed that the film as a whole would 'go far indeed toward placing this youthful producing house in the front rank of English manufacturers'. The reviewer felt that the story was handled in a skilful way and he enjoyed the picturesque location work. He found the acting to be 'entirely satisfactory', with special praise reserved for Fred Paul, whose representation of Jefferson Hope was considered to be a 'very clever character study'. *Kinematograph Monthly Film Record* acknowledged the fact that Sherlock Holmes was already no stranger to the screen, and would always be made welcome. This dramatic interpretation, however, had the ability to attract the public with or without the great detective due to 'striking pictures of life among the Mormons'. Although the detective's amazing deductions were entirely lost in translation on the screen, the drama of the piece ultimately won through, keeping the audience 'intensely interested' even though they might 'not be fully convinced'.

The casting of Sherlock Holmes was in itself a problem, as much depended upon his physical appearance, build, height, and mannerisms the public would expect from reading Conan Doyle's novels. By a stroke of remarkable good fortune Samuelson had an employee in his Birmingham office that absolutely fitted these requirements. 'With his long and lean figure, his deer-stalker hat, cape-coat and curved pipe', James Braginton looked every inch the part and played it 'excellently' according to George Pearson, who claimed that Braginton's inexperience as an actor was matched only by the director's faith in his own abilities to coax a performance. *The Bioscope* reviewer agreed, declaring the story to have been handled skilfully and the acting 'entirely satisfactory'.

A *Study in Scarlet* is one of the many films on the British Film Institute's Most Wanted list. It's not known when it was last seen after its initial release, perhaps just a matter of months. Films deliberately destroyed, scrapped or lost litter the history of British cinema for a number of reasons, often because of bankruptcy where the early cellulose nitrate prints were melted down for the small amount of silver they contained, or once sound films arrived their silent predessors were deemed to be of little value. When the motion picture pioneer Cecil Hepworth went bankrupt in 1924, for example, his entire back catalogue of negatives joined the 80 per cent of British films shot since 1901 that went the way of scrap merchants or were sacrificed to assist king and country as more worrying events in Europe were fast unfolding.

2
The European War and Other Adjustments

Every early film-maker had his own method of working. George Pearson's was dependent on the script, planned as a series of master scenes with an allowance for any spontaneity during filming. At lunchtime, the supporting cast went off to the Royal Oak, still sat today beside the Duke of Northumberland's River about a quarter of a mile down the Worton Road, while the principals and crew ate in the canteen set up in the big house, where there was an opportunity to review the morning's work. The afternoon filming went on until tea-time, when there was a short break for a cup of tea and a cigarette. The day usually finished at six o'clock, with no question of overtime payments unless the extension was lengthy. No matter what the hour, the cameraman would often go straight to the laboratory to check the results of the day's shoot, while Pearson and his assistant would go over the record kept of the day's filming, calculating the amount of actual screen-time captured.

The job description for producer or director was yet to emerge. In the early years it was the same person frequently required to originate the story, write the scenario, design the sets, choose the locations and the actors and direct the cast and crew on the stage-floor or on location and then edit the completed film. The only area over which they had no direct control was in the laboratory, where the link would have been the cameraman. George Pearson was well-off compared to others. He had an assistant who was required to make copious notes throughout filming, the job of continuity a long way off in the future. He wasn't required to source the stories or to write the scenarios, or design the sets but was hands-on in all other areas of production, ready to get stuck in with his cameraman, electrician, carpenter, painter and handyman to help out as required, carrying furniture, removing a heavy lamp or assisting the property man. Even the artistes would dress themselves and put on their own make-up, the luxuries of having people do that for them years away, for almost every aspect of early film-making was driven by the theatre.

Set design was often a matter of painting windows, doors, mouldings, curtains, and even bits of furniture onto canvas-covered flats. Writing about these experiences in the 1950s, George Pearson is perhaps too harsh on himself and his fellow pioneers in railing against such 'abominations', especially given some of the less proud moments in British television more than half a century later. It's doubtful if many among the wide-eyed and fascinated film audiences of 1914 were quite so discerning about a wobbly backdrop or a shaky piece of scenery as he.

For Jessie Lobjoit and her sister Grace on neighbouring Worton Farm, however, the film company brought great interest and excitement into their lives, as well as offers to act in various productions. 'This, Mother firmly refused, greatly to our disappointment, for we were both quite good at acting.' On one occasion the film company was granted permission to use the tennis court to film a scene. 'This was before "talkies" and we watched with great interest.' The scene involved a marriage proposal over the tennis net, but no sooner was the ring about to be placed on the girl's finger, than came the command: 'Cut!' The girl would go off to the end of the lawn for 'quick rearrangements of make-up in front of a screen covered in silver paper' before the performance would be repeated. Jessie and her sister held their breath with excitement, only to hear repeated cries of 'Cut!' Having lost interest, they never saw the ring put on the finger.

With *A Study in Scarlet* completed, Harry Engholm immediately prepared for the screen *A Cinema Girl's Romance*, a comedy with Minna Grey cast in the role of the heroine. But no sooner had the camera begun rolling than the grim news was announced that Britain was at war with Germany. Georges Pearson and Samuelson were in London at the time wrestling among the excited crowds making for Buckingham Palace, shouting that the German navy would be at the bottom of the North Sea in a week. Caught up in the fervour, Samuelson moved that he and Pearson make for 32 Oxford Street to take a room for the night at Frascati's, the sumptuously elegant venue highly regarded for its international cuisine, where they would write a suitably patriotic scenario. While the fashionable elite and the country's foremost businessmen sat musing over *les coeurs de palmier l'Orientale* or *la parfait de foie gras*, the two moving-picture men occupied a little room where they were sustained by pints of tea until daybreak concocting a startling new venture, a fictitious newsreel brought bang up to date with material provided by the headlines of the daily press. Samuelson decreed that *A Cinema Girl's Romance* would be put on hold and that filming on the new venture would begin on 7 August, leaving just two days to get everything ready.

Jack Clair was dispatched across London to book every out-of-work film actor he could find and hire every bit of conceivable military uniform to hand, no matter its nationality. Again, in the days before the internet and the mobile phone, he managed to assemble a veritable arsenal of swords and rifles, as well as medals, decorations, flags, wigs, and all manner of props. For two days Worton Hall was like 'a disturbed ant-hill' with a hundred 'supers' (extras) arriving in batches and wandering round the grounds. Vans were arriving with food, costume-skips, props, furniture, camp-beds, crates of beer, crockery, timber, paint and all manner of things required to shoot Samuelson's mini-epic. The hundred-and-more actors engaged for a week needed to be housed and fed either in the mansion, its grounds or in nearby cottages and inns. And it was probably in the Royal Oak where a couple of extras dressed as German soldiers went for a drink after filming had finished. The bar was empty save for what Pearson describes as an 'unsuspecting yokel finishing a pint', who turned, saw the uniforms and bolted for the door crying 'uns!'

Unadulterated fictional reportage might have brought nothing but ridicule, so Samuelson and Pearson decided to exploit the highly charged emotional mood of the people over cold reason. In this they decided on a technique of brevity in the content of each scene and overall speed in the narrative flow, with each brief flash of fiction cut abruptly, bringing with it a sense of rushing history in the making, integrated by swift moments of patriotic symbolism; a flag unfolding, a lion rampant, German hands tearing a treaty to pieces, a newspaper headline, an emotionalism that gave no time for the facts to mar the story. Many casting problems were solved with the use of lookalikes drawn as much from Samuelson's already overworked staff as from the acting agencies. The extras, too, found themselves as either French soldiers in one scene and Germans in the next, or in morning coats and top hats for the House of Commons. Even George Pearson was conscripted, cast in the part of a bomb-throwing extremist entering a filthy hut down an angled staircase to suggest an underground hide-out furnished only with a stool and a rough table. Here, suitably made up to look the part of a frenzied fanatic, Pearson was required to shoot down the stairs to collect his bomb (a rubber ball painted black) from the evil mastermind, played by Fred Paul, before making his exit back up the stairs.

Samuelson had also decided on a dramatic opening title: *The Spark that Set the World in Flames*, spelt out by petrol-soaked cotton wool on a stiff wire frame that was set alight against a black background. Unfortunately, when the combustible caption was lit, a draught directed the flames on to a nearby drape which in turn ignited the set, prompting one studio hand to suggest a change of title: *The Spark that Set the Studio in Flames*.

To catch up with current news meant squeezing the key events leading up to the outbreak of war into the first two days of filming. This included the Czar's court, Serbian Peter's discussion with his military chiefs, the Kaiser gloating and Sir Edward Grey's ominous warning in the House of Commons, which was crucial to it all. All of these scenes and more required not only actors that looked like the main protagonists, but convincing scenery and props to boot, the most challenging set of all being the House of Commons. The ballroom and dining room in the mansion had been earmarked as potential studio space, but were for some reason not used. Perhaps they were too large to fill with too little in so short a space of time, or possibly lighting was an issue. Indeed, any idea of a replica chamber was out of the question, as the studio boasted little in the way of scenery flats, only two door-pieces and one sash-window and even less furniture. All of the materials used for *A Study in Scarlet* had been broken up, but Pearson's solution was as inventive as it was ingenious.

His idea was for cameraman Walter Buckstone to set up his camera in the roof girders of the glass studio, bolting the camera in place to face directly down. This offered the largest area of clear floorspace possible without revealing any part of the studio walls. The marked off area below was then filled with every seat, form and box available placed in long tiers to represent each side of the chamber. Battens fixed behind these improvised benches were draped with the heavy red curtains taken down from the Hall. A suitably covered rostrum was set between both tiers of benches and on it placed a plaster mace, fashioned by Samuelson's handyman-cum-scenic designer, Bernisconi. Odd bits of dark linoleum covered much of the floor between Government and Opposition tiers, with waste paper camouflaging the odd spaces, mimicking the usual litter of the House in session. The chamber was then filled with a hundred extras, all respectably dressed, some in top-hats and all arranged in individual poses. When the principals took to the benches, the scene that unfolded beneath the camera took on a reality that Pearson declared to be 'truly remarkable'. Nevertheless it was vital in his opinion to end the scene before too much close inspection by the audience. The tight squeeze in the glass studio would have left precious little space for any standing lighting, and Walter Buckstone's situation up the rafters must have been highly precarious, if not potentially lethal from the heat alongside any suspended gantry arcs.

However it was achieved, the effort paid off and a fortnight or so after the marathon session at Frascati's, *The Great European War* was trade-shown and released to packed audiences. The flagrant symbolism of Britannia rising majestically with her long sword heavenward brought forth rousing cheers from the patriotic and emotional crowd. Pearson explained that 'this was film-making forged in the heat of the historic moment. Posterity might find the trenchant symbolism all a little ridiculous,' he added, 'but posterity was not there at the time, and in any case posterity does not – we fear – have the chance to see it.' Shown as a short preceding the release of *A Study in Scarlet*, *The Great European War* shares the same fate, long since lost to celluloid recycling on an epic scale.

British films at this time were gradually giving way to more foreign imports, especially from the United States where the star system was already in place and the end product was more adventurous, imaginative and exciting. Such was the situation in Britain that all imported films were to be subject to a special tax and British exhibitors forced to show a minimum quota of home-grown material, as much as 33 per cent. The exhibitors' response was to blame the producers, arguing that the public should not be penalised for their failings. As well as a lack of choice these restrictions represented a potential reduction in their revenue. But then the exhibitors were not blameless, 'blind booking' films as much as a year in advance, long before they had even been made. They argued that they knew best what audiences wanted and that this method saved the exhibitors time and money. One major downside to this practice was that an unexpectedly good new film either threw the system out of gear, or failed to get the bookings it deserved.

Newsreel and documentaries of the war was one area where there was considerable innovation and excitement. While the British military authorities at first prohibited any reporting or recording of action on the Western Front, so Samuelson's dramatised war reporting pre-empted the Government's later fulsome propaganda agenda. *The Cinema* trade magazine reported in October 1914 that Samuelson had struck an original vein by deciding to produce in instalments incidents from the Front in his *Incidents of the Great European War* (or *The Great European War Day-By-Day*), which 'reminded' the public 'in an entertaining manner of the various important occasions which belong to this present historical epoch'. Each instalment was billed as an exclusive controlled by the Imperial Film Co. The second edition set out to follow up the events across whole weeks introducing here and there 'very well-produced imaginary scenes at the front', starring all of the well-known military leaders of the day, such as General French and Winston Churchill. Every major event in the period was covered, including the king's visit to the wounded and General Botha raising a troop of his fellow South Africans.

Together with 'very striking tableaux of Agincourt, the Armada, Sebastopol and Ladysmith', all of Samuelson's 'inspiring' scenes of British troops advancing in an orderly manner took place on the flat nursery land adjoining the Worton Hall Estate. On the same ground where today 690 million litres of sewage arrives daily for treatment, lines of Tommies launched themselves at the Hun during the making of these 'patriotics'. Playing to record audiences and boosting the volume of British films shown in the home market to 25 per cent, so successful were they that other producers began to saturate the market, seriously threatening Samuelson's box office receipts. As the audiences responded to the traumatic effects of the conflict, so the acceptance of the cinema grew to become a predominant form of leisure in British social life, and in this Samuelson decided to call a halt to his pioneering effort and concentrate instead on the core business of his film studio.

A Cinema Girl's Romance was resurrected and a few more scenes added, only for Bertie's focus to shift again, this time to the making of a patriotic drama with a child as the central figure; a fusion of Gerald Royston, the acclaimed child actor who had earlier that year made his reputation in Kineto's *Little Lord Fauntleroy*, and William Frederick Yeames' painting *And When Did You Last See Your Father?* With the scenario of boyish heroism written by Harry Engholm entitled *A Son of France*, it too was shelved half-way through production when Samuelson was reminded of a short film he had promised the renters called *Xmas Day in the Workhouse*, based on the ballad by George R. Sims. With Fred Paul playing a saddened old inmate who had known better times, the film was made in three days but still attracted praise from *The Cinema* magazine, describing the setting and the photography as 'superb', particularly the snow effects. When *A Son of France* finally saw the light of day as a short, two-reel film, it too impressed the critics with *The Bioscope* enthusing about the absence of 'theatrical artificialities and imitations of war which jar upon one so badly at the present time, surrounded as we are by evidences of the grim realities of battle and death'.

With *A Cinema Girl's Romance* still waiting in the wings, Bertie's attention turned to another new subject, this time a tale of magic and mesmerism called *The Man of Mystery*, only for this too to become victim of another sudden outburst of enthusiasm, ignited by the death of Lord Roberts of Kandahar, who had died of pneumonia at St Omer in France while visiting Indian troops. In this, Samuelson sensed a glorious opportunity to make *The Life of Lord Roberts*, complete with a high-spot in the film recording the famous march from Kabul to Kandahar. *The Man of Mystery* joined *A Cinema Girl* in cold storage, the former never to see the light of day, as the location for the Lord Roberts epic became the subject of much ambition, especially finding somewhere in midwinter England that would pass for the torrid heights of Afghanistan. Dovedale in Derbyshire was eventually chosen, with its winding gorge and narrow riverbed. By placing the camera high up on one side of the ravine, the downward view covered a lengthy stretch of dry, shingle passage that wound around a projecting cliff to disappear behind it. The ground beyond the projection offered an easy route by which troops could encircle the back of the cliff, out of camera view, returning behind the camera to re-enter the march again, thus creating a seemingly never-ending army.

Jack Clair was dispatched to Nathan's, the London costumers, to bag every available piece of military uniform that bore any resemblance to the Kabul period, as well as a few native Afghan robes. In addition to his small armoury of property rifles, Clair included two lath and plaster cannon created at Worton Hall to accompany him on his journey to Derbyshire; only Samuelson's idea of hiring circus elephants eluding Clair's otherwise matchless talent for procurement. He did, however, manage to persuade the Commanding Officer at nearby Buxton of the importance of honouring the memory of the beloved Roberts, or 'Bobs' as the Field Marshal was affectionately known, by offering up 100 trainee Tommies to reproduce the historic march. The light was weak, but not hopeless and fortunately it was dry the following cold, bleak, morning of Sunday 13 December 1914 when the troops arrived, aided considerably by a tough Sergeant-Major 'with a fluent vocabulary' who ensured they made their way double-quick back and forth of the projecting cliff to create the desired illusion.

George Pearson tells us that the scenes shot at Worton Hall also had 'their reality procured by many a stage trick', although sadly offering no detail as to what these tricks were or how they were achieved. Just one month after hitting his studio with the idea for the film, *The Life of Lord Roberts* was screened at the West End Cinema trade show in London to great success. Both *The Bioscope* and *The Cinema* praised the three-reel narrative for its attention to detail reflected in the accuracy of its uniforms and the correctness of the settings. Bertie Samuelson would have been gratified to read that the march from Kabul to Kandahar shot 'in a mountainous and romantic region' was beyond reproach.

Before its eventual completion, *A Cinema Girl's Romance* provided an especially interesting diversion for twenty members of the industry who were invited to Worton Hall to take part in a 'film within the film'. *The Fireman's Wedding*, as the spurious production was called, saw the heroine jump from a blazing building and into the arms of waiting firemen and in so doing revealed many tricks of the trade. The stunt raised one or two eyebrows as to the wisdom of sharing so many trade secrets with the public, but was in reality a lure to screen at Worton Hall his latest two-reel thriller called *The Face at the Telephone*, co-directed by Fred Paul and Pearson's old colleague at Pathé, L. C. MacBean and featuring Agnes Glynne and Gerald Royston.

Samuelson was on a roll. Having just sold *A Study in Scarlet* to America for a four-figure sum, the studio had been working flat-out for seven months on eight films. Unrelenting in his passion to match the Americans at their own game, Bertie's next project began immediately after the Christmas break with a costume drama set in an eighteenth-century France still reeling from the Revolution. *The True Story of the Lyons Mail* was inspired by the famous criminal trial of Joseph Lesurques, an innocent man who was found guilty and executed for the particularly brutal murder of the driver and postilion of the Lyon Mail coach in 1796. The coach was found abandoned at the roadside, the driver dead in his seat with wounds so savage that his head was almost severed. The postilion lay dead on the road with equally ferocious wounds to his head and chest. The French authorities later acknowledged that they had tragically executed an innocent man, but did nothing to assist his impoverished wife and children; the perfect Samuelson vehicle.

Shooting began on 1 January 1915 as mostly a studio subject. Rapid progress was made and so Samuelson decided to schedule in a story he had written himself called *Buttons* about a page boy who unravels a hotel mystery. It was filmed simultaneously with the *Lyons Mail* and with both completed by mid-February. With *A Cinema Girl's Romance* finally done with, all eyes were set on the studio's next and most ambitious effort to date, an elaborate production calling for sophisticated studio sets and sumptuous exteriors in Tewkesbury, a film adaptation of Mrs Craik's famous novel, *John Halifax, Gentleman*.

The youthful John Halifax was played by fifteen-year-old Charles Bennett, who in later years became an author and playwright of repute most notably for his story, *Blackmail*, which Alfred Hitchcock chose for his first experiment in sound. In recalling his part in *John Halifax, Gentleman*, Bennett imagined G. B. Samuelson to have been one of the 'first British film producers ever' to send a unit 'onto actual – far distant – location shooting', although Tewkesbury's 111 miles from Isleworth hardly constitutes exotica by today's standards, making Samuelson's previous expeditions to Southport, Cheddar Gorge and Derbyshire all the more remarkable.

George Pearson recollects long and happy hours working on this film, offering him a greater opportunity for characterisation over thrills and spills. Fred Paul played John Halifax (the elder) with Harry Paulo as Abel Fletcher. The love interest in the form of Ursula March was provided by Peggy Hyland, making her screen debut. In Pearson's opinion she was an actress of rare quality, capable of emotional response exactly tuned to the situation and who never overacted and was never forced. 'The performance of Peggy Hyland, in the inconsolable scene by the bedside of the dying John Halifax was so truly emotionally played that even our studio-hardened hearts were moved', Pearson recounts. Peggy Hyland subsequently went on to make forty films up until 1925 when she mysteriously disappeared from the scene.

Among the plethora of rave reviews for the film, *The Manchester Guardian* claimed never to have seen a novel better screened, taking exception only at the trade show where a running commentary was delivered by 'a gentleman who declaims as the pictures go by'. This, according to the reviewer, was a frank confession of the superiority of the stage. Another novel touch employed by Samuelson was at the London trade show early in April 1915, where he set up a cameraman on the roof of a cab opposite the cinema exits to record the expressions of audience as they came out. *The Bioscope* needed no such prompting. In its opinion it was 'entirely to the taste of a British audience' and one that succeeded in preserving the atmosphere of the period, greatly assisted by the judicious selection of the surroundings reproduced with artistic taste and fine technical quality, with Buckstone's photography 'absolutely perfect and especially his pleasing soft tones'.

The success of Bertie's films and the profits they were netting led to many improvements at Worton Hall. The original glass studio was extended in length to 65 feet and with plans for another. But George Pearson, Samuelson's key cohort and patient coordinator of his ambitions had quite simply had enough. He was exhausted. His one-year contract was coming to an end and he was no longer able to sustain the frenetic pace. While always acknowledging the debt he owed to Samuelson, Pearson left Isleworth after completing *John Halifax, Gentleman* to become the chief film director at Gaumont's crystal palace at Lime Grove.

This was a serious blow to Samuelson, although he did have waiting in the wings the actor Fred Paul with a burning desire to direct. He had some experience, co-directing with L. C. MacBean the drama *The Face at the Telephone* and then *The Angels of Mons*, another two-reeler based on the urban legend of a host of angels said to have appeared in the sky between the advancing German and retreating British armies on the Western Front. His next co-production with MacBean was *Infelice*, a six-reel adaptation by Harry Engholm of the novel by Mrs Augusta J. Evans Wilson about a country girl deserted by her young husband and plotted against by her father-in-law but who overcomes all to become a great actress.

Samuelson wasn't sure if the story would appeal to the public. With Fred Paul playing the pitiable husband (as well as co-directing), Peggy Hyland once again excelled in portraying the heroine's progress from hapless country girl to grand celebrity. And praise for Samuelson's film manufactory at Worton Hall came courtesy of the *Kinematograph Monthly Film Record*, declaring the film to be a clear indication that British producers were beginning to work on an altogether improved scale in skilful staging and elaborate sets, especially the theatre setting, which it considered particularly well done. As one of the villains, an area of performance in which it seems he tended to over-egg, Fred Paul was meanwhile gaining more appreciation for his direction than his acting. *Infelice* proved financially to be one of the Samuelson Film Company's most successful films, booked by 681 cinemas, each of which reported exceptional business.

The Adventures of Deadwood Dick comprised six separate two-reel tales featuring the adventures of Englishman Richard (Dick) Harris, who journeys to the Wild West for adventure and proves himself as tough as any true Westerner. Rachel Low has this film down as the only clear adaptation of a 'penny dreadful' made in Britain, praised for the 'magnificent photographic grandeur of its scenery' on location back in Derbyshire. Unusually it was welcomed by the trade press as rare instance of a film that would appeal to a juvenile audience, a sector of the cinema audience yet to be exploited.

The Dop Doctor, a drama set during the Boer War, was the last Samuelson production of 1915. Directed by Paul and MacBean and adapted by Engholm from Richard Dehan's 1911 novel, the story revolves around the Siege of Mafeking and the regeneration of an alcoholic doctor, although Engholm modified the scenario for the heroine, played by Agnes Glynne, to take centre stage. The Samuelson family's biographer Harold Dunham recounts the story of actress Vivienne Tremayne on her first day of filming at Worton Hall going down to the meadow on the side of the estate where Fred Paul was directing the scene. Jack Clair, his assistant, told her to make for a heap where a Boer soldier was going to try and molest her. She was told to break away from him and jump over the heap and 'then run like hell' because there was 2½ pounds of dynamite stashed in the heap. The actress imagined Clair to mean stage dynamite and so offered up a 'very dainty jump'. She regained consciousness some time later.

By the end of 1915 the war in Europe had reached epidemic proportions. The conscription of all able-bodied men for the fighting services was draining skilled manpower from the film studios just as it was from industries elsewhere. According to George Pearson, with London suffering much from Zeppelin raids normal studio life was dislocated and production ceased at Worton Hall. But this was by no means the case. During October and November, three more planning applications for 'temporary' buildings were submitted by Ideal Films, a subsidiary of Samuelson Film Manufacturing. Walter Buckstone had left to become a forces cinematographer, handing over the reigns to former works manager Sydney Blythe as chief cameraman, with Alf Tunwell his assistant. While Fred Paul remained to direct for Ideal, so Samuelson transferred to Birmingham where he threw himself into the war effort, raising a 300-strong Brigade of St John Ambulance volunteers and money for fifty motor ambulances for use at the Front. Worton Hall, meanwhile, was in good hands.

Fred Paul was busily following in his mentor's footsteps, producing and directing screen adaptations of well-known stage plays, including *The Second Mrs Tanqueray*, scripted by Benedict James with the approval of the play's author, Sir Arthur Pinero. Shot in February 1916, it starred the celebrated actor Sir George Alexander in the Aubrey Tanqueray role he had created on stage. Despite the 'dreary pauses' and the 'unfamiliar surroundings', Sir George took the keenest interest in the working of a film studio.

Ideal then acquired the film rights to Oscar Wilde's *Lady Windermere's Fan*, generating a good deal of discussion as filming began in April as to how it was possible for a film to do justice to Wilde's famous witticisms. With

Benedict James's script somehow succeeding, the film starred the husband-and-wife team of Milton Rosmer as Lord Windermere and Irene Rooke as Mrs Erlynne. *The Bioscope* declared that Fred Paul and the Ideal Company added 'a brilliant feather to the cap of the British producer' and the film 'an unqualified success'. Even before its official release, scheduled for August, *Lady Windermere's Fan* was booked into 173 theatres, something of a record for the company. Fred Paul followed through with Oliver Goldsmith's *The Vicar of Wakefield* and an original work by May Sherman called *Whoso is Without Sin?* about a clerk's suicide reforming an extravagant wife who then saves a prostitute.

Plans for Worton Hall's own purpose-built 'dark studio' were submitted in March 1916 by 'Messrs Chancellors' (the construction company). Measuring a very respectable 93 feet by 45 feet, it was probably similar to Will Barker's third studio at Ealing, an 85-foot by 30-foot structure with workshops and prop room below a glass roof and studio stage on the first floor, making use of available as well as artificial light. The original glass studio was probably blacked out by this time, with lamps suspended from the steel gantries. Additional planning applications included a temporary building 'to develop photographs' and for an 'adequate additional electrical supply to the studio'. Due to the prevailing conditions, extensions to the electricity supply could only be granted for munitions work unless the applicant was prepared to pay for the whole cost of the extension to the public highway (£220). In presenting the proposal to his fellow officers, the local authority Electricity Board representative explained that the studio had been modernised to make use of artificial light, which meant its use could be extended practically all day, 'so that an excellent revenue may be expected'.

The lighting system at Isleworth at one time consisted of the industry-standard Westminster enclosed arc lamps, which were a distinct improvement on the earlier illumination method of mercury-vapour tubes. These lamps burned a violet-coloured arc, or as the liquid rushed up and down its glass tube issued long, perpendicular lines of greenish light which turned the colour of human flesh a deathly pale and the lips an eerie purple. All-white clothing had to be tinted a primrose colour and pale complexions caked in dark brick-red Leichner No. 5 theatrical grease paint to make the skin glow white.

Harold Dunham notes that those artistes playing the title roles of *The Angels of Mons* were filmed against a black velvet background representing the night sky. Unfortunately they had neglected to apply make-up to their bare legs, which made them appear as though the spiritual beings in their flowing white robes were wearing black stockings. Michael Johnson, who acted as a boy of twelve in a later Samuelson film, *Two Little Boys* (shot at Gladstone Road studios, Southall, where Samuelson set up business in 1927) recalled an earlier experience of the lighting used at Worton Hall in the form of Klieg lights, 'which were a horrible blue colour'. They were set out in bands of six or eight vertical lights, looking 'rather like yards of ale'. Bertie Samuelson warned him not to look at the lights, sensible advice which the young Johnson chose to ignore and got 'a dose of Klieg eye'. Samuelson sent him a box of crystallised fruit to aid his recovery.

Technically, the highly actinic glow of these lamps was good for the negative film stock used at the time, although achieving a high contrast could be a problem. A softer artificial light could be obtained by replacing the mercury-vapour tubes with hundreds of ordinary filament bulbs, supplemented with a few arc lamps. The definition was good, but there was still an absence of grey intermediate tones, and the overly intense black-and-white contrast remained. Even a mixture of sun and lamplight all too often proved disastrous with the changing strength of sunlight coupled with the unpredictable nature of the British climate. So to offset these variables the early cameraman's preference was for stage sets to be painted in shades of grey, creating a gloomy and dismal workspace for cast and crew alike, and only with better control of lamp illumination and improved concentration on interior design did a more civilised workspace gradually emerge.

George Pearson credits Samuelson as no slouch when it came to creativity, pushing as he did the boundaries of flexibility and mobility beyond the studio's resources, all the while adding to the quality of his productions. In assisting the development of the camera's dramatic technique, Samuelson was clearly studying developments across the pond and in particular the pioneering work of D. W. Griffith, with the introduction of techniques we today take for granted, such as the actor's point of view and changes in camera distance and angle, usually left to the discretion of the director during filming but now planned in advance as part of the production scenario.

By 1916, the public was becoming indifferent to British cinema in general, partly because of the poor quality of the product, offering little in the way of originality. Most films were bland scenarios written for the screen, or poor representations of well-known novels or popular stage successes. Bertie Samuelson was an exception. By May of that year he was back in production at Worton Hall. Ideal had moved out, having purchased the Neptune Film Company's studios in Borehamwood with its single 70-foot windowless stage, thought to have been the first dark stage in Europe. With the directing partnership of Fred Paul and L. C. MacBean a thing of the past, Samuelson now looked to Alexander Butler, an actor/director who had begun his prolific career on stage, touring South Africa and Australia before returning to England in 1913 and joining Will Barker to direct a dozen features for him. He went back to Australia the following year to direct a couple of films and then came back to England towards the end of 1914.

A difficult and fractious individual, Samuelson's faith in his new director took a bit of a knock with his first film at the newly extended Isleworth studio, a screen adaptation of Sir Sydney Grundy's famous stage comedy, *A Pair of Spectacles*, about a disillusioned rich man whose outlook on life becomes jaundiced after wearing his brother's spectacles. Reviewers found the film disappointing, mostly because the essential humour of the piece needed to be in the spoken word to be fully appreciated. But Samuelson's instinct was well rewarded with the next effort, the second Sherlock Holmes story to come out of Worton Hall, *The Valley of Fear*.

Similar in many respects to *A Study in Scarlet*, the audience has to wait until the later stages of the story before the famous detective makes his appearance. 'Well done, Samuelson!' boomed *The Bioscope*, with *Kine-Weekly* stating that there had rarely been more unstinted applause at a trade show. *Films (Birmingham)* admired 'the smoothness of the continuity; the force and virility with which the story was told', and all reviews remarked on the excellence of the photography, with its delicate tinting and toning, and the splendidly chosen locations, primarily as a means of telling the story.

After the trade show of *The Valley of Fear*, F. E. Spring, *The Cinema*'s representative, and several other 'provincials' were invited by Samuelson to visit his 'busy studio an hour's journey from London'. The party arrived at 'the old palatial mansion' to find two of the most eminent music hall artistes of the day waiting for them, Miss Clarice Mayne and 'That'; the latter being one James W. Tate, Miss Mayne's husband who composed all of their songs and accompanied her at the piano. She would announce the songs as being sung by 'this' (indicating to herself) and composed by 'that' (pointing to Tate). Both were perspiring freely when the press men arrived, having just shot an outdoor scene for *Nursie! Nursie!*, a straightforward comedy about a man falling in love with a nurse.

The two-reeler was being produced by a Mr Walters, a man described by Mr Spring as better employed conducting operations on the Western front. 'What a General he would make! – stern, adamant, and yet when you converse with him as gentle as a lamb – in fact, you would think he could not say boo to a goose'. But then things changed. An interior scene was being filmed with the wretched 'That' bathed 'in a pale and sickly make-up, monocle in eye, dressed in the proper Piccadilly style, strenuously endeavouring to consume a sufficient quantity of liquid out of a blue bottle labelled strychnine'. In order to obtain the necessary dramatic effect, quantities of soap were 'masticated with great reluctance and pain' to obtain the necessary foaming at the mouth for the climax to the scene. 'When finished,' Mr Spring concluded, 'this comedy should be a regular scream, and Mr Samuelson's enterprise in paying these two artistes a very high fee should meet with its true reward. In fact, I look forward to the day when Clarice and 'That' will be more popular on the movies than they are on the halls.'

F. E. Spring admitted to writing his notes in a desperate hurry to catch the London post. It had only just dawned on him that his watch was an hour late and he was therefore only able to offer the reader the most casual impressions of his day's outing.

> The old house and gardens which Mr Samuelson has taken over are delightful. They contain fruit trees in hundreds – massive old trees which must have been growing for a generation or two – beautiful flower gardens, and in the midst of this Paradise, brick-setters, joiners, and plumbers are busy at work erecting additional studios. The completed buildings, I should think, will be the best in England, and when one thinks that, say, a few years ago an English-produced film of any length would have been laughed at, we all felt mighty proud of the enterprise of our host in his earnest endeavours to beat his past successes, and they require some beating – *Sixty Years a Queen, Study in Scarlet, John Halifax, Infelice* etc. In these times one can only speculate on the future of films and the picture business, for many of us may have sterner work in another sphere in the future, but if the war comes to that happy and quick finish which we hope it will, your readers can have every confidence that the English film trade will be kept well to the fore while we have in it such men of light heart and smiling face as our happy host, Mr Samuelson.

Just A Girl was a film that clearly benefited from Alexander Butler's own Australian experience, achieving credibility in the first part of the film which takes place down under, the action shifting back to England and concluding back in Australia as the story follows the fortunes of Esmeralda, an orphan roughly brought up in a mining camp who inherits a fortune, enters English society and eventually finds happiness with a young nobleman. Butler also appeared in the film under his stage name of Andre Beaulieu, playing the part of Esmeralda's protector in Australia. Once again, the trade papers were impressed. The *Kinematograph Monthly Film Record* reported hardened trade show reviewers who forgot what they were there for, applauding vociferously time and again; *The Bioscope* reviewer remarking that Samuelson films were always notable in the 'care and elaboration of production, the consistently good quality of the photography and for the evident determination on the part of the producer to secure the best available talent for their representation'. The *Films* representative went further: 'we have never seen more gorgeous interiors ... beautiful garden scenes, often toned in exquisite taste'.

The public, however, had largely acquired a prejudice against British films in spite of the improved quality. American producers were backed by large corporations and banks that sensed the profit to be made in this new and exciting medium, whereas British films were dependent on individual entrepreneurs. Towards the end of 1915, duties were imposed by the Chancellor of the Exchequer on the import of both negative and positive film as a means of calming American competition. *A Pictures and Picturegoer* editorial in October 1915 urged British producers to get a move on before the winter made exterior work more difficult. The *Kinematograph Monthly Film Record* in January 1916 claimed that the industry had never been stronger, but was worried about the consequences of conscription. Film historian Roy Armes has it that Hollywood did not so much destroy a flourishing film production industry as replace the French, which controlled over 80 per cent of the market. The opportunity for British film-makers to address this imbalance was lost even before the war, except for a few producers, of which G. B. Samuelson was one. And he intended to keep it that way.

Still raw from her experience in 1902 when she was persuaded to be filmed singing 'The Midnight Sun' at the London Hippodrome while her voice was being recorded simultaneously on a gramophone, Vesta Tilly found the whole experience 'not entirely satisfactory'. In her autobiography, she recalls the approach from Samuelson for her to make a silent film; 'the talking picture not progressing too well'. The terms on offer were very good, as was the scenario for *The Girl Who Loves a Soldier*, taking the title of her most popular song, and so she accepted the offer. Thus began the hardest weeks of her working life.

'I had to be at the studio at Isleworth early each morning, and spend the whole day there.' For the first half of the film she appeared as the daughter of a multi-millionaire and the second as a hospital nurse. In between she took on the role of a British Tommy. Billed by Samuelson as 'the greatest vaudeville artiste of the age – unknown only to the unborn', Tilley's talent rested on what we might term today as that of a 'gender illusionist', or even a 'drag king', where a woman performer dresses and acts like a caricature man. According to the film's publicity, Tilley starts out as a young girl and then takes on the full persona of a 'smart, dapper little figure with her close-cropped hair and well-shaped boyish head'. Remarkably, at the age of fifty-two, Tilley not only retained the same jaunty walk that charmed theatregoers of the day, but was able to undertake all of the exacting physical requirements of the part. She had to 'gallop about madly on a restive horse', ride a motor cycle, carry dispatches at breakneck speed, and dive into deep trenches to bayonet German soldiers time and again before the tyrannical director, Alexander Butler, was happy.

In her memoirs of life on the farm next to Samuelson's studio, Jessie Lobjoit witnessed this valiant episode where time and again the hapless rider came past the same place in the lane near her house.

> There would be a bang and smoke from a simulated blast, but nothing more happened and we grew tired of watching … During the summer holidays, we saw much of it, including the star, Vesta Tilley … playing the part of a boy hero – although she must have then been about eighty.

As well as the slight adjustment to Miss Tilley's age, Jessie Lobjoit erroneously credits *The German Retreat and the Battle of Arras* as the film in question, although this was filmed at Worton Hall the following year, in April 1917, by the Topical Film Company for the War Office Cinematograph Committee. Produced by William F. Jury and photographed by Geoffrey H. Malins, it was one of three official Western Front 'big battle films' and the least successful.

For *The Girl Who Loves a Soldier*, Worton Hall and the Lobjoit farm was spread about with two bus-loads of the Queen's Own Westminster Rifles, a batch of German prisoners of war and several wounded soldiers from the West Middlesex Hospital. 'I can see these men now,' Jessie recalls.

> Lying about the yard on stretchers, outside our old granary which was used as the field dressing station, with Sisters of Mercy from Gunnersbury House in attendance. We also had some German prisoners, who were housed in the stables at Redlees, Worton Road. They were guarded by a middle-aged Sergeant, who had fought in the Boer War. He walked beside his charges as they marched in double file to the farm each morning. Most of these men

needed little guarding; they came from Schleiswig Holstein, which had only recently been annexed by Germany. They were definitely pro-British, and glad to be out of the War on that account.

Two lines of opposing trenches were dug across the neighbouring Vincent's Farm where the British and German soldiers were placed. 'It was a marvellous day's outing for them, but too realistic for some of the onlookers, to be in the middle of a simulated battle in which so many thousands of British and French soldiers had lost their lives.'

On her final day of shooting Vesta Tilley was looking forward to the comparative ease of the wedding, only to be informed that the gruelling motorcycle sequence had to be re-shot. Bumped, battered and bruised, the music hall star was changed into her bridal dress and the film completed. Thanking heavens that the ordeal was over, she and the other performers celebrated the event with high tea in the studio that afternoon. That is until it was discovered that it was against regulations for the king to pin the Victoria Cross onto the hero's breast and so that scene had to be redone. One of the Lobjoit's older men, who had lent a hand in arranging the scene-setting, was later called up and found himself at Tunbridge Wells. Feeling very homesick, he wandered into a cinema where the film was being shown, and to his amazement saw on the screen a stack of wooden vegetable boxes bearing the name W. J. Lobjoit & Son, which had been overlooked when arranging the scene filmed on the farm. 'Whatever the general effect of the film, certainly that scene brought a modicum of comfort to one lonely man,' Jessie Lobjoit concludes.

The *Films* magazine reviewer felt *The Girl Who Loves a Soldier* was worthy of the Samuelson stamp, 'which stands for the best in the world of film production'. *The Bioscope*'s expectation that the 'wholesome sentiment, humour, magic ... and very effective battle scenes would bring success' proved to be something of an understatement, with theatres inundated with bookings and enjoying record receipts. Samuelson's terms agreed with Vesta Tilley included a lump sum and royalty payments. 'And from the splendid results,' she recalls, 'the film must have booked well ... Still, it made me vow that it would be my first and last appearance as a film star, and [writing in 1934] I have kept my word.'

Adrian Brunei (sometimes Brunel) was then starting out in the world of film rentals at the offices of Moss Empires in the Charing Cross Road, where he came into contact with many of the famous names of the day and those yet to be. In one of his autobiographies, *Nice Work*, he cites

G. B. Samuelson as the 'most spectacular' producer of all. 'He was only about twenty-five at the time and weighed at least seventeen stone, and had the assurance, as well as the appearance, of a man of forty.' Brunel explains how Samuelson would make a film for, say, £3,000, and when it was finished would give it a trade show, inviting critics, exhibitors and, of course, the renters, or distributors. These men would lurk at the back of the theatre where Bertie would work his magic, often securing a sale long before the last reel was shown (invariably to Moss Empires) for a profit in the region of £1,000.

Relentless in his pursuit of added value, Bertie called upon a childhood acquaintance with the now famous stage actress Phyllis Dare, persuading her to star in his next production, *Dr Wake's Patient*, a romantic comedy about an eminent London physician who is mistaken by a high society lady for a country yokel, with all the resultant comedic twists and turns. Hailed by *Kinematograph Weekly* as another example from a film company 'striving to place British films on top', Samuelson's pictures, particularly the more recent ones had, in the opinion of the reviewer, reached a high degree of excellence with a good deal of artistic merit. The exterior work was always 'remarkably fine', invariably containing 'exquisite scenic effects'. Both *The Bioscope* and *The Cinema* much admired the hunting scenes, the hunt breakfast and ball scene contrasting with a well-executed London train station enveloped in a thick fog. Phyllis Dare was delighted with her screen debut, assisted by a distinguished cast drawn from the Savoy and Drury Lane theatres.

In *A Fair Impostor*, Samuelson's next production, Madge Titheradge, described as one of the finest and most versatile actresses of her day, proved equally content to go before Samuelson's cameras, giving an excellent 'artistic performance in the extreme' with 'fiery vigour and sincerity as the especially convincing slum-girl'. But it was towards the end of 1916 that Bertie would embark on a truly prestige production, a film of the hugely successful play by Arnold Bennett and Edward Knoblock, *Milestones*, which ran for a phenomenal 607 performances at the Royalty Theatre in London. In this, Samuelson looked beyond Alexander Butler as director to Thomas Bentley, who had directed the highly acclaimed Dickens trilogy *Oliver Twist*, *David Copperfield* and *The Old Curiosity Shop* for Cecil Hepworth. Although he had also written the scenarios for these films, Harry Engholm was considered the right man for the job on this occasion.

Milestones was shot alongside *A Fair Impostor* in October and November 1916, when a representative of *The Cinema* magazine paid a visit to Worton

Hall, reiterating that atmosphere, fidelity to story and artistic finish was always the hallmark of a Samuelson production. The reporter found the head of the studio not in his office, as might be expected, but on the studio floor 'busily superintending in conjunction with Mr Bentley' on the third period of *Milestones*. The reporter found Samuelson to be a modest man on the subject of his productions and his patriotism, but one as ever committed to giving the public good, original pictures and variations of themes, together with scenes of local colour instead of a surfeit of foreign productions. Bertie showed the reporter around his new 'dark' studio, described as an 'enormous building fitted with the most up-to-date appliances' that was ready and waiting for the 300 extras due to arrive the next day.

Milestones was a story that traced the repetition in three consecutive generations (1860, 1885 and 1912) of the age-old conflict between the conservatism of middle-age and rebellious youth, with the overall production embellished with numerous historical allusions. It was a mini-epic, later hailed as Bentley's finest achievement in its meticulous accuracy and attention to detail. The typewriter used to illustrate the transition from quill pen to machine, for example, was an original Remington No. 2 built in 1883 and the telephone used was said to have been the first instrument ever installed. Many scenes of Old London recreated at Isleworth included a milkman carrying his pails on cobbled streets, an early motor car following a man waving a flag, a horse-drawn bus, the interior of a cinema with a film being screened, and glimpses of Dickens and Disraeli. Jessie Lobjoit recalls being much amused to see Her Majesty (Queen Victoria) during a break, sitting back in her brougham, complete with black silk bonnet and widow's veil, enjoying a cigarette before the launching of the first iron-clad naval vessel HMS *Warrior*.

Kine-Weekly went so far as to declare that 'more consistently good work from a technical standpoint has never been filmed'. After the trade show, in addition to a handsome bonus cheque, Samuelson presented Bentley with a gold-mounted Malacca cane engraved 'Thomas Bentley from GBS. A Souvenir of "Milestones" December 7th 1916'. Hailed as 'the greatest British production of all time', *Milestones* was a particular triumph for cameraman Alf Tunwell, whom Thomas Bentley thanked publicly. In thanking Samuelson, Bentley declared that the success of the film was down to his ungrudging assent to all the requirements necessary for the production, his many helpful suggestions and his readiness to assist in the interpretation of the scenario, a feature that would always remain a happy recollection of a very pleasant engagement.

In his next production, *Sorrows of Satan*, Samuelson introduced the famous stage beauty Gladys Cooper to the delights of Worton Hall, her only other encounter with the world of film apparently a miserable affair for Cunard Films in 1914, which deeply soured her perception of the new medium and possibly accounts for the difficulties experienced by cast and crew alike at Isleworth. Eventually the toxic fusion of her fractiousness and the 'choleric, unpredictable Alex Butler' threatened the production.

It was nine o'clock and the studio was set up and ready to shoot a big ball scene. Miss Cooper waltzed in ten minutes late and was reminded of this by Butler. 'Miss *Gladys* Cooper, if you please,' she spat, to which Butler exploded: 'I don't give a * * * * if you are Gladys Cooper or the Queen of England – when I say nine o'clock, I mean nine o'clock, not ten past!' Waving his hand he dismissed the crowd, telling them to go and collect their money and to return the following day at nine o'clock. 'And you will be here, Miss Cooper!' And she was. This episode must have cost Samuelson hundreds of pounds, but according to Harold Dunham 'that was the sort of thing that producers did and he let them get away with it. In the event, *The Bioscope* was impressed by Alex Butler's direction but felt that it was unlikely to be greeted with much appreciation by the general public.

Eight feature films and one two-reeler had come out of Worton Hall during 1916; a successful year shared by the whole industry, although one shared with too many foreign inputs despite the hostilities according to *Kinematograph Monthly Film Record*. *Kine-Weekly* bemoaned the lack of investment in British films, believing that the industry was not taken as seriously by investors at home as it was abroad. 'Only when the right people here take a hand in the financial end of the game,' it suggested, 'will British pictures come into their own … the excellent work of the few producing companies – London, Ideal, Hepworth and Samuelson – is equal to, if not in some cases superior to, our rivals.'

There was, however, an element of mistrust of the City among British film producers in so far as the considerable amounts of money it could bring would threaten to dictate the industry; independence over dependence being very much the order of the day. Added to this was an entertainments tax introduced in 1916 on all theatrical and sporting events, which amounted to an extra half-penny on the ticket price, which hit the poorest hardest and was responsible for the closure of hundreds of picture houses. But as the war progressed, so the propaganda value of the cinema became apparent and film producers were invited onto the War Office Topical Committee with the intention of getting official cameramen to the front. Geoffrey Malins was one of the first film cameramen to come under fire filming *The Battle of the Somme*, which was released as a full-length feature within four weeks of the action. Shots of troops being mown down by enemy fire shocked film-goers, but even the king felt that it was important for the public to see for themselves what was happening across the English Channel.

Then there was the battle against state censorship in which Samuelson became closely involved. In April 1916, the Home Secretary, Mr Herbert Samuel, proposed that an official censor should be appointed and an advisory board set up made up of local authority representatives, public figures, authors and a trade representative. British film-makers in response sent a deputation to the Home Secretary urging that the system of voluntary censorship be maintained, with the Home Secretary having the power to appoint the president of the board. Following a special trade conference held on 18 September 1916 and a joint trade conference on 1 November, which included representatives of the Incorporated Society of Authors, Playwrights and Composers, G. B. Samuelson was appointed to a special committee representing film manufacturers known as the Cinematograph Trade Council (CTC), which comprised a standing committee composed of members of the Incorporated Association of Kinematograph Manufacturers, the Incorporated Society of Film Renters, and the Cinematograph Exhibitors' Association. The intention was to seek a test case as to the power of local authorities to impose their own conditions on the exhibition of films. But then the Asquith coalition fell and was replaced by the new Lloyd George government. Herbert Samuel was replaced by Sir George Cave as Home Secretary, who decided not to proceed with the plans for censorship, at least for the time being.

A prime candidate for the censor's snip would have been Ruby Miller, who shocked a generation by revealing a glimpse of knee in one of her celebrated roles as Maimie Scott in the W. W. Ellis farce *A Little Bit of Fluff*. She epitomised the woman of the Edwardian era who used her sexuality to pursue a career that marked her out as modern and liberated in an age when marriage and family was the prime expectation. Samuelson wanted her for his next production, an adaptation of the Berta Ruck novel *In Another Girl's Shoes*, about two girls who change identities. He had already engaged the well-known stage actress Mabel Love to play the part of the other girl, but the production was not to be without its difficulties.

Miller later wrote,

In the opening scene, Mabel Love and I meet in a railway carriage and decide to swap places in life. In order to depict the moving train, Bertie [Samuelson] decided to build the interior of the carriage on the back of an open lorry, with the camera crew crowded alongside to film us as the lorry bumped along.

Samuelson drove ahead in an open car shouting instructions through a megaphone as the cavalcade made its way through the lanes of Isleworth. After a short time, as Samuelson's car disappeared around a bend, the lorry died and nothing the driver did could get it going again. Some minutes later, Bertie's car reappeared and instead of being furious he roared with laughter. The lorry was towed back to Worton Hall and the scene played out with the 'carriage' rocked up and down as painted scenery was wound past the window. Happily the result was quite realistic, 'and Bertie was delighted'.

Unfortunately *The Bioscope* did not share Samuelson's enthusiasm, declaring that a production of so supreme a masterpiece as *Milestones* imposed obligations on a studio not to lightly disregard its future work. 'The public has a right to expect that every successive effort, however unambitious in design, should carry something of that distinction which has been attained by its predecessors,' it maintained. Even the photography and general production values were deemed to have fallen below par. The *Kinematograph Monthly Film Record* was less scathing, reporting the trade show audience to have been generally most appreciative of the historic visions introduced into a dream sequence, and especially a skit on film studios, but otherwise it felt that the film was undistinguished. While Alex Butler is credited for the direction, it is clear from Ruby Miller's account that Samuelson shared some of the artistic responsibility. Despite her appearance only in the opening sequences, with events of her past shown in flashback, Miller alone won approval from the reviewers as the 'most interesting personality', playing the film star who forces her young travelling companion to swap places with her.

Her performance in *Another Girl's Shoes* justified Samuelson's decision to cast her as Jo Marsh in *Little Women* from the Louisa May Alcott novel. 'I loved working at Worton Hall,' she later recalled.

It was a beautifully picturesque place. Working there was like being at a country house party among friends – it was a wonderful, easy atmosphere. We would often, after a long day's shooting, stay at the Hall, where there was a suite of rooms at our disposal. Bertie always thought of everything. To me and all the other actors and actresses at the studios, he was the 'Papa' and with his mother a frequent visitor, taking her lunch with the company in the large dining room.

Miller also recalls Samuelson's love for and respect of theatricals, once telling her that he 'must have people who can hold an audience with an expression. Faces in a close-up must be convincing – not laughable ... if he ever heard an over-zealous director browbeating one of his artists he was quick to intervene and have a quiet word'. Samuelson was almost always on the set during the production and quick to put forward helpful suggestions to the director. Long before Alfred Hitchcock acquired the predisposition, Bertie took to appearing in his own films, allegedly to make him feel closer to the picture and bring it luck. In *Little Women* he took the part of a bespectacled doctor when Jo goes to visit Beth in hospital, and in *Edge o' Beyond* he blacked his face to play a native servant in a Rhodesian farmhouse.

Little Women was well received, with the quality of Samuelson films back on track as far as the trade papers were concerned. But then there were wider problems facing the industry in 1917 in the form of a recession that would see film production reduce to a trickle compared to the previous year. The huge Gaumont studio at Lime Grove closed down. Other studios were ordered to black out after three o'clock to save on fuel and there was a shortage of actors and technicians, now called upon to serve overseas. But in a letter to *Kinematograph Weekly* published on 17 May 1917, Bertie Samuelson concluded that things were not as bad as they might be. The film industry was 'passing through troublesome times' but he was sure it would be able to keep the flag flying. He urged his colleagues in the trade not to criticise American films for the simple reason they were 'too good to be eliminated from the programme' and the exhibitors needed them to retain standards. In a sentiment that would in the years ahead become a reality, he warned that 'American films have made the Kinematograph trade in this country what it is' and that it would be a bad blow for industry if the importation of their films was prohibited. He, in common with every other British film producer, looked to see British films at the top of the game, but that demanded hard work, not 'trying to kill the hen that laid the golden eggs'.

With Samuelson's confidence in British pictures undaunted, Gladys Cooper was persuaded to return to Worton Hall despite her strong dislike of the film-making process. *My Lady's Dress* was a notable stage success by playwright Edward Knoblock that offered a staggering array of settings from Mayfair to Italy, Siberia to Whitechapel; the South of France to seventeenth-century Holland. The film ran for two and half hours, following the story of a young woman who, in order to further her husband's career, flirts with an elderly roué, and as part of her plan buys an unusually expensive dress.

In a dream, she is made to realise the trials of those who have contributed to the making of the dress in its various stages and the sufferings caused by personal vanity and infidelity. Samuelson had 'done the trick again' and made the play into 'almost a film masterpiece' with the trade press likening Alex Butler's authentic representation of seventeenth-century Holland to an old Dutch master. Gladys Cooper and her co-star Malcolm Cherry fell short of overall praise, but after the war the film went on to be distributed in France, Italy, Spain, Norway, Sweden, Denmark, Holland, Egypt, Africa, China, India, Ceylon and Burma, and was re-released in Britain in 1922.

Hindle Wakes was a stage play that had reached almost 4,000 performances since 1912 and had been seen by an estimated three million people. It was one of the earliest films directed by Maurice Elvey, now considered Britain's most prolific film-maker with over 300 feature films and innumerable shorts to his credit between 1913 and 1957. Described by his biographer, Linda Wood, as 'a sympathetic and imaginative craftsman whose role in shaping British cinema has been unjustly neglected in favour of more flashy and less experienced contemporaries', Elvey rose from extremely humble beginnings to direct Gaumont's first talkie, *High Treason*, in 1929; the first British colour film, *Sons of the Sea*, and would go on to mentor Carol Reed and David Lean as well as directing Gracie Fields in her first and phenomenally successful film *Sally in Our Alley* (1931). *Hindle Wakes* was produced by Diamond-Super, a company specially formed to make the film version of the play, which was then contracted to G. B. Samuelson to make and distribute through his rental agency. The story of an indiscretion on holiday of the heroine with a mill-owner's son took the film world by storm. *Films* devoted its editorial to 'A Great Picture', doubting if anything entirely British-made had been 'illustrated or produced and enacted so superbly as this'. Elvey had accomplished 'a difficult task with excellent discretion, artistic sympathy and great skill', reported *The Bioscope*, and when released in 1918 the film broke all box office records wherever it was shown.

Alexander Butler had by now left Worton Hall to work for Will Barker, thus presenting the opportunity for Samuelson to step up to the plate and direct the next production himself. The chosen vehicle was predictably another screen adaptation of a successful stage play, this time Sir James Barrie's *The Admirable Crichton*, a large part of which takes place on a desert island. Samuelson decided on Cornwall for the location work, where it would be reasonable to expect the beaches to be deserted in January. And so they were, thanks to the appalling weather. Basil Gill, who played Crichton, was later quoted as saying that in his opinion it would have been better to have spent money going to 'an authentic location'. In Gill's opinion British film-makers would never truly compete with the Americans 'until we realise that Rottingdean will not do for Brittany or Hastings for the Riviera'.

Playing Agatha was Lilian Hall-Davis, making her first appearance for the Samuelson Film Manufacturing company and another actress who would continue to grace leading roles at Worton Hall in the years to come. Despite his criticisms, Basil Gill considered *The Admirable Crichton* to have been his happiest working experience of his twenty film appearances. This he largely put down to Bertie, which was some consolation. Although the film was not considered to be an outstanding success, *Kine-Weekly* was impressed with the island scenes, the exteriors it considered 'carefully chosen', and the elaborate interior sets well executed. However, while the photography was faultless, the film was hardly up the standards the trade and public had come to expect from G. B. Samuelson.

Sol Levy's renting firm, Sun Exclusives, financed the next film in return for world rights. An adaptation of Ethel M. Dell's novel *The Way of an Eagle* was made for Victor Saville, who would one day become a giant of the British film industry as a producer and director. Saville was working at Sun Exclusives at the time and recalls that it was Bertie Samuelson who was the first producer/director to recognise the merits of turning a popular novel into a film. The budget for *The Way of an Eagle* was a modest £4,000, a good £6,000 less than that expected for a top-quality film – and £36,000 less than Samuelson had lavished on *Sixty Years a Queen* in 1914. Bertie again took on the role of director, while Alex Butler played the idealised all-male hero, Nick Ratcliff. This time the trade press was more impressed with Samuelson's efforts. *The Bioscope* thought that he had 'worked wonders'; the scenes set in India nothing short of 'masterpieces of screen craft'. So convincing was it that an Anglo-Indian refused to be convinced that the whole film was made in a London suburb. *The Way of an Eagle* was the first of Ethel M. Dell's novels to be screened and on release broke all records up and down the country.

Tinker, Tailor, Soldier, Sailor was a seven-reeler scripted by Kenelm Foss, perhaps from an original idea by Samuelson, about the daughter of a mayor who is under pressure from her parents to marry a baronet but who is in love with a shopkeeper. The film then offers three versions of her future; the first, as her parents would have it, the second, she marries as she wishes, and thirdly how it actually turned out. The first Samuelson film to be directed by Rex Wilson, the trade papers made loose associations with *Milestones*, although it was lightweight in comparison. While researching the life and times of Bertie for the Samuelson family, Harold Dunham came across two reels of *Tinker, Tailor, Soldier, Sailor* at the National Film Archive that had been incorrectly catalogued as the 1919 feature *The Right Element*. This chance find offered a rare opportunity to assess first-hand a Samuelson film, which did not disappoint.

Bertie Samuelson was on a roll, following up *Tinker, Tailor, Soldier, Sailor* with *The Elder Miss Blossom*, which was to become his most successful film since *Milestones*. Another adaptation of a successful stage play, this second Samuelson production for Sol Levy proved to be an even greater success than *The Way of an Eagle*. *The Elder Miss Blossom* was seen as markedly superior to the lurid melodramas or sentimental romances generally on offer, *The Bioscope*'s reviewer finding it to be 'in all ways a phenomenal success', while *Kine-Weekly* described a 'clean, well-produced picture, worthy of the effort that is being made to uplift British production'.

Bertie Samuelson survived the Great War in good shape, generally regarded as the doyen of the British film industry. In an interview for *The Bioscope* on 24 October 1918 he called for a concerted effort on the part of all British film producers to seize the opportunity to turn out a succession of films equal to, if not better, than those of other countries. Given all of the constraints over the past three years, it was significant that films produced in Britain had been significantly superior to those produced in previous years. In the same issue other producers and directors expressed similar views, although Thomas Bentley criticised those producers that allowed insufficient time for script development and the organisation of studio time. The great American producer/director, Herbert Brenon, then working in England, saw little wrong with resources in Britain but felt that budgets from £4,000 to £20,000 were unrealistic if the intention was to compete with America. Maurice Elvey agreed, sort of, arguing that producers had been trying to make Grade One pictures with Grade Three staff and technical resources, adding that Britain's inability to manufacture films on the American factory scale was a positive advantage, allowing British producers to develop their originality. Cecil Hepworth looked to the film-maker as an artist with a message to humanity, while Fred Paul was more pragmatic, pointing to the erratic weather conditions influencing delays in keeping to the schedule.

During the course of the war, the government had come to realise the potential of film as propaganda and eventually sponsored two Samuelson films: *God Bless our Red, White and Blue* and *Onward Christian Soldiers*, which typically dripped with patriotic symbolism while actually offering very little propaganda value. By the end of October 1918 all eyes were on the expectation of peace and a return to normality, but with little real hope in the film business for the much longed-for resurgence in the face of stiff competition from abroad. Samuelson had been sometime busy in the formation of a British Screen Association, designed to organise British manufacturers' sales abroad. The results were more muted than resolved and so he concentrated on his core remit of continuing to contribute to a great British revival in film-making, tripping over somewhat with *The Man Who Won*, his last film of 1918. Directed by Rex Wilson, the story set in South Africa concerns a hero in love with a girl above his station who undergoes much suffering until rising above it all to rediscover her lost beau who has also clawed his way to respectability. Normally loyal, *The Bioscope* concluded that 'although Mr Samuelson possess an instinct for pressing just the right emotional button of an audience and can command tears to flow, he lacks a certain originality we would wish to see in our best British producers'. The writing was on the wall.

3

The End of a Dream

In her substantial and near-comprehensive history of the British film industry (1896–1985), a deeply unimpressed Rachel Low sniffily advocates that G. B. Samuelson flew too high, choosing books with little regard as to their suitability for the screen. But at a time when most other British film-makers were suffering from accelerating production costs and foreign competition flooding the home market, Samuelson in 1919 was turning out dozens of successful films to a recognised formula, the most notable being *Convict 99*, which saw music hall star Wee Georgie Wood make his first screen appearance. *Quinney's* starred the celebrated stage actor Henry Ainley and, as well as two more Ruby Miller pictures – *Edge o' Beyond* and *Gamblers All* – *Faith, Hope and Charity* was so successful that it led to an important distribution contract with Granger's Exclusives. *A Member of Tattersall's* was notable for its use of colour; *The Right Element* was from an original story by the celebrated playwright, Roland Pertwee, and *Mrs Thompson*, a story adapted from a W. B. Maxwell novel about the proprietress of a store who is shrewd in business but idealistic in her love for her daughter, represented by no means a bad slate.

With cameramen Alf Tunwell, Jimmy Rogers and Harold Bastick safely returned from the Front, the staff at Worton Hall was augmented by directors Fred Durrant, Albert Ward and Dave Aylott. Samuelson had come up with the idea of teaming specific directors and cameramen, such as Rex Wilson or Alex Butler working with senior cameraman Sydney Blythe on the more prestigious productions. Butler and Blythe were the team allotted the highly controversial *Damaged Goods*, adapted from Eugène Brieux's long-running stage play about the social evil of venereal disease. So contentious a subject was it that Samuelson arranged a private midnight screening of the film, which failed spectacularly to attract the interest of the trade journals. Only the London correspondent of *Variety* turned up to find the film 'distasteful with little dramatic power'. The feeling was growing stronger against 'such propaganda features being foisted on the paying public as items of ordinary programme,' he complained. Rachel Low makes particular mention of an innovative overhead shot in a ball scene, which she derides as one of the earliest examples of a 'self-consciously artistic angle shot'.

Dave Aylott wrote to Bertie Samuelson on being de-mobbed in 1919 and was offered a job. Arriving at Worton Hall with 'the open countryside surrounding the studios and orchards all along Worton Road', he set about directing *Her Own People*, an Anglo-Indian story by B. M. Croker that saw him dispatched on location to Dovedale. But with the weather so appalling he was forced to return to Worton Hall, where he found Samuelson a very worried man, having purchased the rights to Sir George Alexander's play *Gamblers All* and afterwards discovering a clause in the agreement specifying a date when filming was to commence, which was one week away. As the two other directors, Albert Ward and Alexander Butler, were more advanced in their productions than he, Aylott was given the task of transferring a four-act stage play containing only three scenes into a film script with dozens of different scenes in just one week.

Arrangements were made for Aylott to work from home, where each day his copy was rushed to the studio for typing and 'doping', the process where all the requirements for filming, such as cast, wardrobe, sets and props etc., were filleted out. He arrived back at Worton Hall on the Saturday morning to find 'the most wonderful cast assembled that had appeared in British films' and a band of 'extra people' supplied by Sidney Jay, an ex-serviceman who first had the idea of running an agency to supply background artists for film production. They all shook hands and wished each other good luck and the filming started. With the first shots secured and the clause in the contract satisfied, Aylott was sent home for a good rest over the weekend while Samuelson pondered an offer he felt he couldn't refuse.

The 21 November 1919 edition of *Variety* reported that Samuelson had signed a contract with the General Film Renting Company involving $2.5 million for a minimum of fifteen films over a sixteen-year period, including six films in Hollywood designed to promote British films in America. *The Bioscope* was more circumspect with regard to the ambitious new company, which had commissioned Barker Motion Photography as well as Samuelson Film Manufacturing to make films while holding exclusive rights for worldwide distribution. Moreover, General Film Renting announced a further programme for eighty feature films over six years from Swedish Biograph and the Norwegian firm Nordisk, while Worton Hall and Ealing were to be hired out. This in turn led to much speculation of a take-over at Isleworth.

Kinematograph Weekly pondered Samuelson's declaration that he looked to establish himself in America whatever his decision regarding his British interests. While there was no sound evidence for a proposed sale of Worton Hall, there was under the contract with General Film Renters a feeling among staff that things had changed, that Samuelson was to remain at Worton Hall as the producer but without overall control of the output. *Kine-Weekly* erroneously reported on 11 November 1920 that General Film Renters had purchased the Samuelson Film Company 'lock, stock and barrel', but it was never Bertie's intention to sell Worton Hall. This proved to be a wise decision throughout some hard times ahead. The contract with Granger's was drawing to a close with *The Husband Hunter* and *The Last Rose of Summer*, the last films Samuelson completed in Britain before setting off for Hollywood. Arthur Alcott was asked to stay behind and look after Worton Hall, which had been hired out to the pioneering natural history film-maker, H. B. Parkinson, for his *Secrets of Nature* films.

The bucolic setting would have suited Parkinson well. Samuelson took great pride in the beautiful grounds and gardens with 'old Reuben', the gardener, under strict orders as to how they should be maintained, and the several huge cedar trees on the flower-bordered lawns providing a setting for many a film. The orchard and kitchen garden formed an oblong measuring 82 feet by about 160 feet to the south of the estate behind a line of narrow buildings comprising offices, stores and a scenery dock. In front of these were the two studios, the original all-glass structure now measuring 90 feet by about 35 feet, and the later brick building with no natural lighting, measuring some 60 feet by 40 feet and with a dressing room block attached. Next to that was a 100-foot by 20-foot building containing the film printing laboratories, equipment and wardrobe store. The tradesmen's entrance between the mansion and the old stable block remained the main access point into and out of the studio, with the latter now housing the carpenters' shops and stores. A second scenery store was established about 100 yards or so to the south of that, next to the studio's pride and joy, its very own electricity generating plant, believed to be unique at the time.

This state-of-the-art piece of kit was supplied by the General Electric Company to specifically meet the widely fluctuating demands of film production with no reliance on the mains or the potential to overload the circuits, which was not uncommon with film studios. The plant was housed in a solid building divided into two compartments, one containing a motor generator and the other a large storage battery. Paper-insulated, lead-covered underground cables distributed power to the two stages. Assistant lighting cameraman, Alan Lawson, remembers the traction engine continually going – 'you would start off your shot with all the lights on, and by the time you got to the end of the shot, they were a horrible orange colour'. Retired sound recordist Charles Wheeler had been loaned to Worton Hall Studios for a time from Masters Studios, Teddington, as an electrician.

> They had at Worton Hall a huge battery plant which used to light the studios, the likes of which I never saw anywhere else. This overcame the risk of overloading the supply of electricity from the mains, as happened, for instance, at Teddington.

Retired production accountant Archie Holly recalls being tasked with feeding half-crown coins into the electricity meter as the only means of getting the local authority to supply the studio following problems in paying the bill.

There were no such impediments at the Brunton Studios in Universal City, California, said to be among the finest and best equipped in Hollywood and where the owner of Worton Hall was renting space. The first British producer ever to take a company to the States had with him a small company of cast and crew including Alex Butler and Sydney Blythe. William Basson, the general manager, carpenter, scenery arranger and props man, caused much consternation among the American press reporters who declared there was 'no such animal' their side of the pond where the demarcation lines between skills were strictly drawn as they would be in Britain in future years. Cast-wise, Bertie wasted no time in seeking out Peggy Hyland, the English actress who had starred in his films *John Halifax, Gentleman* and *Infelice*. Her contract with Fox had just expired and Samuelson persuaded her to sign a long-term contract to star in his films both in both America and back home. And arrangements were made with the American casting agency, Willis and Inglis, to provide players for supporting roles for the six productions to be completed in four months by the three units of the Samuelson American production company: *At The Mercy of Tiberius*; *Her Story*; *The Night Riders*; *Love in the Wilderness*; *David and Jonathan* and *The Ugly Duckling*.

What impressed the British contingent most of all was the sheer efficiency, organisation and attention to detail the Americans lavished on their film production. Actor Charlie Hallard recalled that if a shot required 250 aristocratic-looking extras, then they were there after one phone call. 'If you wanted Windsor Castle, or a motor cycle, it was there the next day!' It was found that the American studios had more heads of departments than the British had producers, who tended to do everything themselves. Samuelson was clearly impressed, proclaiming on his arrival back in England in April 1920, that he was looking forward to resuming Hollywood production later in the year as well as his hope to one day build a studio there. He had gone to America intending to 'introduce a system of star interchange, whereby players from Great Britain will be seen in pictures made in Universal City and American favourites will be featured in productions made in the British Isles'. Instead he more or less continued to do what he was good at, making successful, entertaining and sometimes challenging British films.

Reaction to his Hollywood output was on the whole very disappointing. Even traditionally supportive *The Biograph* was bewildered by it all and wondered what was the purpose of the exercise. The stories were confused and disjointed and it was 'difficult to gather why Mr Samuelson should have journeyed so far as California ... instead of going to Africa itself'. Overall the results failed to come up to the average American or Continental production. Moreover, the combination of British talent with the advanced technical facilities of an American studio was a wasted opportunity except for the technical gains, some of which were introduced at Worton Hall. Wohl and Wingfield-Kerner lights, for example, were multiple pairs of open carbons issuing a very white light instead of the ultra-violet and very blue effect of the traditional Westminster arcs. These new lights made it easier for cameramen to obtain a true exposure value and greatly improve the quality of the negatives.

From the favourable comments it received from the British trade press Samuelson soon recovered his touch with *A Temporary Gentleman*, the last film made for Granger's at Worton Hall. This wholesome tale of a humble clerk who is commissioned in the Army during the Great War and is too grand to accept lowly employment afterwards but is gradually brought down to earth, was followed by *Nance*, Bertie's first production for the General Film Renting Company since arriving back in England. It was based on a novel by Charles Garvice who enjoyed something of a risqué reputation much favoured by Samuelson. An especially highly coloured, sensational story, *Kine-Weekly* considered the crudity of the original book was 'only magnified by the screen presentation'. If the film represented the author, then there was 'something rotten in the taste of the public', the paper proclaimed. Though 'a morbid misrepresentation of life', the reviewer did, however, admit that the production showed a general advance in its technical qualities, but that it would it would take little 'to turn it into burlesque'.

Aunt Rachel, Samuelson's next film, was one to be congratulated, provided 'a pair of scissors and a modicum of literary ability' was applied to a complete re-titling. He fared better with *The Winning Goal*, adapted from *The Game*, a play by Harold Brighouse, which was the first feature film to utilise professional football teams. The twenty-two players drawn from Bradford City, Tottenham Hotspur, Chelsea, Aston Villa and Bolton Wanderers turned out as the two opposing fictitious teams at Brentford's Griffin Park in the spring of 1920. Samuelson stood in the middle of the ground shouting instructions through a megaphone, but it was a warm day and after some hours the crowd found it too wearisome to summon up any enthusiasm for cheering. As much was shared by the *Kine-Weekly* reviewer, who criticised the direction for lacking 'visual appeal'; a serious problem with a moving picture, whereas the ever-supportive *The Bioscope* urged showmen to 'get a move on before all the dates are booked up'.

Sticking with sport, *All the Winners* (about a young anti-hero who, having suffered betting losses, steals from the body of a tipster killed in a car crash) saw the arrival at Worton Hall of Geoffrey H. Malins, the recent recipient of an OBE for his services as an official cinematographer during the Great War. For the car crash scene, Malins decided to hire a taxi without informing the owner of its intended use and then completely wrecked it. He never directed another film for Samuelson, although he would be no stranger to Worton Hall in years to come. *Kine-Weekly* praised Malins as a film-maker capable of producing very fine drama from a good scenario, although it did condemn the 'gratuitous brutality' as 'a gross lapse in taste'.

Subsequent output from Worton Hall in the form of *The Honeypot* and *Love Maggie* were likewise reviled on the grounds of poor taste, influencing Samuelson to look a little higher than the novels of his choice, and even beyond his commitment to film, as the relationship with General Film Renters gradually soured. The country was in turmoil. Industrial activity was widespread and transport was becoming an issue. This led him to diversify into the coach business, running a daily service of six vehicles between London and various coastal resorts. By July the new enterprise had expanded to a fleet of ninety-nine coaches and fifty-six luggage vans, most of which were acquired on hire purchase. The venture was launched largely in anticipation of a threatened rail strike, which failed to materialise. An attempt to float the company on the stock market proved unsuccessful and the business collapsed within a few months. It was time to put on a grand show, to return to the very beginning of his film career and create another dramatic spectacle, filled with pageantry, processions and great sporting and battle scenes topped with lashings of sentiment and charm. *The Game of Life* was symbolic in its title, taken from an anonymous poem that likened life to a game of cards.

On 9 September 1920 *The Cinema* reported impressive sets constructed at Worton Hall, including a 500-yard length of cobbled London street complete with 100 shops and a tavern. Five hundred tons of cobbles were imported, with timber costing in the region of £2,000 and scenery twice that amount. As many as 4,000 extras had been engaged, reckoned to be the biggest call of background artists in Britain to date and each one at a guinea a day making serious inroads into Samuelson's budget. Being on such a grand scale, several assistant directors were called upon to direct this small army lining the street during Queen Victoria's Coronation, cheering her royal highness at the Derby, fighting at the Battle of Inkermann and standing aghast at the sight of George Stephenson's *Rocket*. Harold Bastick, one of the cameramen, recalls the pioneer engine placed on wooden rails and shot in such a way that the whole length of the train was never seen; the front end being filmed while being pushed from behind.

Both he and fellow cameraman Sydney Blythe were perched on a rostrum at the end of the street ready for the Queen's Coronation and other cameras were placed at intervals along the route of the procession. The weather had turned foul so it was decided to use artificial lights. The cameras rolled, but as the royal coach came within range it was found to be empty. The horses had taken flight when the lights came on and, scared by their prancing, the actress playing the young Queen Victoria had opened the door and bolted. For the Queen's Jubilee the set was completely rebuilt and the Hounslow Fire Brigade called upon to affect the violent rain-lashed thunderstorm that accompanied the actual procession, sending a continuous sheet of water falling over the whole length. But then the foul weather took over for real just as the 1,000 extras had been made up. It was impossible to shoot the scene and they were sent home, paid for a day's work without a frame shot.

The gestation period for this vast undertaking was September 1920 to May 1922 but personal accounts are variable. Harold Dunham records one eyewitness maintaining that the film was shot over several months in between lesser productions and was suspended completely during Samuelson's transport adventure. Others felt sure that the film was completed by April or May 1921. Alex Butler's widow, who was playing minor roles at Worton Hall at this time, was clear that the production was spaced over a very long period, partly because of its epic nature and the constant interruptions due to bad weather. Bertie's second trip to Hollywood in the spring of 1921 might have had a bearing. He'd gone there to sell three of his films, informing readers of *Moving Picture World* that he planned to make films in England during the summer and in California in the winter. Films made in England during the summer were cheaper than could be made in America, he added.

The Game of Life was screened at the opening of the new Scala Picture House, café and ballroom in Leeds on 24 July 1922 as a double-feature programme alongside *The Three Musketeers* starring Douglas Fairbanks; a name that would become closely associated with Worton Hall in the decades to come. The completed film ran for over two and half hours, said to be the longest film ever to come out of a British studio. It was Samuelson's favourite film and should have been the one to have truly made his name. But after the trade show he found it near impossible to find a distributor, doubtless because of its length and the full orchestral accompaniment required for its many special effects. The single offer made for distribution in Britain was dependent on cutting the film down to 2,000 feet, which was not an option. The film had been three years in the making and meant more to Samuelson than simply a film; it was what he had set out to do, to make a British version of D. W. Griffith's *Birth of a Nation*. In holding that everyone was entitled to their opinion, it was his contention that the British public would flock to see *The Game of Life* and so sure was he that rather than mutilate his work he would run it, not on a rental, but on a sharing basis. Each copy of the picture would be sent out with an 'elocutionist' to recite the monologue, exactly as the film had been screened at the trade show and any exhibitor interested in this proposition was urged to write to Bertie at Worton Hall, Isleworth where he would 'be pleased to fix up matters with them'.

The reviews for *The Game of Life* were more warm and admiring than rave. Writing in *The Motion Picture Studio*, producer Sidney Morgan felt that the critics generally agreed the film only just missed real greatness.

We know of scenes postponed a dozen times through weather troubles and eventually not taken at all. We know of the interior of Drury Lane Theatre, done in a studio several times too small ... What an achievement for Worton Hall it was! But what an achievement it might have been for England.

Bertie claimed that he was not surprised by it all, announcing that he had struck a deal with the biggest distributor in America, who had done him the great honour of offering a five-year contract to produce for them in California at 'a salary that would eclipse the combined salaries of all the British directors put together'. At least that's what he said. General Film Renters, however, was suffering gigantic losses. The industry was in crisis and in dire need of reorganising.

The system of exhibitors blind- and block-booking films, often that were not even made, saw producers and renters waiting as long as two years for a return on their outlay. Now, during a slump when money was short and box-office takings low, the high prices agreed in advance with the exhibitors was making the business unsustainable. Samuelson doesn't appear to have taken any great part in attempting to change things. He possibly preferred to hold his own council and wait to see how events transpired. Cecil Hepworth had experimented with a scheme based on mutual co-operation that saw Hepworth Picture Plays reaching the public four months after production, moving on to float a public company in order to finance the redevelopment of his Walton-on-Thames studios, but was strongly advised to wait until the economy settled down. He went ahead and in 1922 went public with a capital of £250,000 and failed. Two years later one of the greatest early pioneers of British film watched his business pass into in the hands of the receivers. But Bertie Samuelson survived, keeping his head and his studio.

Malins-Sabatini films started out at Worton Hall as the short-lived Hardy Film Company had begun, a partnership between the Stoll studio manager, Sam Hardy, and novelist Rafael Sabatini, author of *Captain Blood* and *Scaramouche*. Sabatini later teamed up with Geoffrey Malins, the former chief official war cinematographer, to direct a series of his short stories for the Hardy Film Company at Worton Hall. The first picture, *Bluff*, was trade-shown in January 1922 and unanimously acclaimed one of the best pictures of the year according to *The Motion Picture Studio* magazine. The next picture was *The Recoil*, followed by *The Scourge*, a tale of the Great Plague of London, expected to rank as one of the 'big' productions of the day. According to his biography, Malins aroused great interest in the cinema world with his use of hypnotism. 'Used judiciously in the control of his artists', he apparently reached down to the subconscious to obtain 'more vivid results than by any other means'.

Tilly of Bloomsbury continued Samuelson's policy of adapting popular novels and successful stage plays. The film won trade press approval and a comment in *The Times* suggesting that this latest Samuelson film promised 'hopes of better things to come for British screen comedy'. But in order to maintain Worton Hall and to continue film production there without financial backing, Bertie had little choice but to enter into another partnership, which he did in February 1922, with Sir William Jury and William Firth, a director of Jury's Imperial Pictures. Together they formed British-Super Films. Jury had been associated with the British film industry from its very earliest days, both as an equipment supplier and as a film producer and distributor. By 1914, Jury's Imperial Pictures Ltd was one of the largest renter-exhibitors in the United Kingdom, becoming increasingly involved with the distribution and production of British official films. As chairman of the original British Topical Committee for War Films he was listed as the 'sole booking director' for *The Battle of the Somme*. When the Topical Committee was superseded by the War Office Cinema Committee in November 1916, Jury was put in overall charge of film propaganda, much of which he did unpaid, reaping his reward after the war with exclusive distribution rights for many of the films produced and a knighthood, an honour seen as marking the arrival of cinema as a socially acceptable cultural activity. By 1922 he was also a director of Associated First National Pictures and Provincial Cinematograph Theatres, the first national chain of cinemas, with a picture house established in the centre of most British cities.

British-Super Films paid £21,500 for the freehold of Worton Hall, of which £8,000 was paid in cash and £13,500 by the allocation of shares to Samuelson against its own holding of 10,000, giving him the controlling interest. The main advantage of this arrangement was the guarantee of distribution. In his *History of Worton and Worton Hall*, J. S. Hilton has it that when British-Super was floated, extensive additions and alterations were put in hand. Included in this was the Theatre Block, built on additional land between the estate and the Worton Road, known for some obscure reason as The Factory.

Stable Companions was the first British-Super film made at Worton Hall. From an original story by George Samuelson, the script was by Walter Summers, who would go on to direct *Dark Eyes of London*, Britain's first film to receive the legally enforceable version of the adults-only 'H' certificate. Summers had joined Samuelson to get away from Cecil Hepworth's 'novelette-type productions', only to end up with another predictable melodrama, set in the world of horse-racing where a rich man tests his two nephews by faking his death and leaving one of them his stables and the other his money. It was directed by Albert Ward and photographed by Jimmy Rogers, who bravely, or naively, continued filming when the stables were burning down for real. 'I think I must have been mad,' he later told Harold Dunham, 'but I kept my head down and went on turning. I think the spectacular scene hypnotised me. I certainly obtained some fine shots before the more sane members of the crew dragged me and my camera clear. The entire building collapsed before our eyes'. In the same series of interviews with Samuelson's biographer, Harold Dunham, Walter Summers explained how, for race scenes, the jockeys' coats and caps were hand-coloured by three elderly ladies in a Paris garret using magnifying glasses and tiny brushes. Sadly, when projected the colour spilled from the jockeys' coats and caps onto the rest of the screen, spoiling the effect.

Whereas the special effects were arguably more remarkable than the predictable property, G. B. Samuelson was still sufficient a name in the business to attract quality talent. Director Rex Wilson joined Albert Ward together with camcraman Sydney Blythe with scripts by Roland Pertwee. Clive Brook made one of his earliest screen appearances at Worton Hall before establishing himself as the quintessential Englishman, first in British films, then in Hollywood, playing opposite Marlene Dietrich in *Shanghai Express* (1932) and taking on the role of Sherlock Holmes three times. It was Samuelson who brought back with him from Hollywood Peggy Hyland, one of the most popular British actresses of the day. And Lillian Hall-Davis, the daughter of an East End cabbie who went on to become one of the brightest stars of 1920s British cinema, starred in Samuelson's *Brown Sugar* about a sweet, vivacious chorus girl who battles against the prejudice of her contemptuous and aristocratic in-laws.

Waitress Marjorie Vint might have joined the ranks of these Isleworth lovelies but instead ended up as Mrs Bertie Samuelson. It was while she was working at the fashionable Criterion Restaurant in Piccadilly that Miss Vint found herself engaged in conversation with the kindly gent who was dining alone. He struck up a brief conversation before issuing the most hackneyed come-on line in the movie business from a film producer to a pretty girl: 'I could make you a star.' Explaining that she was the only beautiful girl he had come across in England with an American face, he invited her to come along to Worton Hall for a screen test and she agreed. After successfully fooling her mother as to where she was actually going and what she was really up to she made the 'fairly tedious bus journey' to Isleworth and arrived at Worton Hall 'tingling with excitement'. The studios were just what she had dreamed of:

> extras strolling about in beautiful wooded grounds, dressed in period costumes,
> curious plaster, wood and canvas props – the whole mad scene was heaven to

me. Mr Samuelson met me and handed me over to director Alex Butler, who was to do the test. Mr Butler thrust a piece of script into my hand and in a state of nerves I acted my heart out in front of the cold eye of the camera. I was aware of another eye on the edge of the set – Mr Samuelson's as he stood watching. When the test was completed, he strolled over to me, complemented me on my acting and invited me to his office for tea. I felt terribly flattered by all this attention from the great producer himself.

Miss Vint walked alongside him to the mansion, past extras queuing for their day's pay. He ushered her into his office and while waiting for tea, asked her about herself and her ambitions; 'he was very gallant'. She looked around the wood-panelled, sumptuously furnished study and visualised the tea which would come soon ... 'served in delicate Dresden china cups, set upon a heavily ornate silver tray, by a butler, greying at the temples, making no sound as he moved with dignity between us'. But when the tea arrived it was a strong, sweet brew swilling about in two thick white clay mugs that were unceremoniously slammed on the desk by a motley individual declaring 'Ere's your teas, guv!' Her illusions shattered, she saw Bertie socially on a few occasions, meeting up again years later when she was playing in a theatre in Kingston, Surrey, and he was in the audience. Later still, they would marry.

A string of Samuelson films followed; ten had been the number contracted for British-Super Films over the next decade. 'JAEK', a regular contributor to *The Cinema*, wrote on 4 January 1923 that G. B. Samuelson was not, in his opinion, taken with 'sufficient seriousness'. While very different from D. W. Griffith, G. B. Samuelson displayed 'quite an exceptional sense of dramatic power'. His methods were as British as Griffith's were American. 'In the former, the quality of drama is the strongest and in the latter, the quality of showmanship.' But as Harold Dunham observes, with so little of Samuelson's material surviving, such a comparison is academic, if indeed one can be made at all. For these or other reasons, the partnership with Sir William Jury was already fragmenting and Samuelson was negotiating with Sam Woolf Smith about the formation of another company, Napoleon Films.

The disillusionment was mutual and the separation fully expected. The production cost of a feature film before the Great War was between £2,000 and £3,000. It had risen sharply over the past decade, offering British-Super's capital of £50,000 limited production possibilities. The problems associated with blind- and block-bookings had eased by 1922, but there were still a number of issues dogging the success of British films, not least the domination of the market by American films and the pound's adverse exchange rate against the dollar, which acted as a deterrent to American distributors from buying British films. Moreover, foreign films entered Britain on payment of a duty that represented about one thirtieth of the cost of the average British production, which represented a no-brainer to exhibitors. This aside, there remained a serious lack of application to the new medium by good directors, scriptwriters, actors and actresses still rooted to the stage as their legitimate forum. There was also reluctance on the part of the financial institutions to invest. Throughout, Samuelson's films for British-Super were generally well received and distribution was not a problem, but making a profit was. When Jury announced the company's liquidation he remarked that production was the only part of the whole industry where he had not succeeded, adding that 'while not professing to be really qualified to talk on production, he had never put money in the film industry and lost it so easily'.

Bertie Samuelson and Sam Smith formed Napoleon Films on 22 November 1922, taking the name from its first production, *A Royal Divorce*, an epic following the milestones of Napoleon's life. Aimed at distribution in America and Canada, this mighty roller-coaster blockbuster would travel the length and breadth of Europe, following the emperor's progress from the farewell to his Old Guard in the courtyard of Fontainebleau to his return after escaping from Elba; his march to the Berasina and the retreat from Moscow filmed in the Austrian Tyrol. The burning of Moscow was staged at Worton Hall where, according to Walter Summers' publicity brochure, 'the interior settings were the most immense and elaborate that have yet been erected in Britain – the building of Moscow took a small army of artists and carpenters many weeks to complete and deserved a better fate than that which awaited it'.

Despite the lavish production values, however, the film was condemned as being far too long. It also found itself up against some stiff competition during the week of its trade show against Herbert Wilcox's *Paddy the Next Best Thing* and Rex Ingram's *The Prisoner of Zenda*, both rated higher than *A Royal Divorce*. The *Sunday Express*, however, went so far as to suggest that Samuelson's production 'will probably be the most notable photoplay ever made in this country ... the tremendous sweep of the spectacular accomplishments. These really do invest the film with grandeur.' Apart from its length, criticisms largely rested on too many subtitles, excessive use of close-ups and the inclusion of unnecessary and crude comedy. On its release in Canada and America the film was cut in half and played to capacity houses in Boston, Providence and New Bedford as *Napoleon and Josephine*.

Sticking with the spectacular, Samuelson's next production was based on the one-act opera *Pagliacci*, which required a good measure of ingenuity on the part of Walter Summers, who had to invent an entire prequel leading up to the circumstances at the start of the opera. But this was another triumph that fell short of being a masterpiece. Samuelson threw all he could afford at it, including the complex and hugely expensive Prizma colour process, estimated at six times the cost of printing black-and-white film. On release, things were going reasonably well at home and abroad until a legal claim was placed in France by the alleged owner of the opera who maintained that he had never sold the cinematographic and photo-cinematographic rights to anyone. As a result a series of court cases followed, which continued into the 1930s.

From the visually spectacular to the second of Samuelson's controversial social commentaries, *Maisie's Marriage*, an adaptation of Marie Stopes' landmark sexual partnership manual *Married Love*. A best-seller, reprinted six times following its publication in 1918, the book was banned in America (as was the subsequent film) and proved a key moment in film censorship in Britain. The legal basis on which cinemas operated up until 1909 rested on issues of health and safety in cinemas. The following year a court ruling in London determined that a local council could grant or refuse a licence according to the content of a film, effectively introducing censorship. In order to establish its own system of self-regulation, the film industry formed the British Board of Film Censors (BBFC) in 1912 in preference to government legislation. *Maisie's Marriage* outraged the BBFC on the grounds that a book with the glorification of free love as its main theme had been turned into a film. Scarcely had the controversy regarding this Samuelson film died down than an outraged trade press was reporting on the next. *Should a Doctor Tell* is about a home for unmarried mothers. The doctor running it recognises his son's fiancé as a woman he previously treated as an unmarried mother. Where does his first duty lie, with the concept of doctor confidentiality or safeguarding his son? But like many a controversial film seized upon by the press, Samuelson's 'thoroughly modern' social document left many a picture-goer wondering what all the fuss was about.

Picture Studio reported on 20 October 1923 that the Commonwealth Film Corporation was working on a feature film at Worton hall called *The Money Habit* and that G. B. Samuelson was gainfully employed at Ealing. Doubtless he was sensing the day when the full ignominy of his reduced situation would be complete, with the landing of the auctioneer's hammer on his dream factory. For when British-Super was placed in the hands of the liquidators on 3 August, Bertie was required to quit the studio he had created. The film historian, Rachel Low, states that Samuelson was virtually finished by this time. While she recognises that there are others who would disagree with her, she believes that his demise lay in the record of his productions. Instead of choosing less famous books with fairly simple plots to adapt, carefully managed so as to fit in with his own concept of a film story, his productions lacked a consistent character; a legacy that would haunt Worton Hall as a studio for the rest of its days. Samuelson was certainly struggling like every other major producer and studio but he was by no means finished.

On Wednesday 16 January 1924, Worton Hall was put up for auction by the firm of Harris and Gillow, the London-based theatrical and cinema property agents. Included as one lot was the mansion and the stabling, which had been used as a carpenters' shop and stores. The studio included the various outbuildings, among them two scene docks, the property and dressing rooms and what were still referred to as the Daylight Studio (100 feet by 35 feet) and the Dark Studio (93 feet by 45 feet). The film printing labs came fully equipped and there was a large quantity of sets and a well-stocked wardrobe. The grounds were described as timbered with cedars, acacias and elms, interspersed with herbaceous borders and winding walks; the whole area comprising 6½ acres. Not included in the property for auction was the electric generating and storage plant, which belonged to the General Electric Company, but could be included in the sale for £3,820.

Bertie was abroad shooting *The Unwanted*, an original script by Walter Summers based on an idea by Samuelson about a man with one legitimate and one illegitimate son. Come the war and the former is commissioned but fails to come up to the mark, the latter makes for a good sergeant. Some scenes had been shot in Canada, following on from another trip to America where Bertie had married Marjorie Vint – three times; he being Jewish and she a gentile that required a ceremony at the British embassy under US law. He chose to shoot the interiors for *The Unwanted* at Worton Hall, which he had filed to sell at auction.

Who is the Man? was the last production under the Napoleon Film banner. Adapted for the screen by Walter Summers, who described it as 'feeble', 'uncinematic' and 'poor', it was made cheaply with the minimum of sets and few exteriors. For the key part of Daniel, the title of the stage play from which the scenario was derived, Samuelson secured the services of one of the theatre's most promising young stars, John Gielgud. 'I was fascinated and horrified by my acting,' he later recalled, 'fascinated because seeing one's own back and profile is an interesting experience usually limited to one's visits to the tailor, horrified at the vulturine grimaces on my face and the violent and affected mannerisms of my walk and gestures.' The esteemed Shakespearean actor, whose obituary sadly hung in several tabloids as the butler to Dudley Moore in the *Arthur* films of the 1980s, detested the process of film-making; the lengthy process of make-up, the erratic work schedule spent on a set littered with the technical impedimenta of a film studio, the retakes and the playing of an emotional scene with an actress who is not even there.

The steadfast Walter Summers was on holiday when he discovered that Napoleon Films was finishing, 'which was cowardly, of course', he later bemoaned, claiming he bore no bitterness as he stoically transferred his skills to Stoll. It's not known why Samuelson and Smith decided to fold the company, but it's likely that it was as a result of financial commitments arising from the production earlier in the year of *She*; the fantasy adventure about three explorers who discover a hidden city ruled by the beautiful and apparently ageless Queen Ayesha, or 'She who must be obeyed'. Worton Hall is sometimes credited as the production studio for this first screen adaptation of the Rider Haggard novel, but according to correspondence held by Samuelson's son, David, the Europäische Film Allianz (EFA) provided the studio facilities in Berlin together with all manual labour and materials. For his part in the co-operative venture, Samuelson provided the artists, technicians, film stock and laboratory charges under the banner of Reciprocity Films, founded to market the film. Samuelson and Summers co-wrote the scenario, deploying Haggard to write the inter-titles. *She* was declared one of Samuelson's greatest films by the ever-loyal *The Bioscope*, while Rachel Low describes the result as 'phoney, cheap-looking and poorly acted'.

Before his death in 1974, Walter Summers gave Harold Dunham an ample account of Bertie Samuelson, including the often chaotic nature of his business and how he conducted it. That he loved film and devoted himself to the business of it was clear. That he loved equally the great sums of money that could be made from the medium was likewise transparent. And it appears that Samuelson was not best served by the people around him, especially those whom Summers unashamedly describes as coming from 'the lower orders', regarding himself as the first 'educated person' employed by Samuelson. All others took advantage of the 'simple, unworldly, good-natured' producer who had 'too little book and practical knowledge to guide him, and he needed guidance'. Summers maintains that Bertie found it difficult to stand up to people. Sam Smith, by way of an example, was not particularly supportive, effectively ruling Napoleon Films and overseeing its demise. While claiming to harbour no bitterness over his sudden severance from the company in absentia Summers is, however, somewhat overenthusiastic in his negative assessment of his old boss, as is Dunham in Samuelson's defence. But Summers' flat assumption that Samuelson's part in creating a British film industry was 'virtually nil' is patently ill-met and without foundation.

Another financial brickbat from the ill-fated *She* was the protracted legal action taken by Samuelson's American star, Betty Blythe, who was claiming non-payment of her salary. This turned into a long-running high-court melodrama worthy of a Samuelson feature, which he eventually survived with his name intact but crippled by heavy legal expenses. He threw himself into *Milestone Melodies*, a set of twelve one-reelers, each featuring a well-known song of yore, and *Twisted Tales*, a series of one-reel original stories that was first begun at Worton Hall then shifted to Bushey in Hertfordshire with Britannia Films before returning to Isleworth for a third series. Finances took another serious tumble when a laboratory error ruined his next feature, *If Youth But Knew*, resulting in G. B. Samuelson Films being wound up a year later. Diagnosed with diabetes, various accusations have been thrown at Samuelson for being guilty of 'less successful production', 'wrong development', 'unforeseen expenses' and that his method of production was 'old-fashioned'. Not that any of this appears to have shaken him or his many admirers. *The Bioscope* published a cartoon showing him dressed as Napoleon standing before a globe of the film world with a caption explaining that someone had once told him that his initials (G. B. S.) stood for Get Busy Sam, 'and he has taken it to heart ever since'.

Following a second abortive attempt to sell the Worton Hall estate in October 1924, it was eventually purchased in December for an undisclosed sum by a company calling itself Worton Hall Estates Ltd, which then set about hiring the studio out to various production companies. Rex Wilson began production there in October 1925 with Albert Ward, both ex-Samuelson employees. Then, at the beginning of March 1926, they were joined by another Worton Hall returnee, Geoffrey Malins, who was starting work on a boxing series for H. B. Parkinson. The first was entitled *The Chicken Game*, featuring 'Bombardier' Billy Wells, the English heavyweight boxer who was British and British Empire champion from 1911 until 1919, defending his title fourteen times.

The First World War had taken its terrible toll on British film-making as it did on every industry. The loss of actors and technicians was further exacerbated by the introduction of the Amusement Tax, which created huge losses at the box office while at the same time allowing American films to flood the market. By 1924, nearly every British studio had closed or was struggling to survive. The Cinematograph Films Act of 1927 aimed to stimulate British film production. The Act obliged American distribution companies to fund a percentage of British films in order to continue with their own Hollywood productions, thus creating a guaranteed market for home-grown films. This saw a rush of speculators eager to hand over wads of cash to film companies looking to make fast returns from what was seen as a potentially large and lucrative market. The Quota Act of 1927, as it was known, limited foreign films to 22.5 per cent of the British market, but brought about unforeseen problems for British film striving for quality. For others it was a golden opportunity to fill limited screen time with speedily produced films made on shoestring budgets that became known as 'Quota Quickies', a slur that later, and better, British quota films fought hard to shake off.

The usual budget for these assembly-line productions was determined solely on length, based on a fixed charge of £1 per foot of screened film. Their average length was between five and six thousand feet, enough for an hour of screen time, sufficient for the Quota. The average cost of a silent feature was around £10,000 with no profit until the bookings had doubled those costs, taking into account the renter's fees, release print costs, publicity, trade shows, and other expenses. If lucky, a studio might have struck a deal with an American distribution company that enabled it to maintain a regular output with an occasional venture of a more ambitious nature. Most studios, however, abandoned any idea of producing art. In accepting the work, cast and crew had to conform to the prevailing conditions, with only the fittest and most capable surviving such a harsh and feverish environment in the twenty or so film production facilities in and around London at this time, each teetering on the edge of disaster from one year to the next.

Gone were the days of purchasing the rights to a published novel. Ideas were now drawn from the piles of stories submitted to film companies by would-be writers bought for a fraction of the price more than a decade before. A week or two's work by the director and dialogue writer (if the budget stretched to it) and the narrative sequence of scenes with their content would be described in detail, with each scene timed to determine the exact length of the film. The setting of the picture and whatever scenery was available had a bearing on the costs, so the fewer sets the better. Dialogue could be lengthened or shortened, depending on what was available to work with. The stage floor was never idle. Only by its constant use could a studio make any profit. This meant round-the-clock filming. As one production finished shooting for the day, so another took over for the night. A degree of quality was maintained in some of these low-budget productions thanks to the similar rigours of 'Weekly Rep', where as soon as one play finished so its set was struck and the next in the series erected as the cast rehearsed another play in the season's repertoire cycle.

In 1928 British Screen Productions purchased Worton Hall for £19,000. Curiously, its managing director was man called George W. Pearson, not Samuelson's old contemporary but the former general manager of British Screen Classics, distributors of the *Empire News Bulletin*. With George A. Cooper as producer and supervisor and Frank Miller as director, the company debuted with *Twenty Years Ago*, an odd satirical compilation of topical pictures shot between 1896 and 1928 that were arranged, collected and edited by Ben R. Hart in association with St John Legh Clowes. Far more dramatic and entertaining was the 'thrilling and unrehearsed incident' reported in the pages of the *Daily Express*. A scene was being shot in which three young lions were to be seen making their escape in an English village street. The butcher's shop was hung with great lumps of horseflesh to tempt the lions from their strong steel cage, which stood in the main studio behind plate-glass walls that opened onto the village street. As an extra safeguard, a 15-foot-high wooden palisade was built round the entire set and joining the outer walls of the studio.

The lion-tamer, Mr Giese, and his wife were at first unable to lure the lions from their cage. Women from the film company and other female visitors stood patiently waiting for the action. Then one lion snarled his way round the end of the village street. The two others followed him, creeping with bent legs as though about to spring. The tamer walked in a leisurely manner towards the beasts, cracking his whip the once. One of the lions then leapt onto the butcher's shop and tore at the meat on the hooks, while the others flung themselves at the glass studio windows. The scene so far had gone according to plan until it became obvious that the lions were becoming bored. Suddenly they disobeyed all calls from the trainer, dashing instead through the street-scene, the largest of the three animals hurling himself with a leap of more than 12 feet through a pane of glass. The other two, after rushing wildly around the palisade looking for a way out, bolted back through the entrance to their cage, where attendants locked them in.

The tamer was nowhere to be seen. A scream came from the building. 'My husband! He's got him!' It was Madame Giese, 'snatching at her long-thronged whip'. There was a mad rush by the women observers for the studio doors, which were closed. They then made for the safety of the offices as doors to the side of the studio were barricaded with baulks of timber. Then the tamer reappeared unharmed, clutching a strong rope net and gingerly making his way back into a studio echoing with the angry growls of the escaped lion. Nothing could be done but to leave the tamer to deal with the situation. Entering the studio and fearlessly approaching the crouching animal, he flung the net over it and left it to thrash about until it became entangled in the mesh, knocking over Mr Giese in the process, who managed to save himself by rolling to safety.

British Screen Productions produced nine comedy and romantic films at Worton Hall, featuring a regular ensemble of light entertainers including Jackie Ray, John Common, Pug Podger, June Potts and Happy Robertson among others whose jaunty names have since become as unfamiliar as the productions in which they appeared. Rachel Low sets out what she calls a 'disagreeable example' shown by the group of companies associated with G. W. Pearson and his accomplice George Banfield, accusing both of looking to the new quota law as their big opportunity. Banfield had acquired Walthamstow Studios from Walter West in 1927 and formed British Filmcraft Productions. Pearson formed British Screen Productions and purchased Worton Hall as the coming of sound presented difficulties for both companies. Requiring a creative approach to financing beyond the studio floor, Pearson launched an £850,000 scheme in 1929 to raise finance whereby the public applied for only 3 per cent of the shares and the underwriters repudiated the rest. 'It looks like a ramp,' said Mr Justice Eve at the subsequent legal hearing, describing the move to increase operations in anticipation of increased demand. Undaunted, Pearson launched a new scheme in the spring of 1930 that drew a furious response from shareholders, which led to the company being dissolved. The pair amalgamated various remaining companies under the name of Audible Filmcraft, only for more legal and financial difficulties to see this company crash in the summer of 1932.

Worton Hall then took on a new lease of life courtesy of Fidelity Films, a company financed mainly by Duncan Stuart MacDonald, whose sound technicians came from British Talking Pictures at Wembley where they had developed a non-royalty sound system invented by a Captain Ryan called 'Fidelytone', which required a camera operator and a sound recordist. MacDonald took a lease on Worton Hall and started business as a service studio and manufacturer of his sound recording equipment, selling a number of fully equipped vans to India and to Spain. Fidelity eventually moved on to the Blattner Studio at Borehamwood in a tie-up with the Ludwig Blattner Picture Corporation. Meanwhile, another new company eager to pick up on the expected production frenzy created by the quota system had opened for business at a small studio in Beaconsfield, north-west of London. It was co-founded by Sam Smith and the prolific crime writer, Edgar Wallace, who had recently been successfully transferring his crime stories to the stage. Wallace was made chairman, Smith managing director. The company's first production was a silent adaptation of Wallace's *The Forger*, directed by Smith's former partner, one George Berthold Samuelson. The company was called the British Lion Film Corporation, a name that would in later years become synonymous with Worton Hall.

4

The Last Word in Talkie Studios

It's one of those things. When asked, most people with an interest in the cinema will reply without hesitation that the first sound picture was *The Jazz Singer*, the part-sound, part-silent motion picture that arrived on these shores from America in 1927. Much debated as the first British part-sound feature is Alfred Hitchcock's *Blackmail*, made for British International Pictures at Elstree in 1929. *A Cottage on Dartmoor* made the same year is another contender. Shot at the British Instructional Films studio in Welwyn, Hertfordshire, it was a silent film to which some music and dialogue was added by the Klangfilm Company in Germany. But it is *The Clue of the New Pin*, made in March 1929 that film historians now tend to agree was Britain's first all-talking feature. It was made at their Beaconsfield studios by British Lion.

Hounslow Heath, a mile or so from Worton Hall, was meanwhile increasingly introducing west Middlesex to the novelty of air traffic. Up until 1919 this surviving expanse of ancient heathland was used as a training area and military airport for the British Flying Corps. Later it gave way to the Hounslow Aerodrome, where the first international passenger flights connected London and Paris. And it was while making *Edge o' Beyond* that Bertie Samuelson used this wild landscape to represent the South African veldt where Ruby Miller and Charlie Hallard were required to play a love scene on horseback. 'It took almost two days,' Miller recalls. 'Every time we drew near to each other and Charlie leaned over to kiss me, a plane would roar overhead, the horses would shy and we had to start again.' In common with all the other British studios, and even some in Hollywood, the managers of Worton Hall were now faced with the need to arrange the complicated marriage of sound and film, which would eventually include soundproofing the stages against an increasingly noisy modern world.

In May 1929, British Screen Productions, with American and German help, formed International Screen Productions with a view to making sound films in five languages. A year later and a further merger with Argosy Films resulted in the formation of Audible Filmcraft Ltd, which then went on to purchase the former British Filmcraft studio in Walthamstow Studios and Whitehall Studios at Elstree, with an option of using Worton Hall for sixteen weeks in the year. It was where Fidelity Films had installed their own sound system, making it one of the best equipped of the smaller studios, and where a reporter from the *Middlesex Independent* came to visit. The 'happy family' at the Isleworth 'country club' were busy filming *Downstream* with Chili Bouchier, Britain's first sex siren, who had entered the British film industry in 1927 at the age of seventeen and who went on to become the country's own Clara Bow, known as the 'It' Girl. In her memoirs, Bouchier cites *Downstream* as a silent film and yet the newspaper clipping she kept as a memento has the newspaper reporter enjoying 'a strange sense of peace about the place that is in direct contrast with the usual turmoil that reigns in most film studios'. Preparations for the 'talkies' were underway, leaving the reporter to make sure that he wore a pair of rubber soles on his next visit 'because ordinary shoes do make a lot of noise, and noise is unforgivable at Worton Hall. If a carpenter drops his hammer, I am sure that he will be given notice!'

Notice was dramatically given to British Sound Films after its two Wembley stages were destroyed by fire and production on *Dark Red Roses* switched to Worton Hall. British Sound was a company formed to develop sound films, having converted the Lucullus Garden Club, part of the British Empire Exhibition, into a film studio. Starring the hugely popular screen actor Stewart Rome as a sculptor who becomes jealous when his wife (played by Frances Doble) comes to admire a young cellist, *Dark Red Roses* was directed by Sinclair Hill and recorded under the British Talking Pictures Phonofilm process. One scene, a Russian ballet sequence, was shot out of doors at night 'under the spreading cedar tree in the grounds of Worton Hall'.

London Melody was the first full-length talking picture made at Worton Hall. A musical co-written by Donald Stuart and Geoffrey H. Malins, who also directed, it starred Lorraine La Fosse, Haddon Mason, and Betty

Naismith and was distributed by Audible Filmcraft. Shot in November 1929, *London Melody* was also the last British Screen production before the company ceased trading in 1930. Rachael Low condemns its output as 'a handful of inferior silent films', but makes no mention of its pioneering the talking picture at Worton Hall. British Screen Productions had been heavily criticised by its shareholders on the issue of sound conversion, which the directors believed would double the studio's value. But the entire process of working in this new and complex environment represented a complete sea change for everyone. Even a simple two-shot of Lorraine La Fosse and Haddon Mason was no longer a matter of positioning the duo suitably lit before an appropriate backdrop and turning the camera. Before the advent of the 'boom operator' holding a suspended microphone on a long pole above the heads of the actors, capturing voices and the accompanying orchestra, microphones were strategically placed as close as possible to the source of the sound. Scenes shot on location had the dialogue recorded later and synchronised with the actor's lip movements, a hugely difficult and tedious process in the early years. It wouldn't be until 1933 that music could be added separately to a film soundtrack after the editing had taken place. Until then music and speech had to be recorded simultaneously.

Directors of silent films mostly only ever considered multi-camera shooting for big action stunts that could not easily be repeated. But now with the arrival of sound, two or three cameras would be the norm for even the simplest of scenes. The actual business of recording the sound was reasonably straightforward insofar as whatever was picked up by the microphone was sent by a wire to the disc-cutting equipment where the recording was made. In the days before directional microphones, the noisy cameras were muffled inside large boxes on wheels, covered in heavy blankets and known as 'blimps'. With a door at one end and a small window at the other through which the camera lens poked out, the camera operator was placed inside this confined space, made all the more unbearable by the heat from the studio.

The lighting for Malins' simple duet also required tweaking. On a silent film, close-ups were lit separately and with care to create artistic facial shadows and romantic backgrounds. But with the whole scene shot in one go it was now difficult to place spot lamps for close-ups behind or beside the actors and not be visible to one or more camera. As the cameraman had to light for more than one camera, so a new technician entered the payroll, the director of photography, an experienced cameraman who could separately supervise the lighting crew. The actors, too, were greatly affected by this new technology. Not just those whose voices failed to match their screen image, but the lack of direction during a take. Now they had to motivate themselves and not rely on a third party talking them through the action and telling them how they should react. They needed to deliver their lines with unnatural precision to accommodate the crude sound recording technology. This transitional period was relatively brief, no more than a couple of years, but enough to put the whole of the industry into disarray.

The advent of sound had the added effect of impeding foreign distribution where the received language was not English. European governments responded by establishing trade barriers to protect their own domestic film industries, which resulted in the 'Quota Quickie' debacle. Prior to 1930, foreign markets for American films generated around 40 per cent of a picture's worldwide gross. Of that, almost half came from English-speaking countries, mainly Great Britain. During the Depression foreign revenue halved and while the Europeans looked to rebuild their shattered nations, Hollywood producers capitalised on all-year-round weather and a huge domestic market enjoying a high standard of living. Hollywood producers controlled domestic distribution, leaving their European counterparts unable to compete. Moreover, American distributors used subtitling and foreign-language versions. Paramount established a studio outside Paris to produce versions of its films in French, German and Italian. Dubbing soon became accepted practice, but led to claims of unfair competition, and so France and Germany passed laws barring films dubbed outside their borders, which led to American film companies constructing dubbing studios in each of these countries. Not only were dubbed releases cheaper to produce than foreign-language versions, but they also retained the commercial value of the Hollywood stars. The combination of these factors restored foreign distribution to its former profit levels.

By 1930 the number of films entering Britain from Hollywood had increased, with United Artists looking to strike a balance with more British pictures. In October of that year Audible Filmcraft purchased its own recording equipment from Vienna for the purpose of adding sound to *British Screen News* and *Tatler* newsreels. At the same time, United Artists were looking to organise a production schedule of six low-budget Quota Quickies in Britain for the summer of 1931. Worton Hall and Walton-on-Thames were chosen. The American chairman and managing director of United Artists, Murray Silverstone, was joined in October 1930 by Captain the Hon. Richard Norton, later Lord Grantley, a former officer in the Brigade of Guards. Complete with requisite monocle and permanent stoop as a result of a war injury, Norton was an aristocrat with the very highest connections. Rachel Low describes him as 'gay, witty and influential'. Maintaining a high-society lifestyle and working largely behind the scenes in the film industry, his name is more associated with Pinewood studios than Isleworth. The six United Artists films made at Isleworth and Walton cost between £3,000 and £7,000, an indication as to their dubious quality. Norton felt that a few had 'some box office value' and others were 'disappointing', an adjective sadly emblematic of the product typically associated with Worton Hall at this time, Reginald Fogwell Productions being a prime example.

Unsubstantiated information circulating on the internet has it that Reginald George Fogwell was the son of actor/director Francis Ford, the brother of the legendary American director, John Ford. This would-be impressive lineage to one side, Fogwell was a reasonably prolific film-maker, having worked at Ealing, Walton and Elstree before coming to Isleworth where worked with some of the most respected screen talents of the day including Madeleine Carroll, one of the first English leading ladies to carve a career in Hollywood. *The Written Law* was Fogwell's first film made at Worton Hall in 1931 and starred Carroll alongside Percy Marmont in a drama about a Devon doctor cured of blindness, but with reasons to conceal his renewed sight from his wife. Next was *Madame Guillotine*, a romance that takes place during the French Revolution that also starred Madeleine Carroll alongside Brian Aherne, a notable actor of stage and screen who also later found success in Hollywood. The pair then appeared in *Guilt*, starring James Carew as a playwright whose wife, played by Anne Grey, conducts an affair with an actor under the pretence that it is part of the play.

Betrayal, released in 1932, saw the return of Stewart Rome to Isleworth in a drama about a girl who marries him for money and who saves him when he is tried for shooting her lover. Released the same year was *The Temperance Fête*, the last Reginald Fogwell production at Worton Hall. A comedy starring the legendary George Robey as a work-shy Cockney who laces the lemonade at a temperance fête, this versatile artist had made his first appearance on the music hall stage in June 1891 with his saucy country parson character with big black eyebrows. Robey became known as 'The Prime Minister of Mirth' and made his first film appearance in 1916 in several shorts before playing more substantial roles, primarily for Stoll in the twenties. With a long career and popularity that would spill over into the television era, he was eventually created a knight in 1954.

Sharing the facilities with Fogwell at Worton Hall were Macnamara Productions and New Era National Pictures Ltd. The former was responsible for *Birds of a Feather*, a drama about a painter's daughter (Dorothy Bartlam) who falls for a young artist with a dubious reputation, and the latter *Q Ships*, which was re-released as *Blockade* in 1932 as a semi-documentary set around the attempts to combat the unrestricted activity of German U-boats in World War One by using armed merchant vessels as bait for the stalking menace. The film intercuts with some obvious model shots (created by Edward Rogers); an area of expertise that would soon become something of a speciality at Isleworth. After *Q Ships*, New Era then embarked on a series of films directed by a once formidable figure in the industry only now emerging from a string of personal disasters and just plain bad luck that had reduced him to little more than a perceived liability, and worse, one who attracted bad luck.

Forced into personal bankruptcy and rapidly removed from the mainstream of film-making, George Berthold Samuelson returned to the 'directorial fold', as *Kine-Weekly* put it, with *Jealousy*, starring Gibb McLaughlin, Malcolm Keen and Mary Newland, about a guardian madly in love with his ward who skilfully stages a robbery to discredit the girl's sweetheart. Recorded on the Fidelytone sound system, *The Cinema* reported that 20,000 feet of film had been shot without a single retake required, reflecting the Samuelson approach to the school of no-budget film-making. If he shot 50,000 feet of film at a cost of £1 a foot, which after cutting and editing was reduced to 6,000 feet, then the cost of the production would be about £8 a foot or £7 added to the budget. This to Bertie Samuelson represented poor supervision and inadequate preparation. He had learned the hard way as an independent producer to shoot fast and within a small budget and not to shoot film that would never be used.

Part of Samuelson's deal with New Era was for a series idea conceived as a means of raising capital. Entitled *Spotting*, twelve short features were produced, each on a lavish scale and each including a number of deliberate mistakes to be spotted by members of the audience lured by the promise of a major prize. *A Touching Story*, for example, was set in the mid-nineteenth century and included the use of a petrol lighter, a current banknote and a picture of the present Prince of Wales. With Lord Askwith, Field Marshal Lord Milne and the Marchioness Townshend of Raynham appointed as adjudicators, it would cost cinema-goers sixpence to enter the competition, which would raise something in the region of £300,000 if just 5 per cent of the audience took part over the run of the series. Equal shares of the revenue would go to the Cinematograph Trade Benevolent Fund, the British Charities Association and to New Era as the organisers. Of the total prize money of £100,000, there was to be a sliding scale of lucky recipients ranging from top prizes of £10,000 to consolation prizes of £100, as well as additional cash prizes for each for each individual film. Despite these massively attractive sums, a total outlay of six shillings proved too rich for the average cinema-goer and the scheme folded. Two years later and New Era followed suit.

The company's financial situation was tenuous from the start, and with no money to produce on a large scale, it looked to Samuelson to produce cheaply made quota films for the American distributors. United Artists and Warners had to fulfil their annual quota and only a producer with the depth of experience such as Samuelson could approach them with a script, a cast and a director (himself) for a film ready to shoot. Coming away with a deal for 30 shillings a foot, he would make the film for half that, resulting in a profit of £1,750 on a seven-reel 'pound-a-footer' feature. The more economically he shot, the greater the profit, which enabled him to assemble stronger casts and better technicians, resulting in better pictures. Dallas Bower was in charge of sound at Cricklewood Studios at the time and was loaned to Worton Hall to work on four Samuelson quickies. She remembered Bertie doing anything from six to seven minutes of screen time with complete cover in a day. At this speed, cameramen and sound recordists especially had to be on their toes, with no room for technical errors. The lab had to prepare duplicate negatives should one become damaged. Samuelson knew exactly what he wanted, never allowing for a shooting ratio of more than 3:1, compared to the 'safe' ratio of as much as 15:1. He supervised his own editing, rehearsed efficiently, never turning the camera on a scene before he was sure that every element was ready. In keeping with his other quickies, *Jealousy* was shot in just over a week. Normal starting time was 8.30 a.m., finishing often after midnight – and without overtime payments.

The Bioscope found the film 'gripping'. *The Cinema* declared it to be 'above the quality usually associated with quota films'. *Kine-Weekly* credited Samuelson with 'many fine points of production'. His second film, *The Wickham Mystery*, was also positively received. The tale of a crook who steals pearls and a plan for a helicopter boasted a strong cast, including Lester Matthews, Eve Gray and Sam Livesey and location shooting in Cornwall, all in one week. *Inquest* also found favour with the trade reviewers. Starring Mary Glynne and Campbell Gullan, this was a crime thriller where a biased coroner suspects a widow of poisoning her husband and where the town and country settings were provided by the mansion at Worton Hall and its gradually disappearing environs. *Collision* was the last film Samuelson made for New Era at Isleworth before moving with the company to Cricklewood. He'd purchased the film rights to the stage play for £250, which gave him sole rights of production, adaptation, distribution, exploitation and publicity; subject to a provision in the contract that the film should be no shorter than 5,000 feet and that it should be made 'of the highest class'. Falling short of that, however, *The Cinema* felt that the 'alleged France in the earliest scenes' failed to achieve 'the fullest conviction'. The other trade papers essentially followed *Kine-Weekly*'s assessment of a largely 'slow, listless, unimaginative' production where a 'welter of words' lessened the dramatic possibilities of the lurid melodrama, 'the theme of which has some claim to originality'. On the technical side, Samuelson continued to display his constant striving for innovation by replacing the studio's Fidelytone sound system with Marconi's revolutionary Visatone that printed sound on film; a method soon to become the industry standard. This Bertie achieved by means of hiring a location van from Stoll's at Cricklewood to create a mobile sound suite at Worton Hall; something that had never been done before.

It must have been a melancholy experience for Bertie Samuelson as he clocked off after completion at the old dream factory he had created and nurtured and where he was now an employee. He no longer enjoyed the luxury of his own car, let alone a chauffeur. Instead, he would rely on a friend called Jock to give him a lift to and from Hendon, where he was living at the time. Worton Hall was now just another workplace, another studio close to the capital, doing what it could to survive in the harsh economic environment of the Great Depression, a time when putting bread on the table was for millions more important than going to the pictures. And yet that's the curious thing, films were among the rare beneficiaries of the economic slump. After 1929 when the bottom fell out of the global economy, bankrupting millions of people and prompting mass unemployment and years of hardship, cinema entered a golden age wherein the advent of talking pictures re-energised the medium. People desperate for some form of diversion began flocking to the picture houses in unprecedented numbers to lose themselves in the company of others enjoying a double bill and a newsreel for the price of a packet of cigarettes. And this is where the Americans came up trumps.

Most British output was light entertainment and romantic fare, whereas a new mood of gritty cynicism was coming out of Hollywood that matched the bleakness of the times. As well as the overly elaborate Busby Berkeley dance-based extravaganzas, there was James Cagney and Edward G. Robinson honing in on the social realism of the times played out by anti-heroes determined to get the better of those in control. Comedies too could be sardonic and angry, with the Marx Brothers attacking all that the world hitherto held sacred. Even so, the Hollywood studios were ramping up enormous debts and by 1933, as the Depression's grip tightened and mass unemployment took hold of America, cinema attendance began to fall along with the studios' revenues. British studios and producers, meanwhile, continued to face exactly the same economic constraints but with the added competition from over the pond.

It would have taken great courage for any sane, business-minded person at this time to look at the sale catalogue for a very tired and dated film studio in Isleworth and to consider spending the considerable sum required in not just bringing it up to standard, but worthy of competing with Hollywood itself. Such an individual was film importer Edward Gourdeau, who, in 1933, bought Worton Hall through his father-in-law, J. W. Almond, whose sons George and Arthur worked at the studio. In an interview with David Blake in 2004, former studio accountant Archie Holly believed that the studios were bought from the liquidator and that Almond, as well as being an 'importer and exporter of old films in a smallish way', was actually a bookie. 'He wasn't much of an exporter because there wasn't much to export,' explained Holly, 'but he imported independent films and sold them. I don't know if he sold them lock, stock and barrel – he was an agent and he sold to the other distributors'.

In January 1934 the local authority was considering plans submitted by Almond for 'a studio' at Worton Hall. Just as it was in Samuelson's day when the studio first opened, these plans were subject to approval on condition that the proposed buildings did not stand for more than five years. Come April, more studio plans were submitted under the name of Almond and Gourdeau's company, Interworld Films Ltd, and a month after that more plans were submitted by A. J. Cripps & Co. Ltd, a local construction company specialising in steel-framed buildings, for an engine house, a workshop and machine shop. On 8 June all of these plans were approved, including a boiler house and lobby, a mill and additions to the dressing room block. And then in August 1934 Interworld Films was made a licensee of Western Electric, the proprietors of the sound system that had by now become the industry standard.

Warner Brothers and First National had made the change from sound-on-disc to sound-on-film recording by 1931, but for years to come Vitaphone's dominance in cinemas meant dual versions of films were made and distributed using both processes. The future lay clearly in the sound-on-film method where projectors could read an optical soundtrack laid out on the edge of the film strip created when the film was shot. RCA Photophone and Western Electric were the two major American systems seeking to resolve a complex patent dispute involving an Austrian challenge. In May 1930, Western Electric won an important lawsuit that brought about an agreement on cross-licensing and full playback compatibility. Between 1932 and 1935 Western Electric and RCA created directional microphones, which increased the frequency range of film recording and reduced extraneous noise. New casings suppressed camera noise, boom microphones hovering just out of frame allowed the actors to move, and noisy arc lights gave way to quiet incandescent illumination, which in turn required more expensive film stock, giving directors the freedom to shoot scenes at lower light levels.

In the British trade papers, Mr R. M. Hatfield, managing director of Western Electric Ltd, announced that as soon as the installation of the new recording equipment at Worton Hall was complete, the studios would be available for use on a service basis to producers wanting to use Western Electric equipment. Edward Gourdeau explained in the trade press that he had built two entirely new modern production stages, the larger of which was approximately 130 feet by 45 feet, and in addition, one of the existing stages, measuring 100 feet by 75 feet, had already been completely renovated and modernised. Facilities available consisted of these two large stages and one 'smart' production stage, all of which were intercommunicating, with up-to-date cutting, reviewing, dubbing, scoring and re-recording facilities. The new dressing room building now comprised over forty rooms, which were centrally heated with hot and cold running water and all modern conveniences. In addition there were a number of new executive offices for the convenience of producers and incoming tenants. Gourdeau reiterated that the new studios were intended primarily for operation on a service basis and it was not the intention of his own company to go into production 'on any considerable scale', adding that Interworld Films Ltd had already received several preliminary enquiries for production facilities.

A local newspaper reporter who was invited to look around described Worton Hall not only as 'the last word in talkie studios' but one that boasted 'England's biggest film stage', which was somewhat misleading. The facility for shooting from one stage to another gave a total floor space of 25,000 square feet, whereas Sound City's six stages at Shepperton could also be united to offer a much greater total shooting area. The two new studios at Worton Hall occupied much of the former kitchen garden and together abutted the rear of the old 'Dark' studio, now remodelled and fitted. Samuelson's original glass, or 'Light' studio was now replaced with a production and administration block. The reported £100,000 enterprise was a hive of industry on the August Wednesday afternoon when the *Middlesex Chronicle*'s representative called by. A team of workers were hauling from a lorry one of the two 550 hp Ruston Hornsby Diesel engines used to drive two 325 kilowatt generators capable of providing 10,000 amps; mighty replacements for the old traction-driven unit. And dozens of other workmen were hard at work soundproofing the interior of the main studio roof-space, designed to accommodate 50 tons of lighting equipment and scenery.

Within the former 'Dark' studio, the newspaperman found Harry Hughes busy directing *The Broken Rosary*, a musical about an Italian opera singer who altruistically loses his sweetheart to a best friend. Singer and actor Derek Oldham, best known for his tenor roles with the D'Oyly Carte Opera Company, was playing the part of the singer, Giovanni. And appearing as herself was the celebrated Vesta Victoria, the Yorkshire music hall singer and comedienne who adopted a Cockney persona on stage touring America in 1907, where she became one of the most highly paid stars of vaudeville. *The Broken Rosary* was made under the banner of Butcher's Film Service, originally a rental and equipment company that first went into production in 1909. Hughes clearly decided that he liked the new facilities at Worton Hall, moving on to establish the City Film Foundation there with Basil Humphreys in 1934, producing what Rachel Low describes as indifferent light entertainment quota films.

Harry Hughes started his film career making modest quota quickies but was being given more prestigious assignments with British International Pictures at Elstree before regressing to Isleworth. Basil Humphries was producing *Money Mad* for Champion Productions, the tale of a government official who attempts to prevent a financier from inflating the value of the pound. The film starred the American actress, Virginia Cherrill, best known as the blind flower-girl in Charlie Chaplin's *City Lights* and who went on to marry Cary Grant when finishing filming at Isleworth. The Hughes and Humphries partnership lasted less than year at Worton Hall before moving on to make films at Nettlefold, Walton-on-Thames, Ealing and Sound City studios in subsequent years.

Before wandering through the old mansion, the newly created artistes' green room and the modern restaurant, the *Chronicle* representative came across the man 'in charge of the camera' who happened to be the brother of Len Harvey, the British champion middleweight, light-heavy and heavyweight boxer. The camera equipment was in keeping with 'the most modern and completely equipped studio in the country'. Edward Gourdeau had purchased the studio's first Vinten camera in November 1933, a Fade Model 'H' No. 19, more often sold abroad where the unique in-camera fade feature was more popular with cameramen who preferred its use over chemical or optical fades.

In October, a second reporter from the *Middlesex Chronicle* was lured back to Worton Hall by talk of its becoming 'the biggest studio in the world'. The question on everyone's lips (at least within a stone's throw of the facility) was whether Isleworth was destined to become 'the Hollywood of Britain'. The cost of all the great changes was now reduced to a more modest £10,000; a little less than the £100,000 reported two months previously. Included was a large water tank planned to be built in 'the extensive grounds'. This was eventually dug into the floor of one of the larger adjoining stages and was until very recently at least still *in situ*, worryingly under a large wooden board straddling the void. The artistes' green room was now fitted with a well-stocked bar, where all kinds of refreshments could be obtained. Catering for it and the new restaurant was in the capable hands of Mr Mark Barnett, a member of 'the well-known London family of licensed Victuallers' who had become a universal provider at the studio. And to kick it all off, a new film was in production starring the legendary American movie star, albeit with the best of his phenomenal career behind him, Buster Keaton.

The famous 'frozen faced' comedian began his career in 1899, performing on stage with his parents at the age of three, learning to take the trick falls that would one day make his fortune. He made the transition from stage to film in 1917 as co-star and gag man to Roscoe 'Fatty' Arbuckle, which soon led to his own success. *Steamboat Bill*, *The Navigator*, *Our Hospitality*, *Sherlock Jr.*, and *The General* have made him one of the greatest actor-directors in cinema history. Foregoing his independence as a film-maker to join Metro-Goldwyn-Meyer, Hollywood's biggest studio, coincided with the coming of sound and mounting personal problems including a brutally failed marriage, which led to a destructive period of alcoholism and eventually institutionalisation. In 1936 the former silent star's life and career had reached rock-bottom, signing for an upcoming young producer called Sam Spiegel for the second time. The first occasion was in 1934 when Spiegel arranged for Keaton to star in a British film to be made at Wembley but which never came about. This time it was for a film called *The Invader*, written by Edwin Greenwood, the author of *Love on the Dole*, which centres on a young woman who pretends to love a wealthy tourist to make her husband so jealous that he murders the tourist and is arrested, thus leaving her free to be with her lover. For his leading lady, Spiegel chose Lupita Tovar, considered Mexico's Vivien Leigh because of her role in the epic film *Santa*. Physically, she was ideal to play Lupita Malez, the cantina beauty who feigns love for Leander Proudfoot, the rich American tourist in Spain played by Buster Keaton. But the project came with its problems. For a start it was under-financed. Keaton was paid $12,000 to play the lead, and the full budget was just $120,000. According to Spiegel, Keaton spent most of his paltry fee on alcohol. Two birthday cakes were lined up one morning when the star would be celebrating his thirty-ninth birthday. The cakes were delivered at 8 a.m., just as Keaton was vacating the bar.

Intercontinental drifter, shyster and schmoozer extraordinaire Sam Spiegel began his film career as a story translator in Hollywood in 1927 and soon after moved to Berlin, where he worked on French and German versions of several Universal films. He arrived in London just as *The Private Life of Henry VIII* was reaping rewards for its producer, Alexander Korda, who was to make a lasting impression on the itinerant American. Korda was the antithesis of Spiegel; every inch the European gentleman, possessing all the requisite trappings of the social elite with aspirations beyond the film business. Spiegel's ultimate ambition was that of Korda's, to become an international statesman, a man of influence, easy with politicians and opinion informers. But whereas Korda was already established as the acceptable face of British cinema, Spiegel had only recently arrived, having fled the Nazis with just the clothes on his back, the tale of his 'heroic' escape serving to win him the necessary support and sympathy, and more importantly, money. With an apartment in the West End where his voracious sexual appetite was sated and his legendary social networking ability thrived, he won over a wealthy young man, Laurence Evans, a leading agent who had a passion for making films. With Spiegel, he floated the British and Continental Film Corporation Limited, with offices in Lower Regent Street.

Spiegel persuaded Evans to accompany him to Paris to meet Buster Keaton, then filming *Le Roi des Champs-Élysées*. Saddled with debts and a fading reputation, Keaton represented an inexpensive addition to the cast list of *The Invader*. The choice of studio was therefore crucial in so far as it had also to be cheap. In this, Archie Holly, the accountant at Worton Hall, was given a list of what was wanted, which determined the rental fee. 'Being a service studio we were in competition with all the other service studios.' The studio manager kept his ears to the ground and any producer looking to make a film would be offered a variety of services. 'We would quote them a price for the studio; so much a week for the use of whatever was there – all the props and all the lighting equipment and there was a time when there were cameras there.'

The client had the use of whatever was in the prop room, but they would bring in anything extra. They had use of the cutting rooms every week of their tenure if the editor cut as the filming progressed, or a week after the shoot sometimes free as part of the deal. They would also supply their own make-up, wardrobe, hairdressing and production department, with the studio supplying the craft labour in the form of carpenters, painters and plasterers who came in by the week or the day. It was always the studio's job to build the sets to the instructions of the production's art director, draftsman and master carpenter. 'In the very early days they took them from the door,' recalls Holly. 'If they were freelance and they got to know there was a film going to be made at Worton Hall or whatever, they would come to the gate and try and get taken on.' Later on, with unionisation, the craftsmen became weekly employees. They knew the number of weeks the studio was going to be in use for and for what purposes. For example, once the sets were built there was no more need for carpenters. The studio was obliged to offer two hours notice and an hour's 'grinding money', that is once a carpenter had finished work on the film he was paid extra time to sharpen his tools ready for the next job.

Archie Holly, as the studio's production accountant, attended as many as five production meetings with the producer to establish what was wanted based on what the picture was all about and how long it was going to take. On receipt of the script a check was made with the art director as to what he needed. Mostly it was basic stuff and rarely came in on budget. Holly had an awful job trying to get money out of Sam Spiegel, but this was made up for by the fact that Buster Keaton was one of the accountant's all-time favourites. As he told film historian David Blake,

> I wasn't connected with the picture directly, but I used to try and sneak away sometimes and watch him work. I remember very well there was a tank in the dark studio, built for water scenes and he was in some scene with a girl. It was beneath the floor. I can't remember it being used very much – it was used very, very little. It could only ever have been used once for this Buster Keaton film.

Although Spiegel had managed to persuade the eccentric Sir Francis Cook, one of the richest men in England and a patron of the arts, to finance the film, by the time shooting was underway at Isleworth, much of the money had already gone on Spiegel's extravagant lifestyle. He was assisting a penniless John Huston, at that time sleeping rough on the streets of London while writing a script. The two men would dine at the film's expense at a small restaurant in Mayfair where Spiegel once encountered his financier trying to convince the French actor Maurice Chevalier to play the lead in *The Invader*, rather than Keaton.

Although Spiegel had warned the film's director, Adrian Brunei, not to let Keaton drink, the silent star was often paralytic. And the Frenchman was having other difficulties coping with Spiegel's 'financial recklessness, writing phoney cheques, police charges, lack of sexual control, and other disturbing addictions'. Nor did he appreciate Spiegel's 'creation out of conflict' methodology, which followed that any production that ran smoothly was 'colourless' and only those born of strife had any outstanding merit. A man of mild temperament, Brunei resented losing his rag and moreso when Spiegel congratulated him whenever he did. The misery of a pneumatic drill constantly spoiling the outside takes was no less galling than the hiring of cameraman Eugen Schufftan, whose dark and atmospheric signature photography had little to offer a light-hearted comedy. Spiegel's rapacious sexual appetite added to the farce with a troop of showgirls hired for the dance sequence but who had never danced a step in their lives. 'Much time and money had been wasted,' bemoaned Brunei.

Spiegel was noticeably absent on pay day. The director only received a third of what he was due because there was no money, although roses were delivered daily to Lupita Tovar at the Dorchester. The Westmore brothers, the most significant figures in film make-up, were drafted in from Hollywood for her, with Jo Strasser to design her costumes. Such was her list of benefits that it confounded Yves Mirande, who was co-writing the French version of the picture, and who demanded to know, naively perhaps, what it was she had that made Spiegel behave in such a manner. Spiegel, meanwhile, was living in luxury, enjoying extravagant evenings at the Dorchester which was far more tolerant of credit than a lesser establishment reliant on prompt payment. Besides, Spiegel's high-profile parties were good for business. His biographer, Natasha Fraser-Cavassoni, records one occasion where he took advantage of the banquet room to acquire some cash. It was being prepared for Alexander Korda and some fifty guests of his. Spiegel rearranged the seating plan to have him sitting opposite Korda. At the end of dinner when the host asked for the bill, Spiegel insisted on paying. Korda declared he wouldn't hear of it but eventually agreed to split the bill, handing over a cheque on the understanding that Spiegel would settle the whole amount. The cheque, however, was immediately cashed, solving another cash-flow problem. The director Billy Wilder maintained that Spiegel was a modern-day variant of Robin Hood, but one 'who steals from the rich and steals from the poor'. Sir Francis Cook, however, eventually instructed his lawyer to trim the budget, as he was no longer prepared to subsidise Spiegel's extravagance. Spiegel left the Dorchester for more modest lodgings and began issuing worthless cheques in order to complete the editing of the film.

The Invader had taken less than one month to shoot and was rejected for distribution due to its brevity. As a result it had to be completely re-edited. Luckily, Rudi Fehr was in town and provided a cheap editor, albeit one without a visa and so he had to take the ferry to France in order to be readmitted into Britain with the requisite work permit Spiegel had arranged. Brunei had already complained to Spiegel that he hadn't sufficient material to shoot for the seventy-five minutes running time Spiegel was under contract to deliver. No matter what he did, Fehr's edited version ran for only sixty minutes and so he was left with no option but to use whatever scraps of footage were left on the cutting-room floor. The result was that when a door slammed shut, it remained shut on the screen for five or six seconds. The next shot would be of Keaton on the other side of the door in the process of slamming it shut. These were the only comedy moments in the film, and all unintentional.

Spiegel's various financial misdemeanours eventually caught up with him. He was arrested for obtaining money under false pretences and forgery. Released on bail, he was committed for trial at the Old Bailey where he failed to turn up, instead throwing a lavish champagne and caviar party for his wealthier friends and associates at the Dorchester. When arrested, he excused himself by declaring, 'I am temporarily the guest of His Majesty's Government.' Laurence Evans attended the trial where Spiegel was sentenced to three months' imprisonment, followed by deportation. It was the end of the British and Continental Film Corporation. *The Invader* (also known as *An Old Spanish Custom*) flopped in Britain and in the United States and was a disaster for all concerned. Evans blamed Buster Keaton who, years later, observed that the day had passed, 'when the public would come to see a movie with inferior props, camera work, and generally poor production'.

Two decades previously, George Pearson had railed against these same 'abominations' when he and his fellow pioneers were working at the same studio finding their feet in film. With all the subsequent advances made in technique and technology, this poor showing would have been all the more galling for Pearson's old boss, Bertie Samuelson, who was quietly going about his business in one of the other Isleworth stages directing his last film for New Era, *The Crucifix*, a talking remake of the silent feature *In Bondage* about a badly-off woman who steals a valuable crucifix from her dying mistress, unaware that she had been left everything in her will. Being the ebullient character he was, Bertie possibly rubbed shoulders with Sam Spiegel in the newly refurbished green room bar, perhaps making himself known to the loud American with a view to future work. The forty-five-year-old former studio boss may have swapped stories with him and Keaton about his times in the States when he made movies in Hollywood, or back in the day when his name meant something in the industry. More likely he kept his own company, preferring that to the role of the bore at the bar.

Spiegel was at that time more a Johnny-come-lately whose future would have appeared bleak. He failed to emulate in any way, shape or form the rising fortunes of the thirty-eight-year-old Hungarian film-maker he had fleeced at the Dorchester and who was risking everything on a lavish production based on the life of Henry VIII. And into this equation came Richard Norton, who was now on the board of British & Dominion Films, bringing to the table his vital connection with the principal distributor of British films in America, United Artists. As solely a distributor and not a financier of films, UA did not have to give top priority to its own product and so was always in search of quality material to include in its programme. For a few years all British & Dominion films were handled by UA, and it was due to Norton's intervention that Alexander Korda was able to finish *The Private Life of Henry VIII* when he was running out of money. In so doing he established the reputation that would revolutionise the British film industry and revitalise the fortunes of Worton Hall.

5
The Korda Years, Take One

Sandor Kellner was born in Hungary on 16 September 1893, the eldest of three sons. His sight was damaged as a young boy, which left him having to wear thick glasses throughout his life. Despite this impediment he mastered half a dozen languages and became a journalist, adopting the pseudonym 'Korda'. His film career began in 1911 in Paris where he spent several months working in the Pathé studio, the most advanced film factory in the world. On his return to Hungary he joined a film company in Budapest, going on to become one of the most important figures in the emerging Hungarian film industry, building the Corvin (today Mafilm) Studio, where he directed and oversaw all production. Although not a party member himself, Korda assisted the Communist government's effort to create the first nationalised film industry in the world, but fell foul of the right-wing 'White Terror' regime when it came to power. He was briefly imprisoned before leaving Hungary in 1919, vowing never to return.

Adopting the Christian name Alexander, Korda first joined the Sascha Film Company in Vienna and then moved to Berlin, where he formed his own company, Korda-Film, directing vehicles for his actress wife Maria, which were well received and led to an offer from the First National Studios in Hollywood. The films he made there were met with indifference and so, disillusioned, he returned to Europe where he made several films in Paris and Germany before moving to England in November 1931, where he had agreed to make two quota films for Paramount at the British & Dominion studio. The first, *Service For Ladies* with fellow Hungarian Laszlo Steiner (better known as Leslie Howard) made it plain that Korda was no mere quota producer but one of talent, who believed passionately that the only way forward for the British film industry was to start producing quality films.

Another director was delegated to undertake the second of the two Paramount pictures, *Women Who Play*, while Korda determined to set up his own production company. He was introduced to Leopold Sutro, a prominent banker, who liked Korda's global ideas and agreed to back him. Together with screenwriter Lajos Biro and a third fellow Hungarian, Stephen Pallos, Korda registered London Film Productions in February 1932 as a private £100 company. It took as its trademark the Big Ben clock-face, as befitting Korda's Anglo-centric leanings and as a trusted monument recognised throughout the world. When asked why the clock always struck eleven, Korda explained that eleven was when the sun had come out, which allowed them to get the shot. Joint-managing directors of London Films were Alexander Korda and the Conservative MP Captain A. C. N. Dixey. The chairman was actor and writer George Grossmith, with whom Korda had worked in America. Impressed by Korda's flamboyant lifestyle, complete with chauffeur-driven Rolls Royce and a suite at the Savoy, backing came from other highly placed contacts, as well as international banker Leopold Sutro. Zoltan and Vincent Korda joined their brother's enterprise as production supervisor and art director respectively. Vincent had graduated from the Budapest College of Industrial Art and London's Academy of Art before studying painting in Vienna and Florence for twelve years. He also worked as a painter and designer in Paris.

The first production, *Wedding Rehearsal*, was made at the ASFI studio at Wembley and in all the company made seven quota quickies under a distribution deal with Paramount for the films to be delivered at a fixed price. Even though these pictures had to be made cheaply and quickly, Korda strove for something better than his contemporaries, which he achieved, and in so doing won acclaim and serious attention from the industry, culminating in *The Private Life of Henry VIII*, which went into production in May 1933 at the British and Dominion studios. With Charles Laughton in the lead role, Alexander produced and directed, Vincent designed the sets and Zoltan supervised production. The film was an instant success both in England and America, breaking all box-office records, winning an Oscar for Charles Laughton and launching Korda's reputation into the realm of movie genius. More importantly, it inspired confidence in the British film industry.

Korda's flirtations with the quota system had taught him a lesson in British distribution, but he wanted to create a global market, which meant finance on the grand scale. This arrived in the form of wealthy Australian Montague Marks, who had just arrived in London from New York and who was looking to invest in film. Marks had recently done some business with the Prudential Life Assurance Company and he knew that they had to invest their large capital at a certain monthly or annual rate. As Korda's representative, Marks met with the Prudential and put to them the huge success of *The Private Life of Henry VIII* and his confidence in its producer realising substantial returns on such investments. Well outside of its comfort zone, the usually staid and steady institution agreed to back this new departure from their regular portfolio. For his efforts, Marks was made general manager of London Films and handsomely rewarded.

Then there was the matter of American distribution. United Artists had a large and costly distribution organisation, but its founding members, Charles Chaplin, Mary Pickford and Douglas Fairbanks Sr, were unable to supply sufficient product to cover the overheads and were badly in need of a supply of films. United Artists' management in Great Britain was in the hands of two men: George Archibald, whom Douglas Fairbanks Jr described as 'a wiry Scotsman', and Murray Silverstone, 'a transplanted New Yorker'. Together they persuaded Fairbanks Sr and through him the other UA partners to admit to their ranks a British producer who would make high-quality quota pictures, thus increasing both the profits and the prestige of the company. There was only one contender at this time and that was Alexander Korda.

It was during this time that Fairbanks Jr first experienced big-time movie negotiations at close quarters. In his memoirs he falls just short of calling Korda slippery, preferring to centre on the Hungarian's tremendous charm and intelligence that overcame most obstacles in his pursuit of success, prestige, and power. The deal for Korda to become a partner in United Artists was rapidly finalised, with the cost of his partnership a staggering $2 million, which he was allowed to pay from the expected profits of his films. In the end he managed to pay virtually nothing and the story goes that he later sold the same shares for a substantial profit. Fairbanks Sr declared 'unbounded faith' in Korda, even looking forward to being directed by him in future productions. These negotiations were successfully concluded at the end of 1933, and on 1 January 1934 it was announced that Douglas Fairbanks Sr had joined the board of London Films, followed by a statement that closer co-operation between United Artists and London Films was established.

Right: 1. George Berthold (Bertie) Samuelson. (Samuelson Archive)

Below: 2. Worton Hall *c.* 1914. (Samuelson Archive)

3. The grounds at Worton Hall *c.* 1914. (Samuelson Archive)

4. The official opening of Worton Hall Studio in July 1914. From left to right: George Pearson, G. B. Samuelson, his brother Julian Wylie and seated, Walter Buckstone. (Samuelson Archive)

5. Monday 6 July 1914, the first day of shooting at Worton Hall. Note the taped field of vision on the floor running from the camera lens. (Samuelson Archive)

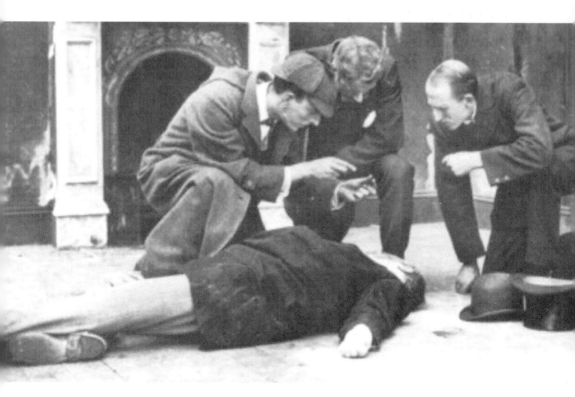

6. Interior scene from *A Study in Scarlet*. (Samuelson Archive)

7. James Braginton as Sherlock Holmes. (Samuelson Archive)

8. Scenery department at Worton Hall, *c.* 1919, hard at work on a royal setting under the supervision of Samuelson's scenic designer-cum-handyman, Bernasconi, possibly the central figure. (Samuelson Archive)

9. Two scenic artists painting a classical backdrop to one production. (Samuelson Archive)

10. Here the task is to create a brick house frontage on a piece of canvas. (Samuelson Archive)

11. Shooting an incident of *The Great European War*. (Samuelson Archive)

12. A still from *John Halifax, Gentleman* with left to right: Harry Paulo, Lafayette Ranney, Fred Paul and Peggy Hyland. (Samuelson Archive)

13. Quite probably the theatre setting from *Infelice*, which the critics declared to be 'particularly well done'. (Samuelson Archive)

Above: 14. The new 'Dark' studio sits behind the original 'Light' studio. (Samuelson Archive)

Left: 15. H. A. Sainsbury as the second Sherlock Holmes to grace Worton Hall in *Valley of Fear*. (Samuelson Archive)

Above: 16. Wounded servicemen at Worton Hall. (Samuelson Archive)

Right: 17. Publicity sheet for *Milestones*. (Samuelson Archive)

18. Production still from *Little Women*. (Samuelson Archive)

19. *Game of Life* cast and crew at Worton Hall. Rear: Harold Bastick (cameraman smoking), Arthur Alcott (behind camera), Sydney Blythe (camerman behind camera on right). Seated: Wyndham Guise, Dorothy Minto, Tom Reynolds. (Samuelson Archive)

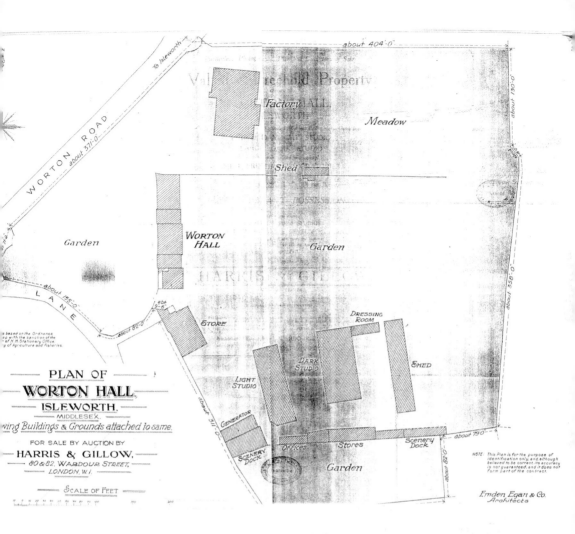

PLAN OF
WORTON HALL,
ISLEWORTH,
MIDDLESEX.

wing Buildings & Grounds attached to same.

FOR SALE BY AUCTION BY

HARRIS & GILLOW,
80 & 82, WARDOUR STREET,
LONDON, W.I.

SCALE OF FEET

NOTE: This Plan is for the purpose of identification only, and although believed to be correct its accuracy is not guaranteed, and it does not form part of the contract.

Emden Egan & Co.
Architects

Above: 20. Plan of Worton Hall Studios, *c.* 1920. (Les McCallum)

Right: 21. Gwylim Evans as Napoleon and Gertrude McCoy as Josephine in *A Royal Divorce.* (Samuelson Archive)

"A ROYAL DIVORCE."

22. John Gielgud as Daniel in
Who Is the Man? (Samuelson
Archive)

G. B. Samuelson.

Urbane, smiling and genial—with cloth cap and mackintosh. A real test for tip-ups !
He has made many outstanding films—" If Four Walls Told " and " A Royal Divorce,"
to mention but two, as diverse as the Poles. He has now made " She "—that is to say,
he has now made it immortal, a lasting tribute to a great British author whose loss
we mourn. " G. B. S." has artistic sense, precision, a brain that conceives and works
quickly. He is one of our greatest films. He is the Napoleon of public sentiment—and gets there
every time. Somebody once told him that his initials stood for Get Busy Sam—and
he has taken it to heart ever since.

23. Bertie Samuelson, *The
Bioscope*'s Man of the Week.
(Samuelson Archive)

24. Worton Hall Studios, *c.* 1920. (Samuelson Archive)

25. *Jealousy*, with Henrietta Watson, Sam Livesey, Gibb McGalughlin, Mary Newland and Harold French. (Samuelson Archive)

26. Sunday Wilshin and Gerald Rawlinson in *Collision*. (Samuelson Archive)

27. The newly equipped Worton Hall Studio complex. (London Borough of Hounslow Local Studies)

28. Alex and Vincent Korda.
(David Blake Archive)

29. *Things to Come.* (Tony
Hillman)

H.G.WELL

Things to com

A LONDON FILM PRODUCTION   DIRECTED BY WILLIAM CAMERON MEN

PRODUCED BY ALEXANDER KO

DISTRIBUTED BY ···

Opposite page: 30. *Things to Come* poster. (David Blake Archive)

Above: 31. Alexander Korda and H. G. Wells. (David Blake Archive)

32. Paul Robeson and Nina Mae McKinney, *Sanders of the River*. (Tony Hillman)

33. *The Man Who Could Work Miracles*. (David Blake Archive)

34. Robert Donat and Peggy Martin in *The Ghost Goes West*. (David Blake Archive)

Left: 35. Douglas Fairbanks
Jr with Dolores Del Rio
and Captain Alec Stratford
Cunningham-Reid at Worton
Hall Studios, 1935. (David
Blake Archive)

Below: 36. The Regency
portico of Worton Hall
mansion, used as a backdrop
in *The Last Days of Dolwyn*.
(Tony Hillman)

37. *Accused* brings a spot of glamour to Isleworth. (David Blake Archive)

38. The Palais de Justice recreated at Isleworth for *Accused*. (David Blake Archive)

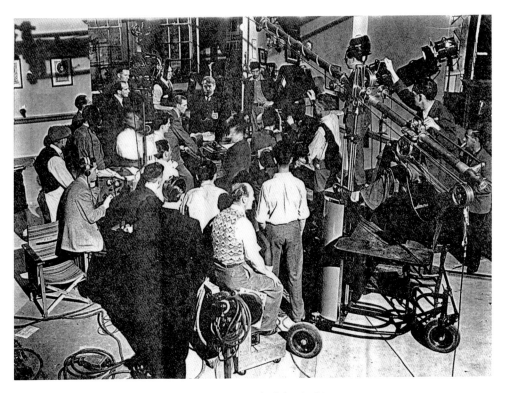

39. On the floor with *Shop at Sly Corner*. (David Blake Archive)

40. Michael Wilding (right) in a scene from *Piccadilly Incident*. (David Blake Archive)

41. *Mine Own Executioner* with Burgess Meredith (left) and Jack Raine (centre). (David Blake Archive)

42. Royal visitors to Worton Hall in June 1947. (David Blake Archive)

43. David Niven as *Bonnie Prince Charlie* (left), failing to take advice from Lord George Murray, played by Jack Hawkins. (David Blake Archive)

44. Vivien Leigh (right) wandering the 'shocking deficiency' of a highland setting. (David Blake Archive)

45. Vivien Leigh and Ralph Richardson in a scene from *Anna Karenina*. (David Blake Archive)

46. Ned Mann (centre, below the camera) and his special effects team at Worton Hall. (David Blake Archive)

47. Royal visit to Worton Hall in June 1947 with a rare glimpse of the giant stage in the background. (David Blake Archive)

Left: 48. Inside H Stage at Shepperton. (Author)

Below: 49. From the outside, with 'DONLON LMSFI' barely discernible after half a century. (Author)

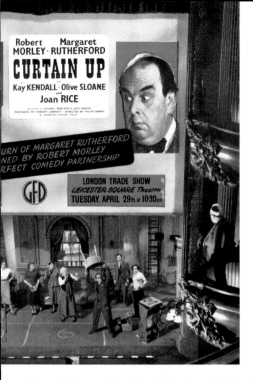

Above left: 50. Press book for *Curtain Up*. (David Blake Archive)

Above right: 51. *The Small Back Room*: Kathleen Byron and David Farrar endure a troubled relationship. (David Blake Archive)

Below: 52. *State Secret* with Douglas Fairbanks Jr. (David Blake Archive)

53. Humphrey Bogart, Lauren Bacall and their son Stevie in the grounds of Worton Hall. (David Blake Archive)

54. Robert Morley in the Isleworth Kungdu Methodist mission. (Les McCallum)

55. The watery backlot, complete with cut-out fort. (Wisconsin Center for Film and Theatre Research)

56. Aboard the German gunboat, noting the rooftops of neighbouring houses in Worton Road. (Wisconsin Center for Film and Theatre Research)

Above: 57.
Hepburn taking
a soaking on
the exterior rig.
(Academy of
Motion Picture
Arts and Sciences)

Left: 58.
Katherine
Hepburn in *The
African Queen*
with Worton
Hall in the
background.
(Academy of
Motion Picture
Arts and Sciences)

59. Richard Attenborough and Bernard Lee in a scene from *The Gift Horse*. (David Blake Archive)

60. Worton Hall, 2011. (Author)

61. Sites of the original silent stages, the 'Light' studio on the left and the 'Dark' studio to the right. (Author)

62. The dressing room block. (Author)

63. The two big sound stages, now workshops and offices. (Author)

Korda had obtained two of the three elements he sought in order to achieve his ambitions; financial backing and American distribution. Now he needed his own studios. As investment money poured in and confidence in him and the future of British films was high, he purchased an annual lease on Worton Hall for the not inconsiderable sum of £35,000. Korda's biographer, Paul Tabori, describes the studio as 'cramped and old-fashioned' but technically it was a match for any other British studio. Among the many improvements undertaken at Isleworth, the facility was hugely expanded in April 1935 to include the largest film stage in the country. Korda had ambitious plans for an epic production of H. G. Wells' *Wither Mankind? (The Shape of Things to Come)* and needed a vast enclosed area for the fantastic sets to match the famous writer's futuristic fantasies.

As incredible as it seems today that such a monstrous structure could suddenly appear on the local landscape without a hint of local noise, so was Monty Marks' simultaneous announcement that it would make more economic sense for Korda to quit Worton Hall and build his own studios from scratch. Based on estimates according to the interest on the capital involved, but with no mention of the construction outlay incurred thus far, it was reckoned that a considerable saving could be made. Despite all the expense and effort put into upgrading Worton Hall, Korda agreed and gave Marks authority to look for a suitable site, announcing in the trade press that the 'gigantic studio' recently erected was to be demolished by the end of May at an estimated cost of £1,500. It would then be transported to Denham in Buckinghamshire where London Films had acquired a 165-acre site to build the biggest studios in Europe at a cost of £300,000.

Paul Tabori makes a solitary passing reference to Worton Hall, as do most other biographers of Britain's only movie mogul. Yet the small Middlesex studio provided the essential grounding for Korda's future ambitions, the framework for what he and hundreds of others would go on to achieve, while Denham almost immediately became a financial millstone. Korda would later tell the film critic Caroline Lejeune that it was only built at a time when London Films was ready for it. 'A studio without a 100 per cent staff is nothing but an empty shell,' he said, going on to explain that for three years the company had been 'collecting' staff, getting them used to working together, 'sometimes apparently doing nothing with them but training them and waiting'. At the right time there were 200 fully trained experts on hand. From the minute he took over Denham they would be able to work at full pressure. In reality, Denham would last just three years, whereas Worton

Hall would continue active for another seventeen, with its giant stage in place awaiting the return of its creator.

The *Middlesex Chronicle* reported that the stage was known as the 'hush hush' stage because only studio employees were allowed admission when Korda's magnificent epic was underway. Indeed, there was an element of paranoia on the set of the Wells epic. In a *March of Time* newsreel for March 1936, entitled *England's Hollywood*, cinema audiences were informed that

> At the present time, there are great general interests which oppress men's minds – excite and interest them. There's the onset of war, there's the increase of power, there's the change of scale and the change of conditions in the world. And in one or two of our films here, we've been trying without any propaganda or pretension or preachment of any sort, we've been trying to work out some of those immense possibilities that appeal, we think, to the everyman. We are attempting here the film of imaginative possibility. That, at any rate, is one of the challenges that we are going to make to our friends and rivals at Hollywood.

These are not the words of Alexander Korda, but the writer H. G. Wells.

Shown as part of the supporting programme to *Things to Come*, the newsreel documented armies of workers and craftsmen busily going about the creation of the most ambitious British film to date in England's newest and largest studio. It centres on the ant-like colony of the new Denham complex, showing elaborate sets being built, gigantic black-painted flying bombers constructed and teams of technicians occupying the vast new stages. The supporting commentary was not in the broken English of the debonair Hungarian émigré owner, but in the clipped tone of the pinched-faced author, freshly returned from inspecting America's studios, despite having no experience whatsoever in the film industry. 'British films with proper British taste and accents' was the remit of Denham and its creator, Alexander Korda, featured replete with tortoise-shell rimmed glasses, cigar in one hand and the script of *Things to Come* in the other. Standing with him is his brother, 'the designer of settings', Victor Korda, the director of photography, Georges Perinal, and the film's director, William Cameron Menzies. But no mention is made of Worton Hall, where many of the dazzling interiors and all of the special effects were shot.

Published in 1933, *Things to Come* is a precursor to the myriad post-apocalyptic science fiction films so familiar today; a story of ruin and resurrection set in Everytown, Wells' Utopian city of the future. Beginning with the warning of an impending war, there follows a century of conflict that leads to a regressive society governed by a brutal dictator. By 2036, a new order based upon reason and technology has emerged and eventually rebuilds the city underground. Production on the film actually began in 1934 at Consolidated's studios at Elstree, formerly the Whitehall Studio, later moving to Worton Hall and using Denham for exteriors after May 1935.

As Karol Kulik explains in her biography of Alexander Korda, the first two phases of the story posed the fewest problems to the production team. The 1940 scenes were simply treated as contemporary sequences, with modern-day London serving as the model for Everytown with its massive office buildings, cinemas, and department stores. The bombing of the city and the symbolic battle scenes were achieved by the use of miniatures, photographic superimpositions, and back-projection work. The ruinous 1940 set was the basis for the 1970 devastation, complete with horse-drawn cars and costumes made from the remnants of whatever material survived. But it was with the rebuilding of the futuristic Everytown that the special effects men at Worton Hall took over completely. The massive excavation and vast factory machinery were all built to a larger scale but miniatures nevertheless. The giant space gun, for example, was over 10 feet tall.

First in models and finally in actual sets and miniatures, Vincent Korda created the future city of minimalist apartments with functional furniture and giant television screens reached by tubular glass elevators, monorails and helicopters. Anthony Gross started, but abandoned, an animated sequence for the film. Instead the later scenes depended heavily on the special photographic techniques devised for the silent stage, which enabled the actors to be shown against what appear to be huge sets. The lower storeys of buildings were constructed in full scale and the upper storeys in miniature, with the two images united by the split-screen method. Less effective was Ned Mann's use of puppets moved along conveyor belts in miniature sets to simulate the crowds rushing towards the space gun.

Richard Haestier, writing in *The Star* newspaper in December 1935, found a 'strange futurist world' had sprung up at Isleworth when he visited London Films Studios to witness Cameron Menzies shoot the last scenes of the film there. Finding himself in a 'lofty, spacious hall, with no corners, hidden floor lighting, a highly polished floor and beautiful furniture made of thick glass', the people in this strange new world were interesting to look at with their appearances of robust fitness and Raymond Massey looking for all the world a Roman emperor replete in toga and sandals. A sheet of rubber standing broadly from the shoulders formed the mould for a draped outer garment as protection from any electric shock incurred by the miniature wireless set and radio telephone as part of the ensemble. Outside the City of the Future the air was buzzing with new types of model aircraft of the 'pusher type', that is to say with the propellers behind the 'passengers' saloon'. It was eighteen months since the film was first started and six months since the cameras began to roll. And if the newly acquired Denham was being actively promoted as a major employer and a panacea for the Depression, then Isleworth provided something of a social commentary in itself, almost at one with the unemployed mining community of South Wales, whose redundant workforce was recruited as the rag-tag army left devastated at the end of Wells' hundred year's war.

Some of the citizens of Wells' bleak future were afflicted with the 'Wandering Sickness', a disease with no known cause or cure. The novelist had explicitly requested 'cadaverous people' be found and employed as the sick. In his treatise on the making of *Things to Come*, Christopher Frayling quotes Del Strother, a trainee sound assistant working on the film, who was asked to scour the streets of Isleworth to find undernourished extras to play these victims, which he did with ease. Although the industrious house-builders Messrs Wimpey & Co. was busily combining town convenience with country joys in the immediate locale of Worton Hall, there were still pockets of poverty that incomers thought they'd left behind in the poorer pockets of London. Thus, despite his great social conscience, Wells cynically exploited the very people his film vehemently defends.

Korda's choice of director was William Cameron Menzies, an acclaimed American film production designer and art director specialising in special effects who won the Best Art Direction Oscar at the first ever Academy Awards ceremony, held on 16 May 1929, for *The Dove* (1927) and *Tempest* (1928). But Menzies had only ever co-directed films and was considered by one critic to be more interested in the set than what the actors were doing in front of it. Surprisingly, therefore, the vast undertaking that was *Things to Come* represented Menzies' directorial debut. Korda hoped that his visual imagination would compensate for Wells' lack of any, although the novelist was granted complete autonomy over the script, direction, design and editing of the film. A memo dispatched to all concerned with the final phase of the film best illustrates Wells' emphatic and continued need to ensure that everyone was firmly on message with his total concept. Hugely prescriptive, these final scenes presented a higher phase of civilisation where human affairs in that more organised world would be less hurried and afforded more dignity. Structures in general would be great but nothing like 'all the balderdash one finds in such a film as Fritz Lange's [sic] *Metropolis* with its robot workers and ultra skyscrapers'. All of these preconceptions had to be cleared from the mind before working on this film. 'Common people' of the past were to be infinitely more uniform and 'mechanical' than those of the future. Machinery will have superseded the subjugation and 'mechanisation' of human beings. The workers were to be shown as individuals doing responsible co-operative team work. With these guiding rules to observe, 'but within these limitations and style I would say to our designers: "For God's sake let yourselves go"'.

Korda's munificence towards the novelist effectively undermined the project from casting to cutting. From early in his career, Wells sought to better organise society. He had visited the Soviet Union to promote his ideas of Utopia to Stalin and had told the Americans a thing or two about their film business. He therefore had no qualms about telling Korda how unimpressed he was by Menzies, accusing him of being incompetent and having no concept of the writer's vision. He later explained that it was Korda who wanted to make the film as far as was possible exactly as Wells had written it. However the task of transferring such a story to the screen was far more difficult than he had imagined, which is why it took much longer to make. It was only later in life that Wells realised how little he knew about film-making when he came to write the scenario. Many of the sequences which 'slipped quite easily' from his pen were extremely difficult to visualise on screen and some were impossible. The film emerged 'spiritually correct', despite the fact that it embodied many alterations suggested by 'a score of other people'.

In order to evoke his vision of the Utopian city of Everytown, Wells was spoiled for choice. The inter-war years saw new art movements springing up all over Europe, each born of changing social and political structures and new technologies.

Wells also approached Bauhaus legend Laszlo Moholy-Nagy who had left Nazi Germany and settled in London in 1935. Moholy-Nagy's short film, *Light-Play* (1930), an investigation into the qualities of light, had attracted the attention of Vincent Korda who approached him to develop the ideas into a sequence for the rebuilding of Everytown. With the City of the Future created in miniature at Isleworth, the design consisted of transparent cones and skeletal glass towers with a piazza element prominent in the film, articulating the transport networks for people and machines in a combination of models and full-size sets where the actors were able to walk around. At Worton Hall studios, Moholy-Nagy created and shot a montage sequence of futuristic effects, using various coiled glass tubing, bottles, bubbling liquids, back-light effects and smoke to illustrate the profound changes leading to building the new Utopian city. Unfortunately only ninety seconds of his work remains in the final product, but he is not credited, with Wells finally settling on the in-house talent of Vincent Korda and his own son, Frank.

In Ned Mann, Alexander Korda made a shrewd choice in his special effects director. Born in Indiana in 1893, Mann worked as a professional roller skater and driver in his early years, entering the movie business in 1920 initially as an actor but then into the realms of technical and special effects, working on top-flight films with some of the biggest names of the day. In the mid-1930s he swapped the sun-soaked Hollywood Hills for temperate Isleworth, where he developed one of the best special effects units in the business. One of the unaccredited special effects camera operators on *Things to Come* was a young Jack Cardiff who would go on to be chosen as one of Technicolor's first British trainees and win an Oscar for the atmospheric magic of *Black Narcissus* in 1948. Equally versatile in the studio and on location, Cardiff is associated with a dazzling array of directors and stars, achieving recognition as a director in his own right with *Sons and Lovers* in 1960, an OBE in 2000, and a year later another Oscar for his lifetime contribution to the art of cinematography.

When production for *Things to Come* started, all Worton Hall staff working on the film were required to assemble each evening to catch the coach to Denham for the big location ground used for the City Square. Technicians and crew left Isleworth at about 5.30 p.m. for the all-night shoots, leaving behind in charge of the fixed photography sequences a technician whose name even among the most devoted students of British cinema history looms relatively small. According to Michael Powell, Walter Percy Day was 'the greatest trick photographer and double-exposure merchant that the movies have ever seen'. He largely made possible the Himalayas in the Home Counties for Powell and Pressburger's celebrated *Black Narcissus* in 1947, a film that won the Oscar for Best Cinematography for Jack Cardiff who later questioned whether the award might more properly have gone to Walter, or as he was better known to the British film industry, 'Poppa' Day.

Day's career began in 1919 with Ideal Films at Borehamwood, where, having trained as a photographer, he was initiated into the mystic arts of visual effects techniques such as the glass shot and the Hall processes that provide for painted scenes and small-scale perspective pictures to merge with live-action footage. Day had created trick shots for Abel Gance in one of the most celebrated films of the twenties, *Napoléon*. In Britain he shot the visual effects for Alfred Hitchcock's *The Ring* (1927) where he learned the process involving the use of a scale model, painting or photograph and a mirror angled at 45 degrees to superimpose it over live action. Using mattes instead of glass, Day first used the stationary technique on the filming of *Au Bonheur des Dames* (1929), based on Émile Zola's classic novel. Returning again to England from France, Day made his mark directing the matte shots for Korda's classic *Thief of Bagdad*, which contains some of the most memorable examples of his craft. Based at Worton Hall for a number of years, Day remains uncredited as the matte painter not just on *Things to Come* but *The Man Who Could Work Miracles*, *Sanders of the River* and *The Ghost Goes West*. After the war, Day returned to Worton Hall where, working across Korda's new British Lion empire based there and in Shepperton, he was again unrewarded with credits as matte painter on *The Third Man*, *The Last Days of Dolwyn* and the process shots for *Mine Own Executioner*. 'Poppa' Day died in relative poverty and – perhaps worse – in almost total obscurity in 1965.

Things to Come boasted a fine cast headed by Raymond Massey as the Messianic Cabal and Ralph Richardson as the thuggish Boss, a role he modelled explicitly on Mussolini, the reason why the film was banned in Italy. As well as Ann Todd and Cedric Hardwicke, the 'pilot' bit part was played by an up-and-coming George Sanders. Uncredited as 'Man of the Future' was the jobbing cabaret artiste who would go on to make his name as the quintessential upper-class 'silly ass' Terry-Thomas. Critically well received, the film was a flop at the box office, but the music by Arthur Bliss was one of the first film scores to enjoy commercial success in its own right. In this Korda was blessed in his choice of musical director. 'There is one name that appears very frequently in British screen credits,' Caroline Lejeune, the film critic for *The Observer* would later proclaim, 'the name of Muir Mathieson, the musical director. Note that name. Remember it. Honour it.'

6

The Golden Year

In 1933, Alexander Korda asked Sir Malcolm Sargent to quit the Royal College of Music to come and work for him as musical director on *Catherine the Great*. Decidedly unimpressed by the film business, Sargent declined and suggested instead Muir Mathieson, who was about to graduate. Mathieson's work and personality so impressed Korda that he offered him the post of assistant director of music to Kurt Schroder. When Schroder quit London Films in 1934, Korda offered Mathieson the post, at a salary of £7 a week, an incredible opportunity for someone of his age and level of experience. Born just as music specifically written for the cinema came about, with recorded film sound evolving the same year he had entered music school, Mathieson foresaw the need for first-rate film music but not necessarily that he would be making a lifelong career out of it. He could have successfully established himself in other musical fields but fortunately for the medium of film, Korda provided the key to the door to a career made for him, where he would arrange, direct, conduct, and occasionally compose music for almost a thousand films between 1934 and 1970.

In keeping with any field of creative support, Mathieson believed that a cinema audience finding itself consciously listening to the accompanying music was a failure on his part. The cinema experience no longer provided for specially commissioned scores played by live orchestras accompanying films. With recorded sound, music was now an integral part of each film like the lighting or set design, where it was possible to be more subtle, more complex, perhaps more emotionally manipulative in its use. Where

Hollywood studios engaged resident composers, so Korda wanted Mathieson to both compose and conduct all the music for London Films productions. But, as Mathieson later explained to Leslie Mitchell in *The March of the Movies*, 'While I believed in my own ability as a conductor, I was well aware of my limitations as a composer.' In fact, he put it to Korda at the outset that he would only take on the job if he was to guarantee first-rate composers for every score. He determined not to write one note of indifferent music and found it 'ridiculous' to consider spending vast sums of money for the best of everything only for the whole thing to be let down by a poor music score. Mathieson insisted on being allowed to approach the greatest composers of the day to write his film scores and Korda agreed, hiring the twenty-two-year-old music graduate for the princely sum of £364 a year.

For all of the disappointments Alexander Korda endured over the two years London Films operated out of Worton Hall, his music director was from the start as consistent as he was successful. Key to this was recognising his limitations; where and to whom to turn in order to create the place for music in film we today take for granted. The choice of Sir Arthur Bliss to compose the music for *Things to Come* was as audacious as it was inspirational. Educated at Rugby School where he pursued his passion in music and composition, Bliss received degrees in music from Pembroke College, Cambridge, and entered the Royal College of Music in 1913 where he was encouraged by Ralph Vaughan Williams and Gustav Holst. Two of his early works enjoyed their first outings while he was serving on the Western Front where he was wounded and gassed.

Bliss never resumed formal musical study after the war, going on instead to develop his own unique contribution to post-war British music. Briefly holding a professorship of composition at the Royal College of Music, he left for America in 1923 where he settled in California, combining composing with lecturing and conducting on the international stage. When Mathieson asked him to provide the music for *Things to Come*, a subject he felt was ideally suited to the film medium, Bliss was able to demonstrate what was possible. Suites from the film score soon became popular concert items and in 1937 Bliss was invited back to London Films by Mathieson to compose the music for *The Conquest of the Air* where he achieved a similar success, unlike the film, that was to rank among other Korda unrealised dreams.

As music director, Muir Mathieson would have spent much of his time at Isleworth in the smallest of the three stages, specifically designed for musical scoring and recording. Adjoining the monitor room and the stage was a synchronously driven picture projector for scoring musical sequences.

A specially constructed portable soundproof booth was provided for monitoring on any or all of the stages, with either a permanent or portable channel, thus enabling the recording engineer to keep the closest possible contact with floor operation. As well as being able to view the scene in production, the booth was equipped for loudspeaker monitoring, mixer and volume control equipment for three microphones. The sound mixer was also able to talk to fellow technicians on the set by means of a microphone and loudspeaker fixed externally to the booth. Western Electric's recent installation of their equipment came complete with the incorporation of every modern refinement in sound recording technique, as confirmed by *Kinematograph Weekly* following a comprehensive tour of the system.

The three sound stages enjoyed interior acoustic treatment designed to eliminate reflection and reverberation throughout the entire frequency range. The acoustic conditions for recording were fully controllable and could be adapted to the requirements of any scene under production. On each stage multiple-outlet connecting boxes had been installed to enable the cameras and portable monitoring booths to be operated at any position on the stages. The various components were all interconnected, making it possible to transport and operate a sound channel at locations unreachable by any other equipment. The testing equipment also included a special microscope and jig for examining the apparatus used for controlling exposure and film processing. The studio's preview theatre permitted the continuous projection of separate sound and picture tracks with an auditorium specially designed to simulate as near as possible the average cinema.

A Western Electric-standard wax recording machine was also installed to provide for simultaneous or independent recording of disc versions, or for playback and pre-recording facilities, which allowed for reproducing and mixing of sound from three sound tracks, one playing discs at 33 1/3 rpm, and two at 78 rpm. Special equalisers were installed to compensate for high frequency losses, such as that occurring during printing, and additional compensating networks were available to obtain special effects, such as increasing or decreasing either high or low frequencies. Complete power equipment for operating the recording channels was installed and two distributors to drive the cameras, recorders and re-recorders in controlled synchronism. It all sounds highly sophisticated, but sound-dubbing and film editor Bill Lewthwaite remembers it well, with the projected picture thrown up onto a screen via two mirrors, and the workspace no bigger than a toilet. 'The conditions at Worton Hall were not the best. It was really a place you were sent to rather than elected to work,' he recalls, 'with the only bonus being its close proximity to Twickenham Rugby Ground where it was possible to slope off when there was a game on.'

In 1935 the studio saw the best of its productions making their way into British film history. With a modest sprinkling of other proud moments along the way thereafter, it would have to wait until the end of its days to host its final great classic. Even so, what few small references have touched upon Worton Hall in British film history the credit is almost always partly or entirely spread across a host of other studios, most markedly Denham and later Shepperton. *Sanders of the River*, for example, was the first in a series of colonial epics from London Films with Alex Korda producing, his brothers Zoltan and Vincent directing and art director respectively. Alfred Hitchcock was minimally involved during the initial stages of the film, which started out as a project called *Wings of the Jungle*, about a British colonial District Officer, R. G. Sanders, who looks to ensure a spot of fair play in 1930s Nigeria.

Playing the part of Sanders was Leslie Banks, who turned his partially scarred and paralysed face to his advantage by showing the unblemished side when playing comedy or romance and the other side when playing drama or tragedy. In his struggle against gun-runners and slavers, Sanders enlists the support of a native chieftain, Bosambo, played by the African-American entertainer, athlete and political activist Paul Robeson. Living in London at the time studying the roots of African culture through music and language, Robeson was looking for a project that would embrace cultural accuracy and dignity to help audiences understand and respect the roots of black culture. In this he believed he had found it courtesy of the Kordas, impressed by the highly unusual move on the part of film-makers of the day to lead a four-month expedition into remote areas of Africa to record 160,000 feet of traditional African dances and ceremonies to be woven into the studio scenes.

Not for the first time, the publicity from Sound City Studios (Shepperton) offers the distinct impression that the film was shot entirely there. While it states that Korda was 'based at the tiny Worton Hall studios in Isleworth', in reality, all of the interior scenes and post-production work was completed at Worton Hall with a whole trainload of black Cardiff dockers from Tiger Bay shipped in for the studio scenes. Sound City played host to some 300 black extras encamped in an African village constructed on the banks of the River Ash, which forms part of the Shepperton backlot. 'Luckily these belonged to some of the same tribes as their African brethren,' notes Paul Tabori. In an interview with Shepperton historian Derek Threadgall, veteran producer E.

M. Smedley-Ashton confirms that so lucrative was this one rental that Sound City's owner, the dynamic Scottish businessman Dennis Loudon, was able to close the studio for redevelopment, a move that would eventually spell the end for Worton Hall.

Paul Robeson described Zoltan Korda's African footage as 'magnificent', believing that it provided incontrovertible evidence that the continent enjoyed 'a definite culture a long way beyond the culture of the Stone Age … an integrated thing, which is still unspoilt by Western influence'. He was equally delighted by the music Korda had recorded, which Robeson believed revealed much more melody than he had ever heard come out of Africa before. He told *The Observer* newspaper that he had passed up an offer of two performances of Amonasro in *Aida* from the Chicago Opera at $1,000 a performance to play the part of Bosambo. The film, he explained, promised a milestone, the first comprehensive record of African culture, the prospect of which he found enormously exciting. 'For the first time since I began acting, I feel that I've found my place in the world, that there's something out of my own culture which I can express and perhaps help to preserve.'

Even as the film neared completion, Robeson remained confident of its value, with every scene and detail of the story faithfully accurate. He firmly believed that the film would do much towards 'the better understanding of the Negro culture and customs'. His wife, Essie, said that it was 'great fun' working with the Kordas; 'they know their business thoroughly and are human beings'. But, alas, she and her husband were to be bitterly disappointed. Despite objections from Zoltan Korda, who it appears also genuinely harboured the Robesons' desires, *Sanders of the River* emerged as an unwavering celebration of British colonial rule, dedicated 'to the handful of white men whose everyday work is an unsung saga of courage and efficiency'. The film uncritically retained the patronising racism of *Edgar Wallace*'s novel, depicting Africans as children whose natural tendencies towards deceit and violence required moderation from their white British masters. Bosambo came across as little more than a servile lackey of British colonial rule and Robeson was furious, complaining bitterly that he had been duped and that he had unwittingly dishonoured 150,000,000 native Africans; especially the chiefs and members of the various tribes who had taken part. One of the extras on the film, however, was Jomo Kenyatta, the future President of Kenya, who was sufficiently impressed with the film to present Alexander Korda with a silver cigarette case inscribed 'with deep admiration and gratitude'.

Robeson's ignominy meanwhile continued unabated. The New York *Daily News* characterised the film as one glorifying the heroism of one of Britain's empire builders and the *Sunday Times* celebrated 'a grand insight into our special English difficulties in the governing of the savage races [which] could not be improved upon for the respect it displays to British sensibilities and ambitions'. The newspaper's daily sibling added that the film would 'bring no discredit on Imperial authority'. *Sanders of the River* was the only Paul Robeson film shown in Italy or Germany, as it portrayed the black man much in the fascist way of thinking. So disillusioned was he by the picture that Robeson attempted, but failed, to buy back all of the prints to prevent it from ever being shown.

Despite all of this, Worton Hall appears not to have been a place of disillusionment for Robeson, who became a frequent visitor to the studio when it was taken over by Douglas Fairbanks Jr's Criterion film company a year after *Sanders* was filmed. In his autobiography, Fairbanks recalls 'a special glamour' that was added to lunch hours at Worton Hall by the frequent visits of this 'real, though unlikely, fan' of himself and his father. Robeson continued to perform in England, drawing comparisons between all oppressed peoples exploited by the colonial powers of Western Europe, as well as the plight of blacks in the United States. His gravitation towards social activism had already led him to make several trips to the Soviet Union where he wholeheartedly embraced the Russian way of life and the lack of racial bias. Developing a marked leftist ideology, he continued throughout the rest of his life to criticise blatant discrimination.

Of the myriad less divisive projects flitting in and out of Alexander Korda's portfolio in 1935 was a film to celebrate the Silver Jubilee of King George V. For this Korda chose Anthony Asquith to direct, and as the scriptwriter Winston Churchill, then languishing in the political wilderness due to his unyielding anti-Nazi stance towards Germany. His son, Randolph, had been working for some time in the publicity department of London Films and so a meeting was arranged with the politician and Alexander Korda in a pub near the Isleworth studios where the Hungarian entrepreneur bought the film rights to Churchill's *Marlborough* for a reported £10,000. Paul Tabori fails to name this pub. There were only two nearby; the Royal Oak on the banks of the Duke of Northumberland's River, which had served the needs of a thirsty cast and crew since the studio opened, and the neighbouring County Arms. This large Tudorbethan building was erected to serve the tide of first-generation home-owners filling the district rather than beer-fuelled conferences of directors and scriptwriters exchanging ideas, or stars of stage and screen downing a stiff drink or ten at the end of a long day. There was the studio bar for that. There was never a hint of its glamorous neighbour lining the walls of the County Arms like those of the Red Lion opposite Ealing Studios, nor will there ever be, for it has been demolished to make way for more housing.

The Man Who Could Work Miracles was another adventure into the ultra-imaginative world of H. G. Wells, involving a mild-mannered draper who receives the gift of omnipotence from a pair of heavenly spirits curious to know what mankind would do with such power. In a typical Wellsian turn of events, George McWhirter Fotheringay, the draper, naively commands the leaders of the world to create a Utopia free of greed, war, plague, famine, jealousy, and toil, with potentially disastrous consequences. Paul Tabori states unequivocally (but erroneously) that the film was shot entirely at Denham, whereas Korda was still waiting for his plush new Buckinghamshire base to be finished. The special effects facilities at Worton Hall continued to bring forth all manner of delights under the direction of Ned Mann, assisted by Poppa Day and the young Jack Cardiff on fourth camera. In an interview with film historian David Blake, former apprentice electrician Joe Gillnet remembers scenes from *The Man Who Could Work Miracles* shot on the massive silent stage where models were built of St Paul's Cathedral and the Albert Hall: 'The plasterers had a whale of a time, they loved it, it was all intricate work.' The cast of the Albert Hall was turned upside down and then scored all over with fine saw cuts, so when it exploded the whole thing imploded. By reversing the shot it reassembled itself. A number of ex-army huts were erected for the 'tricks department' close to the Big Stage in which papier-mâché work was carried out to create trees and even on one occasion figures for a large crowd scene.

Roland Young stars as the draper who represents the common man, and the infinite possibilities heaped upon this representative of the people to undermine the establishment and create a more just world. Welcoming the return to Worton Hall, this time as one of Fotheringay's antagonists, the blustering Colonel Winstanley was Ralph Richardson. The ultra-urbane George Sanders makes a small but meatier screen appearance, this time as the aptly named 'indifference', benefiting from his trademark sneer. Other faces that would later become familiar on screens big and small include Nigel Stock and Joan Hickson. More whimsical in tone, *The Man Who Could Work Miracles* was less prone to the same degree of author involvement as that endured by the cast and crew on *Things to Come*, but not entirely free of his tyranny. Many of the characters in the screen adaptation were created especially by Wells from a script suffering from his inexpert attempts at screenwriting. His penchant for lecturing resulted in another overly informative film where political and sociological debates swamp the potentially fantastic and romantic qualities of the story. Korda demanded retakes, but when released in 1936, a full year after its initial completion, it still proved too scholastic for most audiences and was another failure.

As Korda's bright new complex at Denham neared completion, the only real success in financial terms for London Films was *The Ghost Goes West*, inspired by *Sir Tristam Goes West*, a short story written by Eric Keown and published in *Punch* magazine. It concerns a Scottish laird, Murdoch Glourie, who shames his family name by dying dishonourably and is forced by his dead father to walk Glourie Castle every night at midnight until he has the opportunity to physically twist the nose of a MacLaggan, the rival clan; an act that will restore the family honour and lay his ghost to rest. Ten generations later and his opportunity arrives in the form of a gullible American businessman who buys the castle and transports it to Florida where it is rebuilt and used to publicise his chain of supermarkets. Once there, the supermarket tycoon's main rival turns out to be none other than the last member of the rival MacLaggan clan. His nose duly twisted, the ghost is allowed to rest in peace.

The story appealed to Korda and so he commissioned a script with Charles Laughton in mind to play the lead. The choice of director was made at a time when the French cinema reigned intellectually pre-eminent. René Clair ranked with Renoir and Carné as one of its greatest directors. Considered witty, stylish, charming and technically accomplished, Clair was admired for his grasp of trick photography. In co-writing a revised script with the American screenwriter Robert Sherwood where the romantic elements were brought to the fore, it was clear that the portly, middle-aged Laughton no longer suited the role, which now called for a younger, more attractive actor. Clair wanted the up-and-coming Laurence Olivier, but Korda's preferred choice was Robert Donat, whom he had brought to screen attention in casting him as the dashing hero, Thomas Culpepper, in *The Private Life of Henry VIII*. Like Leslie Howard, Donat was of Polish descent and with his darkly handsome good looks was ideally tailored for the American market. Indeed the Manchester-born actor had just finished Hitchcock's *The 39 Steps* and was at the height of his career. The romantic interest came in the form of Peggy Martin, the American businessman's daughter. Having made a series of small films for MGM in the early 1930s, Jean Parker was loaned to RKO for her first substantial role in Frank Capra's classic sentimental comedy *Lady for a Day*. This so impressed RKO that they extended her loan to play Beth in *Little Women* alongside Katharine Hepburn, Frances Dee and Joan Bennett. After several starring roles, she made the interesting transition from Hollywood to Isleworth where Alexander Korda cast her in what would become her most popular role opposite her favourite co-star of all.

Robert Donat was as complex as he was troubled. Suffering from a weak constitution, his insecurity could lead to absolute terror, giving way to aggression and antagonism. Like many actors drawn from the theatre, he found the process of filming excruciatingly boring. Despite the financial security, the prestige and the fame, the day-to-day drudgery of the studio turned to boredom and frustration, leading him to wonder what he was doing. Health-wise, his time at Isleworth was relatively trouble-free, with no asthma attacks or other illnesses, except for a short spell in a nursing home where his sinuses were drained. Early in production Clair circulated a formal note to all the cast and crew with regard to punctuality on the set, to which Donat retorted smartly,

> While being late on the set occasionally causes a hold-up, and while I admit to being late myself very occasionally, it strikes me as quite ridiculous to assert that a 9.30 start will ensure twelve takes in a day and an early return home. The truth is that I am heartily sick of being kept waiting on the set due to such stupid inefficiencies as camera trouble, studio noise which of late has been rampant, and the extremely irritating problem of visitors walking on to the set at any hour (including Press people who seem to manage to buttonhole one) just as one is trying to rehearse an important scene: faults which, in my opinion, are entirely due to an organisation which strikes me as puerile. I would remind you that I have been completely accommodating.

Despite this outburst, Donat considered there could have been no finer choice as director for *The Ghost Goes West* than Clair. A 'master of lively detail', he writes in his autobiography; 'suave, unruffled and patient at the end of a long day's shooting as he was at its commencement, Clair's handling of Robert Sherwood's script was inspired'. Donat considered the Frenchman's methodical direction to be largely due to an infinite capacity for preparedness; once on the floor he knew exactly what he wanted from his artists and crew, demanding take after take until he was satisfied that the scene could not be improved. But this came at a price. When location filming began at the superb new set-up at Denham where the façade of the lower half of the Glourie castle had been constructed, staff from Worton Hall were coached up each day, sometimes for very long periods; 'something like 36 hours,' recalled Joe Gillnet. Inconvenience money was paid, known as 'Ghosters', which was equivalent to ten times the normal weekly wage.

Alexander Korda interfered frequently during the filming, demanding the re-shooting of some scenes. But while this conflict damaged his relationship with Clair, the intervention paid off with the film going on to gross £450,000 at the box office and voted the best film of 1936 by the annual ballot of *Film Weekly*. Major contributory factors to its success were Vincent Korda's set designs and the special effects unit based at Isleworth where the Hall process was first tried in a British studio. The film opened Joe Gillnet's eyes as to 'how they got an actor to walk through a wall'. Despite the innovation of computer-generated effects we take for granted today, the first appearance of the ghost of Murdoch Glourie in the film remains magical. Audiences then marvelled at Donat's dual characterisations, skilfully executed in the double-exposure scenes where he speaks to himself and takes his leave of Donald, and again after a gunfight in America where the ghost appears, announcing, 'Father, I don't like America!'

Nor did America much like the film, although it oddly enough triumphed in China where the ghost was erased due to ancestor worship, reducing the seven reeler film to just two. Donat was deeply honoured to be presented to Queen Mary and the Duchess of Kent at the première of the film in London where, among the exceptionally favourable reviews, Campbell Dixon of *The Daily Telegraph* reported on 'a story so flimsy a single false note would have been fatal; but it never came. For ease, strength, charm and good looks Mr Donat is probably the finest young actor on the screen.' Chili Bouchier, the former silent star, had what she described as a 'lovely part' in the film, dressed as Cleopatra for a fancy dress ball aboard the Queen Mary. Her 'torrid' shipboard romance with the ghost, however, finished up on the cutting room floor 'because of overshooting'. During the screening, Miss Bouchier dropped her programme, missing the one line of hers retained.

Miss Bracegirdle Does Her Duty was directed by the acclaimed American cinematographer Lee Garmes, who had worked with some of the greats, including Howard Hawks, Josef Von Sternberg, Alfred Hitchcock, King Vidor and had co-directed two feature films with the legendary screenwriter Ben Hecht. Garmes arrived in Hollywood in 1916. His earliest films were comedy shorts, his career fully taking off with the introduction of sound, winning the Academy Award for Best Cinematography in 1932 for *Shanghai Express*. Now at Isleworth for Alexander Korda he was fashioning the story of a prim and proper English spinster (Miss Bracegirdle) on her first visit to Paris. On arrival at her hotel she is taken to the wrong room. As she opens the door to leave, the handle falls off and turning round she sees a man in bed. The first of many amusing situations during the course of her many misadventures, Miss Bracegirdle has a nightmare that the newspapers are printing scandalous headlines about her. For this dream sequence Garmes took his cameras on location to the *Middlesex Chronicle* printing works, shooting the paper's revolutionary new automatic printing press, the first complete plant of its kind in the country, and obtaining some valuable free publicity at the same time.

The paper duly reported that London Films had almost completed *Things to Come* and that Lee Garmes would be soon working on another big Korda production, an adaptation of the French classic novel *Cyrano de Bergerac*. There was indeed such a plan with Charles Laughton as the nasally endowed hero, but the actor's erratic temperament and crippling self-doubt proved disastrous. Even after meticulously working on the script for a year, he and Korda argued over every point until Laughton pulled out, leaving Korda to declare that he had abandoned the project as being too uncommercial. *Miss Bracegirdle Does her Duty* represented a prime example of the extraordinary lengths that Korda would go to in order to get what he wanted. It was in fact designed specifically for Elsa Lanchester to make her capricious spouse feel at home. Despite later Oscar nominations for *Come to the Stable* (1949) and *Witness for the Prosecution* (1957), Lanchester is best remembered as the wild-haired bride of Frankenstein in the film of the same name. A child dancer with Isadora Duncan's troupe, she made a dozen or so films in Britain before leaving for America, most memorably in Korda's *The Private Life of Henry VIII* and *Rembrandt*, where she played opposite Charles Laughton. Despite his homosexuality, she remained married to Laughton until his death. In an odd parody of her life, just as Miss Bracegirdle did her duty, so did Lanchester hers to Korda. As she heroically puts it in her memoirs, 'I was just a human shoehorn.'

The short film was another concept in which Korda professed a keen interest either as documentary or fiction. In this, Bernard Browne, an assistant cameraman on the staff at Worton Hall, was called upon to direct and photograph *Wharves and Strays*, a twenty-minute study of dockside London, which failed miserably to compete with *The Private Life of the Gannets*, considered a truly landmark film and one recognised as the world's first natural history documentary, winning an Academy Award for Best Short Subject. Hector Hoppin and Anthony Gross had made a highly successful cartoon in France called *La Joie de Vivre*, which hugely impressed Alexander Korda who was also keen to explore the world of animation. He brought the two men to England to work on a proposed animation sequence for *Things to Come* that failed to materialise but arranged for the two men to set up an animation department at Isleworth, together with cartoonists Spud Murphy and Ronnie Giles. However, the use of colour processes in British animation was constrained by the fact that Disney had a monopoly on the use of three-colour Technicolor until 1934. Thus, although other systems were employed in the early part of the decade, Korda had to wait until 1935 to make the first British Technicolor animated film, *The Fox Hunt*, an eight-minute experiment that represents an end to his interest in short-film production.

Brother Zoltan meanwhile was busy behind the camera at Worton Hall directing *Forget Me Not*, a failed shipboard romance involving a middle-aged opera singer played by Benjamino Gigli, the most famous tenor of his generation. The film lies buried in the mire of other less prestigious productions generated at the behest of Zoltan's big brother, whom he'd followed from Budapest to Hollywood and back again to England in 1930. Despite an obvious closeness, the brothers shared a highly volatile temperament that often spilled out onto the production floor in the form of furious arguments conducted in Hungarian. Alex was a hands-on producer out to impress international audiences, while Zoltan looked to direct exotic but realistic adventures, focusing on social justice. This conflict proved evident in *Sanders of the River*, which was a significant commercial and critical success for Alex. But Zoltan would have to wait until 1939 and *The Four Feathers* for what is considered to be his finest film.

Also at Isleworth at this time was Anthony Asquith, the son of Herbert Asquith, the former Liberal Prime Minister. The younger Asquith had gone to Hollywood for six months after leaving university, where he made some useful contacts in a business not considered at all respectable for a chap of his background. Nevertheless, on return to England he went to work for British Instructional Films, the Stoll Film Company in Cricklewood and Gainsborough before joining London Films in 1935 to direct *Moscow Nights* at Worton Hall, the only film he made under contract to Korda. Based on an unpublished novel by Pierre Benoît, the film is set in 1916 Russia and is the story of a Russian girl who is persuaded by her parents to marry a wealthy middle-aged contractor. It starred the French actor Harry Baur, then considered a colossus of 1930s cinema and once compared to the legendary Jean Gabin, the most popular French actor of the pre-war era. Playing the part of Natasha was Penelope Ward, the elder daughter of The

Right Honourable William Dudley Ward and leading socialite Freda Dudley Ward, who is best remembered as the long-time mistress of the Prince of Wales, the future short-lived King Edward VIII. And making his film debut was a young Anthony Quayle, whose screen career would take off two decades later starring in a series of Associated British films, most memorably the powerful social drama *Woman in a Dressing Gown*, described by film historian Jeffrey Richards as 'the *Brief Encounter* of the council flats'. A pillar of the post-war acting establishment, Quayle went on to play a raft of supporting character roles in films such as *Ice Cold in Alex*, *Lawrence of Arabia* and *Anne of the Thousand Days* for which he was Oscar-nominated. He was awarded a CBE in 1952 and knighted in 1985.

Playing second lead to Harry Baur in the role of Captain Ivan Ignatoff was Laurence Olivier, who made his stage debut in 1922 and acted in films from the early 1930s until arguably the most striking directorial debut in British cinema history with the 1944 film version of William Shakespeare's *Henry V*. Olivier was knighted in 1947 and created a life peer in 1970. While his earlier film roles presented opportunities at the time, they later became more of an embarrassment to the ultimate darling of the stage. *The Conquest of the Air*, for example, was a drama-documentary with re-enacted historical sequences originally planned as part of a grand, although unrealised, scheme documenting the history of transport through the ages. Jointly directed by Zoltan Korda, Alexander Esway, Donald Taylor, Alexander Shaw, John Monk Saunders and William Cameron Menzies, the project turned out to be a disaster and only received a proper release in 1940 when it could benefit from wartime patriotism. Both it and *Moscow Nights* began shooting at Worton Hall, with the latter being the first film to go onto the stages at the new Denham Studios when they opened in 1936.

7

The Fairbanks Flirtation

Just as J. Arthur Rank was planning to open his Pinewood Studios in Buckinghamshire, so building had commenced in June 1935 of Alexander Korda's new complex just a few miles away near the village of Denham in the same county. Designed by Californian film studio architect Jack Okey, who had been responsible for the First National and Paramount Studios in Hollywood, there were to be seven sound stages, two large, two half-size, and three small ones with a total floor area of 120,000 square feet, the largest privately owned electricity generating station in England, numerous workshops for scenery construction, review rooms and a dubbing theatre and scoring stage large enough to take a symphony orchestra. In addition to the hundred or so offices and dressing rooms, a complete film laboratory was built on an adjacent lot and a large water tank for filming water scenes. But no sooner had this magnificent new complex opened in May 1936 than it became apparent to Alexander Korda that it was too big. He feared, and it came to pass, that his ambitious dream factory would be difficult to fully utilise even with tenant producers supplementing his own production schedule. Indeed, it would serve to add to the £330,000 losses London Films had incurred for the previous year.

Over in Los Angeles meanwhile Douglas Fairbanks Jr's long-held ambition to form his own production company was about to be realised. In his memoirs, he asserts that no one questioned his qualifications and know-how. His experience and track record were good and his box-office status better than most. Although not considered a big star, he was a well-rated one. But in Hollywood that meant nothing. Ever since the success of the United Artists concept railed against the 'tyrannical hegemony' of the major studios, the only outsiders allowed into the magic circle were super-rich 'angels' such as William Randolph Hearst and Howard Hughes. With ambitions of entering this elite circle as a player finally extinguished, Fairbanks Jr finally took David O. Selznick's advice and went east, by which he meant Europe, settling on Britain where he looked to create a company to rival Korda's and to show the bruisers in Hollywood the mistake they had made by not including him. With no financing in place, he created Criterion Film Productions and began the search for a suitable script with which to make his first picture.

Murray Silverstone and George Archibald were United Artists' representatives in Britain and therefore useful connections in a world where it mattered who you knew. They offered Fairbanks a distribution contract for one picture with options for more at a later date. They also helped him raise the seed money, but on the strict proviso he shared responsibility with an equal partner who would be responsible for the financial end of things, a clear indication of their personal reservations. In this, Silverstone brought in Marcel Hellman; a producer friend newly arrived from Hitler's Germany, whom Fairbanks describes as 'a nice little man who made many humorous mistakes in the language but none with money'. On the whole, the two men appear to have got along quite well, more so away from work where Fairbanks considered Hellman to be 'a clock-watcher and penny-pincher'.

Born Douglas Elton Ulman, Fairbanks Jr was very much the son of that hackneyed cliché 'Hollywood royalty' and thus the way ahead appeared set for a bright, gifted and devastatingly handsome boy. During his time at military academy in 1919 he excelled in everything and very early on had developed a taste for the arts, becoming something of a painter and sculptor. At age fourteen he was given a contract with Paramount Pictures where he made his screen debut in *Stephen Steps Out* (1923), but the film flopped and his career stagnated despite a critically acclaimed role in *Stella Dallas*, made in 1925. Things picked up when he married Lucille LeSueur, a young starlet who was to become the legendary Joan Crawford. The couple became the toast of the town and screen success followed in *Little Caesar* (1931). After a delayed honeymoon to England, where they were entertained by Noel Coward and the Duke of Kent, Fairbanks became active in both society and politics. Crawford, meanwhile, was far more interested in her career and her affair with Clark Gable and the couple divorced in 1933.

For a young man with his credentials and his ambition it is even more surprising that he should have decided to enter the British film industry when no more than twenty of the 640 film companies registered in England since 1925 remained active. The main problem was the cost of American distribution far exceeding the revenue. Twickenham Studios faced liabilities in the region of half a million pounds, the same amount by which Gaumont-British had increased its overdraft due to its failure to get into the American market. Pinewood studios, partly owned by Rank, fought to keep its stages open and even Denham had gone dark for a short period. But it was not all doom and gloom. This was in other ways a vintage year for British cinema in terms of its infrastructure, with Denham setting the agenda to match the might of Hollywood, and Norman Loudon over at Shepperton reaping such dividends that it was screaming out for expansion.

Loudon had purchased the Littleton Park estate in 1928, churning out numerous quickies unbound by any concerns of aesthetic quality. When the refurbished studio opened in 1936, it boasted seven sound stages (including two of 18,000 square feet), twelve cutting rooms, three viewing theatres, scene docks and workshops, and the Jacobean mansion was refurbished to provide hotel and restaurant facilities. That year alone, twenty-two productions took advantage of the new complex. Whatever adventure Douglas Fairbanks Jr was embarking upon, the bar was now higher in Britain than it had ever been and the competition to stake a claim never more fierce.

Joining Fairbanks and Hellman as a director of Criterion was Captain Alec Stratford Cunningham-Reid, a First World War flying ace and Conservative Member of Parliament. An impoverished country clergyman's son, the war hero had married well. His wife, Mary Ashley, was Edwina Mountbatten's sister and co-heiress of their grandfather's immense fortune. Even so, Cunningham-Reid was renowned for being something of a ladies' man and so the idea of being chairman of a movie company stirred up all manner of prospects under the heading of business. The couple kept a large townhouse in Mayfair, complete with swimming pool and film projection room where they entertained often and well. Fairbanks had typically met them during a weekend with the Mountbattens at their country house. Besides being an avid movie fan, 'Dickie' Mountbatten had always been a keen admirer of Fairbanks Sr, and recognised in the son a similarity of spirit insofar as they were both born of once-famous world heroes, now reduced in rank. According to Fairbanks, Mountbatten became almost a surrogate older brother and his wife, Edwina, always a friend and therefore well-placed in influencing her brother-in-law to support the new venture.

Fairbanks was offered a formal distribution contract with United Artists for four pictures, on condition that he played in at least two of them. With approval on all storylines, UA would also approve the principal players and the director. Not that this concerned Fairbanks. After years of trying to promote his own creativity and being kept out of the running by the Hollywood system, these restraints saw him as more or less his own boss. Besides, the first vehicle had already been approved; an adaptation of Jeffrey Farnol's novel of Regency days, *The Amateur Gentleman*, which succeeded in attracting the playwright Winifred Clemence Dane, who agreed to write the screenplay. The film was shot at Elstree on a modest budget which Marcel Hellman stretched to the limit, visiting the set periodically, conspicuously taking out his watch and considering how to move the game forward. Whereas Monty Marks had advised Alexander Korda to quit Worton Hall and go build his expensive white elephant at Denham, so the cautious Hellman advised his co-directors that purchasing the small but well-equipped Isleworth studio to make all of the Criterion productions there would relieve them of the demands and excessive overheads of other studios. The deal was done on 31 December 1935 and on 9 January 1936 Worton Hall Studios Ltd was registered with a capital of £10,000 in £1 shares. Joining the board was Paul Czinner, who directed Korda's *Catherine The Great* and Edward Gourdeau, the managing director of Interworld Films Ltd, former owner of the Worton Hall estate.

Like much of the agricultural land surrounding London during the inter-war years, that around Isleworth was fast becoming buried under acres of new industry and semi-detached houses bleeding off the new arterial roads striking out of the capital. The journey by car from the exclusive Boltons in Kensington where Douglas Fairbanks Jr resided was now less than an hour away, and a shade more to the heart of the film business in and around Soho. A flavour of how Worton Hall presented itself to the glitterati as their limousines rolled along the surviving country lanes comes from the pages of *Highwayman's Heath*, the collected wisdom of 1930s local historian Gordon S. Maxwell. He describes the mansion at Worton Hall as one of three substantial eighteenth-century houses occupying this tiny enclave of less than 200 souls; the Manor House at the corner of Bridge Road and Worton Road, its fine range of stabling effectively screened by a high hedge surrounding the grounds; Worton Court, distinguishable by its turret, and Worton Hall further along the road. Maxwell describes the latter as one of the finest types of late-eighteenth-century architecture. 'In every sense it is typical of its age, both in the building and in the lawn in front with its fine cedar-tree in the centre.' To the rear was the studios and if the film-makers ever wanted a period scene for a costume drama then they need look no further than the house itself.

Maxwell recalls once standing by the front gate for an hour 'peopling the old place' with visions of his imagination 'as real to me as if I had seen them on the screen – in fact, more so than a good many impossible ones I have seen at "the pictures"'. Some of the mental pictures conjured up included

a post-chaise or a yellow barouche with its bewigged postillions drive up to the old pillared doorway, 'My Lady' descends with her high-powdered hair and hooped dress of fine brocade, handed down by her escort garbed in a flowered coat and silken breeches. Then the scene would shift, a few years pass by, and I would see the old house as it was in the Regency days; a meeting-place of the dashing Corinthians and the Bucks of those stirring times; and even a solitary highwayman prowling round would sometimes come into the picture, for at one time this old mansion stood on the fringe of the Heath. Yes, they were vivid pictures by that gate.

The district of Worton had lately been blessed with a sewage 'farm', destined to blossom considerably into the malodorous Mogden Sewage Treatment Works feared locally today, but apparently of little concern then to Fairbanks and his associates arriving in the wake of London Films. As Alexander Korda settled down to run his more grandiose studio set-up at Denham, so the first Criterion film went into production at his more modest former base. *Accused* was a backstage murder mystery set in Paris. A tale of misinformed jealousy and murder concerning the trial of the wrong person and the revelation of the real murderer, the leading lady was Dolores del Rio, the beautiful Mexican film star of Hollywood films during the silent era. She had taken the surname of her husband for her film debut in *Joanna* in 1925 where Hollywood executives first spotted her appeal as a sex siren, dubbing her the female version of Rudolph Valentino. In late 1926, the acclaimed director Raoul Walsh offered her the role of Charmaine in *What Price Glory*, which saw her become admired as one of the most beautiful women on screen. More success came in 1927 when she again worked with Walsh on *Carmen* and later *The Red Dance*, but then came the talkies. Because of her Latin accent she was almost immediately relegated to exotic and less important roles. By the time she joined the Fairbanks ensemble at Isleworth, Del Rio's once glittering career had declined and her part in *Accused* typical of a series of bland, two-dimensional roles.

Douglas Fairbanks Jr was busily planning two big specials starring himself, as the distribution deal with United Artists called for. The proposed *Bonnie Prince Charlie*, about the young Stuart pretender, and *The Armstrong*, set in the Anglo-Scottish border wars, were both variations on the American Western, but played out in rugged Highland glens rather than Monument Valley. Requiring huge budgets which he was unable to find, Fairbanks 'clearly lacked Korda's persuasive charm and experience in finding financial supporters', he laments in his memoirs. Both ideas were temporarily postponed and having also failed to attract a leading man for *Accused*, Fairbanks reluctantly stepped into what he describes as 'the not very good part'. The highly acclaimed English actress, comedienne and impersonator Florence Desmond was cast as a temperamental French singer who gets murdered and Googie Withers as Ninette, a chorus girl. Withers broke into films in 1934 with *The Girl in the Crowd* but found herself confined to playing mostly second leads like her role in *Accused*. She became best known for a series of melodramas at Ealing Studios in the 1940s, later proving a versatile character player on the big and moreso the small screen.

While Korda struggled to fill Denham's vast capacity, Fairbanks' tiny domain at Isleworth continued to attract business either by design or ill-fortune. *Love in Exile* was a Capitol Film that had begun shooting at Elstree until a fire destroyed the British and Dominion Studio there and the production was transferred to Worton Hall. The story of an abdicated king who outwits two revolutionary oil magnates and stages a surprise return to his throne, this was a wholly unremarkable production with a cast and crew to match, except for the chief cameraman, Otto Kanturek. Either a Czech or an Austrian national, Kanturek began his prolific film career as an assistant cameraman with Pathé and Éclair in Paris in 1912. After spells working in Milan and Vienna, he worked for Alexander Korda in Budapest and in 1920 was in Berlin where he worked on numerous films, including Fritz Lang's *Woman in the Moon*. With the rise of the Nazis, he moved to Vienna and Prague in 1933 and then to London where he worked until the outbreak of war. By 1941 Britain had been at war with Germany for two years. RAF Coltishall in Norfolk was playing a key role, but the planes taking off were not just carrying bombs, but also cameras. Kanturek and fellow film-maker Jack Parry were shooting some aerial footage for *A Yank in the RAF* and *One of Our Aeroplanes is Missing*, when a Hurricane fighter collided with Kanturek's plane, killing him and the crew. His name appears among the war dead who fought and died on British soil and who are buried at Scottow in Norfolk, except to the inscription above Kanturek's name is added 'Twentieth Century Fox Films Ltd'.

Just before Christmas 1936, Douglas Fairbanks Jr was spotted at Heston Airport (Heathrow was yet to be built) shooting a scene for *Thief in the Night* (otherwise *Jump for Glory*), a lame murder melodrama about a thief redeemed through love. The action included a parachute jump, which was made by Mr B. G. de Greeuw, a well-known proponent of the art, doubling for Fairbanks. Watching the action unfold was Roy Parkinson, who had progressed to the position of second assistant director with Criterion Film Productions, and who talked about his experiences to Sid Cole as part of the BECTU History Project in 1987.

Having had to explain to Cole where Worton Hall was, Parkinson recalled being taken on by Marcel Hellman and Douglas Fairbanks Jr. 'Young Doug was a jolly good chap to get on with. He was really good, you could talk to him, he joined in with everybody, he was really one of the boys you might say.' And there's the rub. For as much as Fairbanks fought to claw his way out of his father's shadow and prove his worth to those who undervalued him in Hollywood, he was yet to become the man. His relationship with Hellman was becoming increasingly difficult; although he described the 'little man' as 'personally as nice as could be', their respective views of what comprised a high-quality film grew further apart daily. This, according to Fairbanks affected his judgement and his performance. Matters were not helped by studio labour problems, which slowed production down and discouraged him even further. To make matters worse, his relationship with Criterion's chairman, Alex Cunningham-Reid, was fast deteriorating with Fairbanks becoming apprehensive about his 'slick' ideas for financing the company. With the fight barely begun, Fairbanks was already seriously considering quitting Criterion altogether.

In late September 1936 Fairbanks had been to see a new play in the West End called *Mademoiselle* and was struck by the personality and talent of the beautiful, but then little-known leading lady, Greer Garson. Directly after the final curtain, Fairbanks made his way backstage to her dressing room and introduced himself. 'She was as flustered and fluttery as a young girl at her first dance,' he recalls, after telling her about the part he wanted her to play in *Jump For Glory* as her film debut. Although tempted she felt that film wasn't her medium, adding coyly that she was not at all photogenic. Fairbanks was so taken 'with her evident charisma' that he pestered her for days, eventually tempting her out to Worton Hall for a screen test where great care was taken with her make-up and hairdressing. Criterion's 'top-notch cameraman', Gunther Krampf, took infinite care with her lighting for the agreed scene with Fairbanks. In the view of all the experts who saw it, the result was every bit as fine as Fairbanks had predicted. The only hesitation came from his United Artists overlords who felt that Garson had not yet established herself as a top-name stage star and was completely unknown in films. Although difficult to sell, they would only agree to her hiring provided a well-known male star was engaged to play opposite her.

A few days later, and to Fairbanks' huge disappointment, Garson turned down the offer of the part. Having seen the screen test she thought it 'absolutely dreadful', the whole experience confirming her belief that films were not for her. In a letter she wrote to Fairbanks she wondered how his female co-stars ever managed to perform when faced with his presence and thanked him for helping her out with the test. 'The only moment that didn't make me prickly with shame,' she writes, was when she thought that the test was over and she rushed out of the studio protesting wildly that 'never, no – never, unless your make-up and camera wizards could mitigate the full horror of my countenance, could I think of making a picture'. This, she hoped, did not offend the various technicians too much, but Fairbanks was having none of it and continued to pursue her for his film. Eventually Garson's producer, Hugh Beaumont, wrote to him, making it plain that he had, quite firmly, refused permission to release her. With that Fairbanks admitted defeat and began looking for someone else. A year later and MGM succeeded where Fairbanks failed, signing Garson to a contract to appear in *Goodbye, Mr. Chips* with Robert Donat. It was an instant hit.

Fairbanks eventually secured the services of Valerie Hobson as his leading lady, of whom he has little more to say in his autobiography other than that. Her performance, however, did catch the eye of Alexander Korda, who promptly signed her to a long-term contract. In the event, she made only two films for him, *The Drum* (1938) and *Q Planes* (1939) with Ralph Richardson and Laurence Olivier. A respected leading lady in the British cinema of the 1930s and 40s, Hobson would achieve a second moment in the spotlight as the wife of John Profumo, the Tory minister at the centre of the Christine Keeler affair in 1963.

Engaged to direct the modest *Jump For Glory* 'at a big price' was the legendary Raoul Walsh, who began his career as a stage actor in New York in 1914, switching to film as assistant to D. W. Griffith. He made his first full-length feature a year later, *The Life of General Villa*, and then the critically acclaimed *Regeneration*, arguably the earliest gangster film. This busy year also included Walsh playing John Wilkes Booth in *The Birth of a Nation* while assisting Griffith on the epic landmark film. He directed the 1924 version of *The Thief of Bagdad* for Douglas Fairbanks Pictures, cementing a relationship with the acting dynasty that sadly failed to benefit Fairbanks Jr. In front of the camera Walsh starred alongside Gloria Swanson as her boyfriend in *Sadie Thompson*, and it was while filming on location in Arizona for *The Cisco Kid* that he lost his right eye in a car accident, adding the signature eye patch to his persona. In the early days of sound with Fox, Walsh directed the first wide-screen spectacle, *The Big Trail* (1930), starring a former prop boy he'd discovered called Marion Morrison and whom he renamed John Wayne. An undistinguished period followed, which included his trip to Isleworth, his career picking up after 1939 when he moved back to Hollywood and with Warner Brothers made some of the most iconic movies of the 1940s with James Cagney, Humphrey Bogart, George Raft, Edward G. Robinson, Marlene Dietrich, Clark Gable and many others. Alan Hale was added to the cast of *Jump for Glory*, but still the project was unable to attract a suitable leading man, leaving Fairbanks no choice but to abide by his contractual obligation to United Artists and play the lead himself. Walsh meanwhile spent his time studying the day's racing rather than directing the unremarkable film.

As autumn slid into winter and with a good deal of work still to be done on *Jump For Glory*, there was fun instead to be had elsewhere, with friends at country weekends and especially time spent with the German screen goddess, Marlene Dietrich. By the time the film was ready for delivery to United Artists, Fairbanks' latest infatuation had left London for California, leaving him to ponder his future. Writing to his partner, Marcel Hellman, with a copy to Cunningham-Reid, Fairbanks sought to put on record his dissatisfactions with Criterion's operations. It was his intention either to raise the sights and alter company policies or to resign, stating unequivocally on the advice of his family solicitor that he found his position and activities incompatible with the ideas that inspired him to organise the company in the first place. Tellingly, he makes mention of his partners' 'greater production authority' that had devalued his career beyond recognition; leaving him no option other than to dissociate himself completely from the company's future. There were no blazing rows, but everyone knew that there was no way short of a lawsuit to halt his resignation. Surprised at how well *Jump For Glory* did at the box office, the small profit failed to placate his disappointment with Criterion's record. Having completed his statutory two starring roles, Fairbanks was effectively on gardening leave for the company's third and final film, providing space to sort out the company's corporate difficulties including what he mentions in his memoirs as 'a sort of financial settlement'.

Crime Over London was yet another routine melodrama emblematic of Criterion Films. Googie Withers was invited back to play Miss Dupres in a film that centred on 'Joker Finnegan' and his gang of New York hoodlums who travel to London to rob The House of a Thousand Windows, a large department store. Under the watchful eye of Inspector Gray of Scotland Yard (played by Paul Cavanagh), Finnegan (played by Basil Sydney) forces an American actor named Reilly (Joseph Cawthorn) to impersonate the store owner, who is identical in appearance. The first British film to be directed by Alfred Zeisler, the prolific American-born German producer, director, actor and screenwriter, he had as his cameraman Claude Friese-Greene, the son of William Friese-Green, the early cinematography pioneer who invented a colour film process called Biocolour. A confused patent lawsuit decided by the House of Lords in 1915 meant that William Friese-Greene was unable to fully exploit his system, and after his death in 1921, Claude (cinematographer on more than sixty films from 1923 to 1943) continued his work, renaming the process Friese-Greene Natural Colour.

Despite a generous sprinkling of proven talent including Alan Hale, Barbara Everest, Basil Radford and Roland Culver, the last Criterion production was a box-office disaster. In his anxiety to settle his departure swiftly it was agreed that compensation in the form of a portion of the profits from *The Amateur Gentleman* would cover what Fairbanks had lost on the other films. After that, his resignation became final. By the end of 1936 the company was in disarray. Paul Czinner, who played no part in the running of the company, had resigned. Fairbanks wrote to Cunningham-Reid, 'Our pictures, for what they are, have been disastrously expensive.' No more were made and 'young Doug' returned to America where he was loath to report the news to his father that the company he had started, and of which he had been so proud after such a promising start, was finished. To all others he minimised his disappointment and his uncertainty about the future. But his year away from Hollywood had left him without representation and it was only after the intervention of Marlene Dietrich that he found himself on the books of another agent willing to take him on.

8
Taking the Cue from Hollywood

Alexander Korda had enjoyed a good business relationship with Sam Goldwyn and the two men had talked about buying control of United Artists. By June 1937 arrangements were virtually completed on a deal to buy out Douglas Fairbanks Sr, Mary Pickford and Charlie Chaplin, with Korda sharing in the profits and distribution of his films in thousands of American cinemas. Lord Strabolgi, the chairman of the British Film Advancement Council, stated that the more serious and expensive films made in Britain between 1934 and 1937 simply copied the Hollywood technique and that only a few highly successful British pictures of a specialised kind, such as *The Private Life of Henry VIII* and *The Ghost Goes West* had done well in the USA. On the whole, American distributors found no reason to screen British pictures in favour of American products. 'Only Korda, by his arrangement with United Artists, was able to break this boycott,' he believed.

Goldwyn and Korda each held a 20 per cent interest in United Artists and in November 1937 confirmed their take up of the remaining 60 per cent interest held by the three founders. This meant that Goldwyn and Korda would each hold 50 per cent each, although Fairbanks and Pickford had agreed to leave a substantial amount of their shares in the company. Korda's share was to be guaranteed by a British group, headed by Oscar Deutsch, the creator of the Odeon cinema circuit, who wanted American films for his own theatres. On 15 November 1937, the *Financial Times* reported that the negotiations had been successfully concluded, subject to final action deferred until the legal advisers had fully examined the proposed details. Pending the final contract, United Artists announced that it would show twenty-one new British films throughout America. Murray Silverstone, the British head of United Artists, said that the success of Korda's films had been so great in all countries that his company had resolved to make the world-wide distribution of British films a permanent policy.

Despite all the positive news, talk of a crisis in the British film industry persisted. Korda countered the claim by arguing that all the claims about making cheap pictures for the British market was rubbish. 'This country has a right to the best film industry in the world,' he slammed, 'and will get it only by competing on the world market.' He cited companies that were formed without the proper technical or commercial personnel who had either lost their money or would lose it in the future. This was no reason to slam those who were attempting to build up the industry, he argued. If London Films was short of money then it wasn't because its productions hadn't done well. *Sanders of the River* and *The Ghost Goes West* grossed £450,000, and even the tricky *Things to Come* had eventually taken £350,000 at the box office, although this was neutralised by the very high production costs. Korda spoke with authority when he declared that the real art was in the selling of the product. Exactly the same conditions applied to the cheap British production made solely for the home market as it did the more ambitious productions destined for the international market. In Korda's view, 'the selling and distributing of pictures is an art that England still has to learn'. He had created the finest studios equipped with the best staff in Europe and enjoyed as robust an international distribution deal as any of the biggest American studios. But even so, he was finding it increasingly difficult to tease fresh financial backing from the Prudential. Eventually, he was forced to change tack, announcing that London Films would focus on 'good, entertaining films of comparatively little expense, taking the cue from Hollywood'. These would not be quickies, as such, and the more ambitious production would still have its place.

Korda felt that Britain had not done too badly. With studios equal to anywhere in the world, a number of promising directors, excellent technicians and a wealth of screen talent, there was no reason at all to believe that the perceived crisis was endemic. But there were those who blamed Korda's excessive spending for the film industry's decline, gambling on big returns from the American and the home market and in some cases on projects that barely justified the expense. This led to imitators spending equal sums on indifferent films that had no hope of entering the American market and even less of recouping the costs from British cinemas. But with comparatively few exceptions most of the films coming out of British studios in the second half of the 1930s were at best mediocre, and in this Worton Hall played no small part, continuing to attract an eclectic assortment of films that mostly favoured the indifferent, such as *Under Secret Orders*, shot simultaneously in French as *Mademoiselle Docteur*.

This was originally planned as a German project in 1933 by Georg Wilhelm Pabst, considered by many to be the greatest director of German cinema of his era. But the project was banned by the authorities before production could start. In 1936 it was purchased by Trafalgar Films and placed in the hands of Franco-British director, Edmond T. Gréville, née Max Montagut, née Edmond Gréville Thonger (real name Greville Thong), who was responsible for over forty films between 1927 and 1963, of which none fall under the category of distinguished. *Under Secret Orders* was based on the real-life story of Anne Marie Lesser, who became involved with a German spy during the First World War. Realising that he is being followed by British agents, the spy passes the secret information he is carrying to her. When he is killed, she gives the information to his superiors, and herself becomes a spy, hoping to exact revenge for his death. She is then sent on several dangerous and deadly missions that cause her to question what she is doing.

Playing the part of Marie Lesser was Dita Parlo, a popular actress in Germany who moved easily between German- and French-language films during the 1930s. Failing to establish a career in Hollywood, she returned to Germany at the outbreak of war in 1939, where she appeared in only three films during the last thirty years of her life. Playing a predictably unsympathetic German spymaster who recruits Lesser was Erich Von Stroheim, the Austrian-born star of the silent film age, later lauded for his directorial work and playing arrogant Teutonic characters that made him 'the man you love to hate'. Such a huge fantasist was he that much of what has been written about him is the stuff of fiction. He claimed, for example, to be Count Erich Oswald Hans Carl Maria von Stroheim und Nordenwall, the son of Austrian nobility, but is more likely to have been born to a middle-class Jewish hat-maker. He may or may have not had an uncredited role in D. W. Griffith's ground-breaking film *Intolerance*, but certainly after the First World War he became infamous for his dictatorial and demanding style, considered to be one of the greatest directors of the silent era, best remembered for *Greed*. But it was his unwillingness to compromise, his extreme attention to detail and the resulting escalating costs of his films that led to fewer and fewer directing opportunities.

John Loder, a one-time prisoner of war who stayed on in Germany to run a pickle factory and work as a bit-part player in German films, played the part of the British spymaster. Fox Film Productions set up a German branch after the war with Alexander Korda as their representative. In August 1926 the company purchased the film rights to Clement Vautel's French novel, *Madame ne veut pas d'enfant*. In casting for the film, Korda interviewed the young Loder, who was looking to move full-time into films. Korda told him to forget the idea, as the film business was a mug's game. That said, Loder was asked if he owned a dress suit, which he did, and thus was hired as a 'dress extra' along with fellow newcomer, hired on the same basis, Marlene Dietrich. With the advent of the talkies, Loder tried his luck in Hollywood, appearing in *The Doctor's Secret* (1929), Paramount's first talking picture.

In the autumn of 1931 Korda was working for Paramount and was dispatched from Paris to London to take charge the company's British interests. With no prospects other than two pictures for Paramount, he predictably took offices he could ill afford in Grosvenor Square. From there he immediately set about firming up a future founded on his own entrepreneurial skills, and it was John Loder who was in a position to help out. In one of a series of events that were to have important consequences for the rise of the ambitious Hungarian, Loder introduced Korda to his brother-in-law, the wealthy and influential head of a large brewery, which in turn led to introductions with prominent establishment figures. At the start of the Second World War, Loder went to America where he appeared in a string of B-movie roles.

Playing the thankless role of 'Rene's Girl' is Clare Luce, primarily a stage actress and dancer who appeared in a few films. She starred in many Broadway plays from 1923 until 1952, including with Fred Astaire in the original musical *Gay Divorce* in 1932. Astaire tried to secure her for the film version but was overruled by the studio (RKO Radio Pictures) opting instead for their contract player, Ginger Rogers. In his autobiography, Astaire credits Luce as the inspiration for his legendary Night and Day dance routine. And missing from the credits of *Under Secret Orders* is a young actor who was working with the Birmingham Repertory Company at the time and looking to break into films. Born James Leblanche Stewart, the great-great-grandson of actor Luigi Lablache, his decision not to pursue a medical career led to the West End and his screen debut at Isleworth. After release from military service in 1942, Stewart Grainger landed his first starring role in *The Man in Grey*, the first of many film roles spanning the forthcoming decades.

Success as a playwright for Terrence Rattigan came with the stage play *After The Dance* in 1939, which showcased his determination to write serious social drama. The young Old Harrovian had left Oxford in 1934 looking to make a career as a writer, finding initial success as a playwright two years later with *French Without Tears*. Three years later and his first screenplay was penned for Liberty Films, working out of Worton Hall. A seafaring tale, *Captain's Orders* features a transatlantic race in which one of the captains involved nearly loses after saving an actress from her sinking yacht. The outbreak of war temporarily halted the rich career of the country's most popular twentieth-century dramatist. Netting a CBE in 1958 and a knighthood thirteen years later, direction of his practice-piece at Worton Hall was entrusted to Ivar Campbell, a man who ploughed his way through numerous low-budget productions and quota quickies.

Captain Trent was played by Henry Edwards, an actor who truly encompassed the British film industry from silence to sound, in front of and behind the cameras. Sometimes described as Britain's first male movie star and celebrated as the country's answer to Douglas Fairbanks Sr, Edwards was a principal actor with the Hepworth Company at Walton, starring in twenty-two films, playing everything from an aristocrat to an honest, working man. With the collapse of Hepworth, Edwards began to direct and in 1927 teamed up with Julius Hagen to found the W. P. Film Company at Twickenham, personally spearheading its conversion to sound. In 1931 he and E. G. Norman purchased, rebuilt and re-equipped Teddington Studios, previously damaged in a fire. Seeking a base for their British product, Warner Brothers promptly negotiated a lease for the property. With the industry in recession and a cut in the demand for quota quickies, Edwards finished his directing career with a pair of Stanley Holloway films in 1937 and continued to act, playing supporting roles such as police inspectors, majors and judges, with his last screen appearance in Robert Hamer's *The Long Memory* (1952).

Less than two months after announcing their grand plan, Korda and Goldwyn decided not to buy out United Artists. The reason they gave was the fragile global financial climate. But in reality Fairbanks, Pickford and Chaplin were unwilling to allow Korda's films to be released by any company other than United Artists. Korda needed to make other films for outside release in order to keep Denham Studios running at a profit, so he had no option other than to walk away from the arrangement, but leaving behind a legacy that enabled British independent producers to market their films through United Artists at much-reduced costs and receipt of a share in the profits. Unfortunately, this was only paper thin, as UA didn't own any cinemas in the United States. So the door Korda had opened for other British films in America allowed very limited access and none at all for the likes of George Smith Enterprises, typical of the British producer concentrating on low-budget regional comedies and pulp-novel melodramas. *His Lordship Regrets* was an exemplar made at Worton Hall in 1938 starring Claude Hulbert, the comic actor younger brother of the more successful Jack.

But British cinema at this time was by no means a centre of cultural despair. While the US studio system was continuing to turn out such consistent box office hits as *The Adventures of Robin Hood* starring Errol Flynn, *Angels with Dirty Faces*, one of James Cagney's greatest roles, *Bringing up Baby* with Cary Grant and Katharine Hepburn and *Jezebel* with the incomparable Bette Davis, in Britain Gainsborough had produced Hitchcock's *The Lady Vanishes* with Margaret Lockwood and Michael Redgrave; Pinewood *Pygmalion*, starring Leslie Howard and Wendy Hiller, and MGM at Denham Studios had a handful of hugely successful films, including *A Yank at Oxford*, *The Citadel* and *Goodbye Mr. Chips*. The Cinematograph Films Act of 1938 was designed to provide incentives for British film companies to make fewer films and of higher quality, a move however that in the main failed heroically to affect the industry's output overall. In this, Worton Hall reigned supreme.

The second Ivar Campbell offering for Liberty Films at Isleworth was *Too Many Husbands*, an adaptation of Guy P. Bolton's stage farce *Mirabelle*, which involves a notorious con artist thought to have been killed in a plane crash but who heads for the gaming tables of Monte Carlo to cash in on his new identity. It starred Jack Melford, all but forgotten to cinema history despite a profuse film career spanning forty years and over 120 screen appearances.

Redd Davis was a Canadian film director and producer who made his British debut with *The Spare Room* in 1932 and worked mainly at Twickenham Studios churning out his quota of quickies as he learned his craft. He was booked into Worton Hall for *Special Edition*, the tale of a reporter who helps a surgeon's daughter to unravel a web of blackmail and murder, innocently involving her father. Davis' most successful film was *Underneath the Arches* in 1937, starring the comedy duo Flanagan and Allen, who formed part of the Crazy Gang ensemble. Although his budgets improved, he never completely divorced himself from slapdash, low comedies such as *Special Edition*, starring John Garrick, an actor reputed to have excelled in confounding a director's best creative efforts, and Lucille

Lisle, whose successful stage career was countered by such poor choices of film work.

You're the Doctor was another lightweight capitulation to low romantic comedy gracing Worton Hall. The story of a young girl who pleads illness to avoid going on a cruise with her parents and goes off to a nursing home with a scientist mistaken for a doctor, it starred Bruce Seton, later Sir Bruce Lovat Seton of Abercorn, 11th Baronet, who forwent an earlier romantic objective of regaining the family estates lost in the '45 rebellion to become an actor. A familiar face in films of the 1930s and 1940s, Seton is best remembered for his portrayal of *Fabian of the Yard*, one of the very first British television detective dramas. Googie Withers returned to Isleworth together with an uncredited Michael Ripper, who would go on to provide a plethora of servants, pub landlords, petty crooks or cockney coppers until settling in as a regular face for Hammer Films, one of the most commercially successful of all British film companies. Gus McNaughton was already a well-established character actor who is perhaps most notably seated opposite Robert Donat aboard *The Flying Scotsman* in *The 39 Steps*, mildly horrified by the antics of a travelling salesman who insists on exposing his samples of ladies undergarments.

As the American studio system continued to turn out quality movies the likes of *The Wizard of Oz*, *Gone with the Wind*, *Stagecoach*, *Mr. Smith Goes to Washington*, *Wuthering Heights*, *Only Angels Have Wings*, *Ninotchka* and *Midnight*, so the Prudential Assurance Company was left bitterly regretting its backing of Britain's great Hungarian hope. Both the Pru' and United Artists had loaned Korda too much money to extricate themselves. E. H. Lever, one of the Pru's company secretaries, begged him to abandon managing his company and to concentrate on producing films, but to no avail. Lever wrote in 1938 that 'it is unfortunately true that on account of his temperament and opportunism in financial matters, Mr Korda is a dangerous element in any business, more particularly if he is in a position of control'. A year later and Korda was forced to hand over that control to his greatest rival, the Rank Organisation, taking off to America to supervise completion of *The Thief of Bagdad*. The tiny studio at Isleworth that had once served his purpose was now a dim and distant memory, its fortunes in the hands of film producer Maurice Wilson, who had taken out the lease. Until such time as Britain's war with Germany for the second time that century got fully underway, the production line at Isleworth continued to churn out mediocrity with aplomb.

Shadowed Eyes was a Maclean Rogers offering on behalf of George Smith Enterprises. It centred on a famous surgeon, played by Basil Sydney, who murders his wife's lover while suffering a mental blackout. Following another bout of the worrying condition he manages to successfully operate on the father of his girlfriend, who then helps him on the road to normality. Basil Sydney endured a return visit to Worton Hall for *Miracles do Happen* along with Patricia Hilliard who played Janet Gordon in *Things to Come* and the shepherdess in *The Ghost Goes West*. A comedy based on the discovery of a synthetic milk formula, its loss and purchase by a syndicate anxious to suppress it, *Miracles do Happen* was the last in a string over forty-five mostly forgotten films made by George Smith Enterprises since the company was formed in 1931. Stewart Rome, a major star of the silent era, enjoyed third billing and the film's star was Jack Hobbs, who at the age of sixteen appeared in an early production of *Tom Brown's Schooldays*, which was the first feature film chosen to be presented by royal command at Buckingham Palace in 1917.

Venture Films was another lowbrow company that made use of the Isleworth facility for at least two of its films. *The Body Vanished* was directed by former actor Walter Tennyson, responsible for half a dozen or so lower order productions. This one starred Anthony Hulme as a Scotland Yard inspector on holiday with his newspaper reporter friend. They happen upon a murder that might not be a murder, so it's up the detective to stick around to establish from the range of eccentric rural characters if a murder actually occurred and if so the motive and ultimately the killer. Striking an international note, Venture's next film was *Mistaken Identity*, an Australian production which involved a booking clerk played by Richard Goolden (best known for his stage work as Mole in *Wind in the Willows*) who is dismissed after a mistake and confused with a millionaire in London. Its first trade screening was in July 1939 but was not released until 1942 when the nation was grateful for anything that took its mind off war.

Writ large once more at Isleworth was the name Hulbert, with Jack's own production from the musical play *Under Your Hat*, a lively spy caper where the male half of a married song-and-dance duo moonlights as a government spy and is assigned to monitor a sexy foreign counterpart. It starred the popular musical comedian and his long-time wife, Cicely Courtneige, star of slapstick comedies who would become one of the most recognisable faces on television. Directed by the inexhaustible Maurice Elvey, *Under Your Hat* proved something of a transition film for the husky-voiced leading lady Glynis Johns, who had made her screen debut in 1937 in *South Riding* playing a petulant, foot-stamping adolescent, graduating to her most famous coquettish leading role as the alluring mermaid in *Miranda* in 1946.

Uncredited was party guest Paul Henried who came to England in 1935 after being discovered by the legendary director Otto Preminger. Henried successfully worked his way into the system, becoming an American citizen in 1940 and blossoming at Warner Brothers famously as Jerry Durrance in *Now Voyager* and resistance leader Victor Lazslo in *Casablanca*.

Talking to David Blake in 2004, production accountant Archie Holly couldn't recall if previous owners of Worton Hall before the war had gone broke, stopped making pictures or if their lease had run out. Grand National had taken a lease on the studios from the owners, but he believed that it was still owned by the Almond family and the Interworld group. *To-day's Cinema* in November 1938 announced Grand National's bold plan to open their own distribution company in Britain, with the first year's output in the region of thirty films and rising to about forty. First off the production line at Isleworth was a Jack Raymond production of an Edgar Wallace story tentatively entitled *The Mind of Mr. Reeder*. Distribution contracts were signed with Vogue Film Productions and other 'important British producers' to ensure that Grand National would be in the first rank of renters in Britain within twelve months. At its sales convention in May 1940, the company announced six 'attractive, star-studded box office releases', including *You Will Remember*, which had started shooting at Worton Hall. Another Jack Raymond Production, but one that broke the shackle of low-brow comedy, this biopic featured the turbulent life and times of the once-popular English composer Leslie Stuart, responsible for many popular tunes of the early twentieth century, including 'Lily of Laguna' and 'Dolly Daydream'.

The deceptively pompous Robert Morley starred as Stuart, the bulky, bushy-browed actor having returned to England the previous year from Hollywood where he had received an Oscar nomination for his film debut as the foppish French King Louis XVI in *Marie Antoinette*. Clearly Jack Raymond had ambitions for this film, casting alongside Morley the up-and-coming actor and playwright Emlyn Williams as Stuart's long-time associate, Bob Slater. Williams had worked with Alfred Hitchcock, starring alongside Charles Laughton, Leslie Banks and Robert Newton in *Jamaica Inn* (1934), and was writing additional dialogue for *The Man Who Knew Too Much*. Cast as the young Bob Slater was Roddy McDowall, who by the age of eight had embarked on his already successful acting career. When the Blitz on London began in May 1940, so the twelve-year-old McDowall was evacuated to the United States and never looked back.

The last film to roll off the production line at Isleworth before the studio was turned over to war work was *Spellbound*; not the psychological mystery thriller from the master of that genre, Alfred Hitchcock, but a supernatural drama directed by John Harlow for Pyramid Amalgamated Productions. It was re-released in 1943 and again in 1946, taking the alternative names in Britain and the States *The Spell of Amy Nugent, Passing Clouds* and *Ghost Story*. Described as a strange and compelling tale, it was originally banned by the censors, only just passing when a prologue by the Spiritualist Church was added. Starring Derek Farr, Vera Lindsay and Hay Petrie, the story involves a college student unable to overcome the death of his lover. He attempts to contact her by holding a séance, an experience he finds so frightening that he suffers a breakdown, and it is only through the efforts of a secret love that he is returned to health and finds new happiness. Based on Robert Benson's novel *The Necromancer*, the screenplay was written by Miles Malleson, the abundant screenwriter and actor associated with *Nell Gwyn, Tudor Rose* and *Victoria the Great*, whose chinless wonder looks and bumbling effervescence offered up landmark cameos such as the theatre manager in Hitchcock's *The 39 Steps*, the hangman in *Kind Hearts and Coronets* and the shifty precurer of porn in *Peeping Tom*. Playing the part of Amy Nugent's mother was Irene Handl, the delightful comedy actress of distinction who graced the credits of over a hundred films, specialising in slightly dotty landladies or domestic servants in such landmark films as *Night Train to Munich* and *Brief Encounter*.

Lurking just below Irene Handl on the credits was at the time 'the most dangerous man in the world', according to H. G. Wells, and 'the greatest personality that has walked down Fleet Street' in the opinion of the press baron Lord Beaverbrook. Others described this individual as the most abused, praised, hated and feared of any journalist living. Dubbed 'The Pope of Fleet Street', Hannen Swaffer's acid-penned prose made so many enemies that he often headed his newspaper column 'People Who Are Not Speaking to Me'. The self-confessed inventor of the gossip column was admired as much as he was feared by actors and managers and was at one time banned from twelve theatres. Swaffer freely admitted that his verdicts were capricious. 'I judge people by my liver,' he oozed. And it was as a militant crusader for Socialism that he favoured or reviled his targets according to his bile, which probably included one or two of his fellow artistes sharing the credits at Isleworth. But it was as honorary president of the Spiritualists' National Union that he found séances more rewarding than Socialism; holding his own sessions where he claimed to have established contact with John Galsworthy, Douglas Fairbanks Sr and George V. His old boss, the late Lord Northcliffe, would offer advice from beyond but Swaffer told him that he never obeyed him when he was alive, so why should he now? He once invited George Bernard Shaw to a séance, to which the playwright allegedly replied that he had given up table-rapping in his childhood, causing Swaffer to counter attack, 'I thought that now you are in your second childhood, you might want to give it another go.'

By outbreak of war in September 1939 there were twenty-two film studios operating in and around London accounting for sixty-five stages, or an area of 647,652 square feet. Those requisitioned by the government for war work included Sound City (Shepperton), Pinewood, MGM, ABPC (Elstree), Nettlefold, Islington, Beaconsfield and Worton Hall. In August 1940 came the surprise announcement in the trade press that British Lion had taken over the entire distribution of all former Grand National pictures. The news of this merger was announced 'with dramatic suddenness' by British Lion's managing director, S. W. Smith, during a lunch at the Dorchester. Grand National would continue as a producing unit with any films completed at Highbury and Worton Hall to be distributed by British Lion. *Under Your Hat* and *You Will Remember*, both recently completed at Isleworth, were not yet trade-shown. After August 1940 Worton Hall became a 'ghost factory' manufacturing parts for the war effort. By 1944 that role was coming to an end and the studio's fortunes turned on a decision by British Lion that its requisitioned studio at Beaconsfield was no longer large enough to meet the company's planned production needs. The Crown Film Unit then transferred from Pinewood to Beaconsfield on a twenty-one-year lease, leaving British Lion looking for a new home.

9

The Lion Awakes: The Korda Years, Take Two, 1944–1952

For the third time in its history, Worton Hall film studios presented an attractive proposition to a production company looking to operate from its own base. Under the auspices of a new company called Worton Hall (1944) Limited, British Lion acquired a 50 per cent share with Panton Street Nominees (40 per cent) and Irish entrepreneur The Honourable Frederick Fergus MacNaghten (10 per cent). The first task after derequisitioning from the government was to set about a programme of refurbishment, which was achieved within a year thanks to company secretary Ken Maidment. *To-Day's Cinema* reported in November 1945 its 'Big Plans for Worton Hall', with British Lion putting into operation an extensive schedule of British productions with Victor Hanbury, late of RKO Radio British Productions, appointed as executive producer/director. A large number of top-ranking artists under consideration were core to the company's intention of making big-budget British films for the world market expected to begin production at Worton Hall in February or March 1946. It also looked to equip the giant silent stage for sound to complement the two sound stages used for six months by British Lion and a Mr John Cornfield, who held the other half-year lease.

Then came the sensational news that London Films had acquired control of British Lion. Alexander Korda had stayed on in America during the war to direct *The Hamilton Women*, seen as excellent propaganda for a war-torn Britain. Although severely criticised for having left Britain during these troubled times, it appears that he was in reality something of an undercover courier, having made several transatlantic crossings on behalf of Winston Churchill. Knighted in 1942 for his efforts, he returned to London the following year to set up a merged MGM-British Lion production company. After two frustrating years wherein only one film was completed (*Perfect Strangers*), he resigned in late 1945 and looked to resurrect London Films. Prudential Assurance had kept the negatives of Korda's films and the company foreclosed with Korda owing a vast sum of money. It was delighted with his offer to buy back the negatives (for a modest sum). But not half as delighted as he, going on to enjoy the lucrative proceeds for years to come.

H. Burford Judge and Paul Nathanson resigned from the directorate of British Lion and four new members were appointed: Harold Boxall, Hugh Quennell, Sir David Cunynghame and Sir Claude Dansey. In February it was announced that Arthur Jarratt had renegotiated British Lion's arrangements with Anna Neagle and Herbert Wilcox for a series of films covering a period of four years, which gave British Lion exclusivity 'intended to create an independent organisation of leading producers' (including Alexander Korda). The first Wilcox-Neagle film would be made in Technicolor at Worton Hall, with negotiations for the acquisition of two other 'important subjects of world interest' being finalised for subsequent Wilcox-Neagle productions under the British Lion banner.

In the spring of 1946, British Lion's chairman, Hugh Quennell, outlined the corporation's £1 million expansion plan, looking to create a self-contained production and distribution unit owning its own studios and offering full facilities to independent British producers. The company's old Beaconsfield studios would be sold and Technicolor formally approached. In order to continue what he described as 'the upward trend of success for British films', Quennell also announced further assistance given to the British film industry and independent producers by British Lion with the acquisition of a 75 per cent controlling interest in Sound City (Films) Ltd at Shepperton. With proper investment these studios presented a 'first class' opportunity for Technicolor and black-and-white production. Immediately, and for the second time in its associations with Korda, Worton Hall was deemed to be 'wholly inefficient for the company's requirements'. The company had only a 50 per cent interest in the studio and therefore did not serve its best interest. Worton Hall was declared a 'useful adjunct to Sound City Studios', its historical record thereafter airbrushed from history.

British Lion was now a powerful factor in British film production, with studio facilities greater than those of ABPC and second only to Rank. *Film Industry* reported in July 1946 that Alexander Korda and his newly formed

London Film productions was about to embark on *Bonnie Prince Charlie*, with Edward Black producing and Leslie Arliss directing. Six months later in January 1947 the new era for British Lion was formally announced with production on a modest scale, starting with some 'finger-exercises', as Paul Tabori puts it. The first was a Pennant Picture production for British Lion shot at Worton Hall, *The Shop at Sly Corner*. A long-running West End hit and short-lived Broadway vehicle for Boris Karloff, the story follows the fortunes of long-standing criminal Descius Heiss, who settles in London as a respectable antique shop owner, but is actually involved in the buying and selling of stolen jewels.

Directed by George King, the cast included Oskar Homolka, the stockily built, bushy-eyebrowed quintessential Eastern European in the role of Heiss. Although he was neither Eastern European nor Russian, Homolka fled to Britain after the rise of the Nazis, playing the bomber in Alfred Hitchcock's *Sabotage* in 1936, but is perhaps best remembered for his portrayal of KGB Colonel Stok in the 1960s classics *Funeral in Berlin* and *Billion Dollar Brain*. Kenneth Griffiths, whose film work erred towards the largely unsympathetic and weaselly characters, made his first notable film debut as Archie Fellowes, Heiss's ambitious and unscrupulous shop assistant. Heiss's daughter, Margaret, was played by the diminutive Muriel Pavlow, whose career peaked in the mid-1950s. Rendering 'a competent characterisation' of a young naval surgeon was Derek Farr, the dark, brooding former schoolteacher who worked as an extra, rising to leading man in the 1940s and 50s, usually cast as a good egg falsely accused of murder. Like the plot of a quota quickie, he and Pavlow fell in love on the set of *The Shop at Sly Corner* and were married.

Irene Handl returned to Worton Hall, this time as the colourfully named Ruby Towser. She was accompanied by arguably one of the finest British film character actresses of the 40s and 50s, the homely Kathleen Harrison, who carved a career out of playing overstated cockney mothers, maids and charwomen. It was while playing Eliza Doolittle in Bernard Shaw's *Pygmalion* at the Royal Academy of Dramatic Art that the playwright attending rehearsals advised her to go out into the Old Kent Road and just listen to the women talking, which she did, and found her niche. And securing her first film role was Britain's answer to Marilyn Monroe, Diana Dors. Described by her biographer, Damon Wise, as 'shamelessly peroxided and breathtakingly cantilevered', she 'mixed with gangsters, suffered disastrous marriages, hopeless assaults on Hollywood, bankruptcies and brushes with the law' but remained 'cheerfully unrepentant'.

Born Diana Fluck, the emergent sex siren was approached by one of her drama examiners, Eric L'Epine Smith, to work on *The Shop at Sly Corner*. The part he had in mind was 'the spiv's tarty girlfriend', Mildred. The drama academy where she was studying baulked at the idea, but undeterred by her tender age (she was seventeen) Smith had her tested and she got the part. In her memoirs, Dors recalls having great fun playing the slack-jawed, flighty mistress of the lowlife Archie. In the scene where Heiss visits Archie's flat and stares forlornly at a treasured painting of sentimental value that used to belong to him, she huffs, 'I don't see anythin' in it meself. No glamour. I love glamour, don't you?' Mid-way through shooting the film Smith attempted to own up to Diana's real age but George King wouldn't hear of it. She had made the impression that would become her trademark, except in *Yield to the Night* (1956) in which she played a woman accused of murder awaiting execution inspired by the Ruth Ellis scandal.

White Cradle Inn was booked into Worton Hall because there was no space at Shepperton. Directed by Harold French, the story is set in a Swiss town that provides refuge for a number of French children during the war and where a worthless man saves a child's life at the expense of his own. Produced by Ivor McLaren for Peak Films, Madeleine Carroll played the wife of the innkeeper played by Michael Rennie, a former car salesman and factory manager whose chance meeting with a Gaumont-British casting director led to his first screen job as stand-in for Robert Young in *Secret Agent* (1936) directed by Alfred Hitchcock. Having achieved star status in *I'll Be Your Sweetheart*, released the same year, Rennie would in 1951 be invited to Hollywood by Darryl Zanuck to play Klaatu in *The Day The Earth Stood Still*, his most enduring role and now a science fiction classic.

Under their four-year deal with British Lion, Anna Neagle and her producer/director husband Herbert Wilcox stepped onto the stages at Worton Hall to shoot some scenes for ABPC's *Piccadilly Incident*, a wartime drama about a newly married Wren presumed drowned when her ship is torpedoed and who spends three years on a tropical island before returning to England to find her husband remarried with a baby son. The film was part of the cycle of highly wrought upper-class English melodramas laced with wartime themes of separation and loss that began with *I Live in Grosvenor Square* (1945) and have subsequently become known as the London series.

Anna Neagle began a dancing career at age fourteen and got her big break when Herbert Wilcox first cast her and then married her in 1943, guiding her career towards becoming one of the brightest stars of her time. A sensational box-office commodity for nearly two decades, she played in everything from lightweight musicals and comedies to heavyweight heroines such as Edith Cavell, Florence Nightingale, Amy Johnson, Odette and Queen Victoria, and made three Hollywood musicals in the early 1940s before returning to Britain. Her appeal faded in the late 1950s when she retired altogether from the screen. She was made a Dame of the British Empire in 1969 for her contributions to the theatre. Blessed with dashing good looks, her resolute co-star, Michael Wilding, was 'discovered' working in the art department of a London film studio in 1933, debuting in *Bitter Sweet* that same year. Although he continued in work for the next three decades, his fame ultimately lies in having been the second Mr Elizabeth Taylor.

Herbert Wilcox as both a film director and producer looms large in British film history as one of the country's most important and successful British film-makers for over forty years, producing more than 100 films and directing around half of them. He entered the industry in the 1920s selling American films to exhibitors in Yorkshire before forming his own production company. By 1925 he had established himself as a successful producer/director, making films in conjunction with German companies, pioneering the use of American stars to improve the saleability of British films in the United States. As well as experimenting with colour and becoming heavily involved in creating 'the British Hollywood' at Elstree, he rented studio space in Hollywood in 1929 where he made his first talkie, *Black Waters*, which pre-empted Hitchcock's *Blackmail* by a few weeks. *Goodnight Vienna* (1932) began Wilcox's long professional and personal relationship with Anna Neagle. They spent the early part of the war together in America making musical comedies for RKO, returning to Britain in 1942 to make their acclaimed patriotic and unashamedly escapist semi-musicals. After *Odette* (1950), an accurate portrayal of SOE agent Odette Sansom in occupied France, subsequent films harked back to the successful Wilcox and Neagle formula until his career ended in a series of light entertainment films featuring popular music and singer of the day Frankie Vaughan.

Classed by one critic as 'entertainment only for the unsophisticated', *Piccadilly Incident* contains a five-minute ballet, 'Boogie Woogie Moonshine', devised and choreographed by Wendy Toye, who at the age of five was stooge for Hayden Coffin, a famous music hall comedy star. At age nine she was appearing at the London Palladium in a ballet she had choreographed that enjoyed enormous success and established a huge demand for her talents. Toye made her first film appearance in 1931 as an actress, but found she was more interested in the technical process of film-making, which became the path to her continued success. In 1950 she made a twenty-three-minute film for £3,000 (*The Stranger Left No Card*), which so impressed Sir Alexander Korda that he offered her a contract. She later went to Rank, where her films continued to do well, and continued directing stage comedies until the mid-1990s, when she retired. In a 'Memo to Mr Wilcox', the reviewer John Huntley was unconvinced by the dance sequence in *Piccadilly Incident*. 'We all know Anna Neagle can dance,' he begins, but 'is it necessary to give her a dance routine that takes seven or eight minutes' screen time and holds up the action? The theory that all British films must have a dance scene went out of fashion in 1939,' he concludes.

Another, less celebrated husband-and-wife team arriving for duty at post-war Worton Hall comprised John Clements and Kay Hammond. As a film actor, Clements came to prominence when chosen to star opposite Ralph Richardson in *South Riding* (1938) and again in *The Four Feathers*, after which his film career was somewhat irregular apart from a series of British war films. From less than thirty decidedly dodgy productions in the 1940s, Clements' stage appearances numbered 200 and for which he was made a Commander of the British Empire in 1956 and knighted for his services to drama in 1968. Made at Worton Hall in 1947, *Call of the Blood* represents Clements' film directorial debut with as obscure a film as the 1906 novel from which it was drawn. Kay Hammond is most famous for her role as Elvira in Noel Coward's *Blithe Spirit*, which she played in the original stage production, reprising her role in the 1945 film version opposite Rex Harrison, Margaret Rutherford and Constance Cummings. In *Call of the Blood* ('a tale of heredity with a Sicilian background') she plays 'a woman without beauty, but of lofty character and intellect, mated at the age of thirty-four to a man ten years her junior, as beautiful as a Greek god, and with the faun-like nature of Hawthorne's Donatello'.

Despite a seismic shift in the business of making movies since the days of Bertie Samuelson, where a strong sense of family pervaded Worton Hall, an element remained in post-war Isleworth, apparent from the wedding of Doris Cummings (*née* Joyce), the chief hairdresser. The blushing bride managed to capture more than the usual column inch in the local press due to the many film stars and personalities that attended or sent congratulatory telegrams. One guest was Christine Norden, Britain's 'number One oomph Girl', who was less than two years away from winning a British National Film Award for her performance in *Saints and Sinners*. But for now she was making her screen debut in *Night Beat*, then in production at Worton Hall. 'I sang, danced, got drunk, seduced men, murdered my lover and then committed suicide,' she revealed to the gentleman of the press. When the producers said they were introducing her to films 'they meant it!' she added.

A gritty crime drama about two former wartime comrades who go their separate ways, one joining the Metropolitan police and the other becoming a racketeer, *Night Beat* saw Guy Morgan, former film critic of the *Daily Express*, hired by Korda at a party to work on the script with T. J. Morrison. This was very much a film that Korda wanted to use as a vehicle to 'warm up' his new enterprise. A forerunner of *The Blue Lamp* in attempting to show the police from the inside, it was produced by Harold Huth, a reasonably distinguished former actor and director who populated the production with talent drawn from the entire spectrum of British cinema past, present and future, including Ronald Howard, the son of Leslie Howard, Sid James, who would go on to become one of the country's pre-eminent comedy stars, and Michael Medwin, a bit-part player who would in later years establish Memorial Films with Albert Finney, producing such award-winning classics as Lindsay Anderson's *If* (1968). Michael Hordern was another uncredited star in the ascendancy whose acting career was picking up after six years at war and who would go on to become one of the most familiar faces and voices across all strands of entertainment until his death in 1995, by which time he had picked up several BAFTA and Royal Television Society Awards, and a knighthood.

Operating the camera for *Night Beat* was the celebrated Freddie Francis who first served as an apprentice stills photographer before joining Gaumont-British as a clapper-loader in 1936. After serving in the Royal Army Cinematographic Unit during the Second World War he became a camera operator at British Lion, graduating to director of photography on *A Hill in Korea* (1956), ranking as one of Britain's major cinematographers on films such as *Room at the Top* (1959) and *Saturday Night and Sunday Morning* (1960) and winning an Oscar for *Sons and Lovers*, directed by Jack Cardiff that same year.

Another name destined to loom large in British cinema history, Guy Hamilton, eventually established a foothold as a third assistant director on *Night Beat* after years of trying to get a job in the industry. He had worked before the war at the Victorine Studios in Nice doing all sorts of jobs, from sweeping up the cutting room floor to loading the camera. The director Carol Reed would later prove instrumental in getting Hamilton his first job as a director on a low-budget adaptation of Edgar Wallace's *The Ringer* in 1952 and by the 1960s he would acquire a reputation for directing set-piece action sequences, eventually leading to *Goldfinger* (1964), the third *James Bond* film and the first of four *Bond* movies directed by him.

Guy Hamilton stayed on at Worton Hall to assist Anthony Kimmins OBE, RN (Retd) on a psychological thriller called *Mine Own Executioner*, which the *New York Times* found to be a 'singularly refreshing attribute of depicting its hero as being somewhat less than infallible … a serious, adult and highly interesting film drama both in point of view and execution'. *Film Industry* magazine declared it to be one of the best films to come out of a British studio for many months, with due credit given to Nigel Balchin who adapted his novel to the screen, and to Kimmins and Alexander Korda who supervised the production. The two men knew each other well from the days when Kimmins was working for Ealing Films and later as chief public relations officer at the Admiralty. When the war ended, Kimmins was in the Pacific when Korda sent him a cable asking him to become a director/producer.

Mine Own Executioner is the story of Peter Milne, an unqualified psychiatrist, who takes on the case of an RAF veteran badly wounded in Burma who has attempted to strangle his wife. Things go terribly wrong, resulting in the patient murdering him before killing himself. Milne is played by Burgess Meredith, a former child soprano who became a leading figure in American theatre of the 1930s, making the transition into films in 1939 with the favourably received adaptation of John Steinbeck's *Of Mice and Men*. Going on to feature in many films, he is best remembered for his portrayal as Rocky Balboa's trainer, Mickey Goldmill, and as The Penguin in the TV series *Batman*.

The schizophrenic ex-RAF pilot was played Irish actor Kieron Moore, whose first film role was as an IRA man in *The Voice Within* (1945). Following his acclaimed performance in the West End hit *Red Roses for Me*, Alexander Korda offered Moore a seven-year contract with London Films, with his role in *Mine Own Executioner* confirming his potential. His adoring wife was played by the smouldering Christine Norden, who replaced Rosalyn Boulter after the intervention of Burgess Meredith's wife, Paulette Goddard, who felt that Boulter wasn't sexy enough. Korda signed Norden to a seven-year contract, placing her in stark, dark-edged films as fetching femme fatales. And playing Milne's understanding spouse, whose love and devotion brings him back to psychiatry, was Dulcie Gray, best remembered for her stage work with husband Michael Denison, as well as a string of films in the 1940s.

Mid-table in the cast list playing one of the many doctor roles punctuating this saga is the inimitable John Laurie, whose long career would span over

120 screen roles. First appearing on stage in 1921, his craggy profile, arcing bulbous nose and stern visage was made for Hitchcock's dour, suspicious and miserly Scottish farmer, John Crofter, in *The 39 Steps* (1935). Laurie was sought out by Laurence Olivier for his Shakespearean adeptness and became involved in British experimental television films in 1938, and played the zealous Khalifa in *The Four Feathers* a year later. Throughout the 1940s and 50s Laurie's distinctive face appeared in a huge variety of films, although he is probably best remembered by British audiences as the dour James Frazer in the popular BBC TV series *Dad's Army*, which ran for nine years from 1968.

Richard Winnington, the caricaturist and film critic, described *Mine Own Executioner* as the 'first psychoanalytical film that a grown-up can sit through without squirming'. An interesting choice then for the young Princesses Elizabeth and Margaret when they toured Worton Hall in June 1947. Visiting the art department, they were introduced to the art director, William Andrews, who showed them a finished model of a night club and other miniature sets in the course of construction. In the set construction department they met manager W. McClaren, who explained how the models were translated into the real thing and how the set dresser and chief electrician added to the magic. The princesses then settled down to watch the scene being shot and were afterwards introduced to the various cast and crew members taking part.

In the special effects studio the princesses met Ned Mann, introduced to them as the head of the 'trick' department and who explained how the effect of a man being run down by a train was achieved. Visiting the pattern shop the princesses saw icicles being made from plastic material and were each presented with a paper knife bearing their names, the title of the film and the date of their visit. Finally the royal visitors were taken to the projection theatre to meet the editor and chief cutter, where they watched some of the rushes, including the finished shot of the man being run down by a train. As they signed the visitors' book, Princess Elizabeth remarked, 'It's Friday thirteenth. Well, let's hope it is lucky.'

Korda was lucky. Indeed, he was 'in Clover', according to the headline in one trade journal. London Films was a private company with all but 2 per cent of the shares owned by him and his family, making a profit in 1946–47 of £283,000, although all was not as it seemed. The lacklustre *Bonnie Prince Charlie* was planned as the company's first big Technicolor production. Ted Black had initiated the project with location shooting begun back in August 1946 and Korda taking it over when Black died suddenly.

In her biography of Alexander Korda, Karol Kulik describes a reluctant David Niven loaned by Samuel Goldwyn for the starring part with little else prepared. Leslie Arliss was to be the director with a script by Clemence Dane, but Korda was unhappy with both and so replaced Arliss with Robert Stevenson, taking over the screenplay himself. In the opinion of one anonymous reviewer, Korda's dismay may have been rooted in the period so close to the end of the Second World War, in so far as his staunch Anglophilia moved him to play down the atrocities against the Highlanders by the English and to magnify the German elements of Cumberland's army. Or it might be simply that so much money had already been spent on the film that Korda was reluctant to let it go. Although he was busy directing *An Ideal Husband* at Shepperton, he certainly more than tinkered with the hapless epic.

The vast silent stage at Worton Hall was filled with 150 tons of soil, 6,000 pieces of turf, half a ton of bog moss, bulrushes, osier reeds, and bog iris in an attempt to recreate the Scottish moor at Culloden where the brutal suppression of the Highland Scots by the English took place. But this, and the 'inadequacy' of the other sets, would be seen as the film's 'most shocking deficiency' according to *The Scotsman*. The critic for *The Manchester Guardian* would share the horror of the garish glens and mountains as 'emerald as picture-postcards'. Vincent Korda during production shared these reservations, looking upon the full Highland regalia with utter dismay. 'He disliked the idea of men in skirts,' recalls his son Michael in his book cataloguing the Korda clan, *Charmed Lives*, and hated the colours, the orange and green in particular looking awful. 'On film it will look like a tin of marmalade,' he complained. Although it was explained to Vincent Korda that these were authentic tartans, he had seen others he preferred, but gave way to authenticity.

Returning from America aged thirteen, Michael Korda accompanied his father on his daily trips to work where it is apparent from his recollections some thirty years later that Shepperton and Worton Hall blend into one. The sound stages, the property stores and the cutting rooms were common to either location. Poppa Day, however, was not in charge of the 'carpentry department' at Shepperton but was a fundamental element of Ned Mann's setup at Worton Hall. The hoards of extras seen wandering about the dubious Scottish moor and the aftermath of battle was played out in Isleworth's huge silent stage, not Shepperton, and the Derby Council Chamber was created in one of the sound stages at Worton Hall and in the other craftsmen built the interior of a Derby barn from materials taken from a genuine antique building.

The finished film achieved a veritable pasting by the press. *The Manchester Guardian* condemned 'every postcard scene accompanied by enough chorus wailing of old Gaelic and Jacobite airs almost to turn the film into a slap-up musical'. The Scottish critics considered 'even as a piece of fantasy' it would not do. It was in their view a 'concentration of insipid hokum', the action slow, the photography uninspired, and the accents mixed. 'Bad sets, bad lighting, bad cutting and bad direction' began the *Film Industry* onslaught, its critic finding it difficult to comprehend how it came to be made. The sets were not only 'atrocious' but photographed in such high key that 'every stroke of the paint brush' was visible on the plaster rocks. As an example of technique, 'many a small studio could have done a better job on a £200,000 budget'. The critic Ralph Bond noted that Alexander Korda was slow to realise the extent of post-war changes in the film-goers' tastes. 'The drawing rooms and stately mansions, the vapid meanderings of the idle rich, the affected accents of the public schools had been left behind,' he reflected. Real people and real situations was becoming more the rule than the exception with the public responding to realism over sham theatrical.

By continuing to look to Hollywood, observers such as Bond believed that Korda was losing touch with the British public. Nevertheless, British Lion Studios paid a dividend of 15 per cent to shareholders in July 1947, the first payment they had received in over ten years. The company also showed a respectable net profit of £61,154 and in place was a $14 million American distribution agreement with Twentieth Century Fox. Whereas at the outset Korda's new empire was modest compared to Rank, more than half of that company's best directors, writers and artists had by now crossed over to London Films. *Bonnie Prince Charlie* notwithstanding, quality over quantity was Korda's mantra, pointing out that vast numbers of films was not the issue, but films of the highest possible worth. And as part of his passion for the grand 'international' film, Korda put aside his long-held ambition to make *War and Peace* and instead decided on Tolstoy's other literary masterpiece, *Anna Karenina*.

Utilising Shepperton and Worton Hall for this Russian epic, Korda chose three Frenchmen in the key roles of director, photographer and writer; Julien Duvivier, Henri Alekan and Jean Anouilh respectively. However, Anouilh's treatment placed the story in France in the early 1900s, which was wholly unacceptable and so Korda hired Guy Morgan to work on a new script with Duvivier. As Paul Tabori recounts, these script sessions would begin with a fine dinner flushed down with the best wines, brandy and cigars. Then Korda would change, tearing into the script, swearing and cursing until Duvivier, 'in a towering rage', would gather up his papers, announcing that he would quit the picture and return to Paris. Morgan, meanwhile, would sit on the sofa, taking it all in. Sometimes Korda's doctor would arrive to give him something to calm him down, but the result was always the same; Duvivier would not leave and something constructive would be achieved. This went on for a year, costing £700,000. The film enjoyed a reasonable run but was ultimately condemned as 'big, beautiful, but ultimately boring' compared to Clarence Brown's 1935 version starring Greta Garbo and Fredric March. Korda famously admitted to having 'lost a packet' on the film, conveniently placing the blame for its failure on prevailing conditions.

The British economy at this time was in such a state of flux that the Labour government placed a restriction on imports in order to reduce the outflow of funds to hard currency territories. Using its powers under the Import Duties Act, 1932, the Treasury imposed a 75 per cent customs tax on all film imports, the majority of which came from the United States. Despite a stockpile of as many as 125 films already awaiting a UK release, the Motion Picture Export Association of America (MPEA) ordered an immediate boycott of any further films to British cinemas. This took the Board of Trade by surprise, as the most that the American industry could clear in any financial year was the cost of production and looked to its export trade to produce a profit. This new quota was fixed at 45 per cent, an increase of 25 per cent in the screen time for British films. For Korda and for Rank this was hugely disappointing. As Korda had done so with Twentieth Century Fox, so J. Arthur Rank had gone to the States with a view to arranging wider distribution for his films. All their hard work 'went for nowt', as Rank bluntly put it, 'right down the drain.' Backed into a corner, the British government responded by telling British film producers that they had been granted a wonderful opportunity to fill the screens with home-grown pictures.

Three months after the embargo and those same producers were being blamed for not rising to the challenge, with Rank announcing a programme of forty-seven films at a total cost of well over £9 million, which was nowhere near enough to make the sort of films that people wanted to see. Korda responded with a missive in *The Times* to the effect that more films were being made in Britain than ever before. In America only twenty-four first feature films were in production, and in Britain there were twenty; quite something considering that all of the British studios put together comprised less than one of the major studios, and with the number of people employed in Britain around 15 per cent of that in Hollywood.

By the time Sir Stafford Cripps replaced Dr Dalton as Chancellor of the Exchequer and Harold Wilson took over the Board of Trade, it was clear that the import tax had done nothing to halt the dollar drain, with reissues or new American films already in the country still earning large amounts. The government had little choice but to swallow its pride and negotiate, characteristically doing so without consulting British film producers and distributors. Korda's plan for the quota involving a grading of films according to budget and quality would, however, be adopted with his emphasis on quality still the most important consideration.

In this he promoted the brilliant union between Graham Greene and Carol Reed on three films destined to rank among British cinema's most important. The son of Sir Herbert Beerbohm Tree, the consummate Victorian actor manager, Carol Reed came something of a full circle having once been chairman of the newly formed British Lion Film Corporation in 1927. Switching to the creative side of the business, he became a director at Ealing Studios where he won an Oscar for the Best Documentary in 1946 for *The True Glory*, a compilation of combat footage shot by dozens of Allied cameramen. He made *Odd Man Out* for the Rank Organisation but wasn't happy under the growing influence of John Davis, who had become the most important executive there by the end of the war. Deciding to quit the inclement climate at Rank like so many of his contemporaries, Reed signed a contract for five pictures with London Films in 1947, signalling one of the most successful producer/director relationships in British cinema history.

The first project was *The Fallen Idol*, shot jointly at Worton Hall and Shepperton. Drawn from Graham Greene's short story *The Basement Room*, Korda introduced the novelist to Carol Reed and left the two of them to develop a screen-play that turned out to be one of the most sensitive and original pictures in Carol Reed's career. The story revolves around Filipe, an ambassador's son (played by Bobby Henrey) who struggles to deal with truth and lies, made all the worse when he believes he has witnessed a murder. Playing the part of Filipe's friend and eventual fallen idol, Baines the butler, was Ralph Richardson, fresh from *Anna Karenina* in his fourth film for Alexander Korda. Knighted in 1947 for his services to the theatre, Richardson's portrayal of Baines is generally considered to be his finest screen work, full of detail and craftsmanship.

Jack Hawkins (as Detective Ames) is a name synonymous with post-war British films where quality supersedes quantity. The firm-jawed good-egg-type with the angle-grinder voice made his screen debut in 1921 as a child performer in *The Four Just Men*, with serious fame arriving much later in

1952 in his roles as Captain Ericson in *The Cruel Sea* and the teacher of deaf children in *Mandy*. Dora Bryan, the chirpy blonde of dubious character in numerous films throughout the 40s and 50s, excels as the warm-hearted Rosie who lightens the otherwise ambiguous sexual undertones of *The Fallen Idol* in the police station as an unrepentant prostitute trying to comfort Felipe. Leslie Halliwell, the eminent film historian, critic and encyclopedist, described the film as 'a near-perfect piece of small-scale cinema, built up from clever nuances of acting and cinematic technique'. Forging the important relationship with Carol Reed that would shape his career was second director Guy Hamilton, who would inherit a much-changed world to that of his mentor.

As gritty realism was fast superseding the theatrical, so the politics of film was at this time fast changing. The technicians union, ACT, had secured greatly improved working hours and conditions for its members, effectively creating a closed shop. Korda voiced his fears in the *Times* newspaper in November 1947, believing that the reduction of hours from sixty-six before the war to a five-day week of forty-four hours meant that films could no longer be made as quickly or as cheaply as before. This brought about accusation of Korda being 'anti-labour'. Harold Wilson, meanwhile, was leading negotiations between the British government and the MPEA, proposing that the American companies could take more of their earnings than the 25 per cent left after the duty in return for a genuine commitment to show British films in the United States. This was agreed and led to the Anglo-American Film Agreement that allowed American studios to resume the export of their films to Britain with no limit on the number of films but with earnings leaving Britain restricted to $17 million for two years from July 1948. The balance was to be used for investment in British film production, rights acquisition, prints, advertising and even the purchase of studios and other properties, excluding cinemas. But yet again the British film industry lost out, this time on both fronts, in production and exhibition. For just as the increased production effort of the British studios was ready for release, the marketplace was flooded with the backlog of American films that audiences clamoured to see over home-produced films.

Ever the survivor, Korda arrived at a mutual arrangement with David Selznick to handle a number of each other's films. British Lion and the Associated British Picture Corporation signed a contract under which Korda acquired a long lease of British National Studios in Boreham Wood, designed to increase the production capacity of British Lion by as many as seven big feature films a year. Although British Lion handled films other than those made by London Films, Korda was its most important source. When the new exhibitors' quota was announced, he welcomed it as another safeguard for British films, which, with hindsight, was a little premature. The Rank Organisation had acquired an overdraft of more than £13 million, brought about by producing too many films that not enough film-goers wanted to see and with no world market. In March 1948 the process of consolidation at British Lion began with the decision to shift the giant stage at Worton Hall to Shepperton. The following month *To-day's Cinema* reported the sacking of 225 staff across Isleworth and Shepperton, retaining 1,200. 'We needed a lot of people for the elaborate sets,' a spokesman let it be known. There would be no requirement for such settings in the future.

And then there was the Entertainment Tax, draining £40 million a year out of the film industry. The Labour government decided to do something to assist and so Harold Wilson set up the National Film Finance Corporation (NFFC) to provide £5 million to finance production. But to the horror of the producers, the loans made available from this fund were to be channelled through the distributors. While Rank wanted none of it, Korda had no such qualms. As a producer he had no direct access to the money, but he did through British Lion, which received a massive £2 million long-term loan in November 1948 from the NFFC on the understanding that it would handle eighteen British-made features for Korda and his associated producers. With interest on the loan representing £80,000 a year and bank charges adding to the overheads, Korda declared that production costs would have to be scaled down, which again brought him criticisms from the unions insofar as the Korda group was perceived as becoming a government-subsidised organisation.

The Last Days of Dolwyn represents one of a number of necessary diversions from Korda's emphasis on quality as he saw it. Not that the piece from the pen of the celebrated Welsh dramatist and actor Emlyn Williams lacked value and worth, it simply didn't sit at the same table as the Hungarian's ambitions. Intended to be an offbeat but moving and even humorous picture of Welsh life, Williams was nervous about tackling the whole thing himself, yet couldn't abide interference. Korda famously responded,

> I leave it all to you, my dear Emmaleen, you know what you want, I will give you all the expert technicians I can and please come to me in doubt and trouble, for I have been through the whole bloody mill. It will be a nice film, though of course I know and you know there won't be a damned penny in it, but it's worth doing.

Co-directing with Russell Lloyd, Williams also starred as Rob Davies, a malcontent who returns to Dolwyn, the scene of a childhood trauma, to exact revenge on its inhabitants following the managed flooding of the fictional Welsh village to provide water for an English town. Shot on location in Rhydymain, Llanfachreth (near Dolgellau) and at Lake Vyrnwy in North Wales for most of the autumn, much of the summer was spent filming at Isleworth. The *Film Industry* representative visiting the studio watched cameraman Gus Drisse address a particularly complicated tracking shot that took in the entire village recreated under the vast roof of the giant silent stage, ready and waiting for the effects of the devastating flood to be made real by Ned Mann and Poppa Day.

The studio interiors, picturesquely designed by Oscar-winning art director Wilfred Shingleton, were tiny cottage sets with low ceilings that afforded difficulties both in lighting and camera movement. In one, the man from *Film Industry* watched Dame Edith Evans sitting at a kitchen table talking to two newcomers to the silver screen, Anthony James and one Richard Burton. In another complicated pan, the camera was brought up close up to Dame Edith to allow the table to be dragged away, allowing the camera to pass unimpeded by Burton and James to exit through the cottage window.

Lifted from his working-class roots by Philip Burton, the schoolmaster whose surname he took and who steered him onto the stage in 1943 and then on to Oxford a year later, Richard Burton's first professional acting debut was in *Druid's Rest*, a play by Emlyn Williams, who became his mentor. Having toured several plays around the country, Williams offered Burton his first screen role in *The Last Days of Dolwyn*. Brook Williams (Emlyn's son) recalls that Burton might have quit acting had it not been for his father arranging for a screen test, the producers having been unconvinced by the embryonic screen legend. In the event Burton got the part and was informed by telegram while on tour. He didn't bother to reply, admitting later that he had lost the heart for acting and had thrown the telegram into the waste bin before going for a drink. Williams heard nothing until Burton turned up months later on the first day of filming. Doris Spriggs was a young secretary to studio manager Gerry Blattner at the time and in Gareth Owen's *The Shepperton Story* recalls Burton taking lodgings in the first house on Worton Road (No. 3) next to the cutting suites, now new housing.

In the film Burton plays Gareth, who trades his city life in Liverpool to work in the local shop where he can lust after the local landowner's niece. The part of Burton's foster mother, Merri, a devout woman who loves the village she has never left, is played by the matchless Edith Evans, beyond doubt the greatest English stage actress of the twentieth century who excelled in the classics as much as modern roles in the West End, Broadway, Stratford-upon-Avon and the Old Vic, just as she did on the screen. She was created a Dame Commander of the Most Excellent Order of the British Empire in 1946. Although a fantastic break for him, Burton apparently took his first outing in front of the cameras all in his stride. One of his biographers, Paul Ferris, describes his performance as a 'convincing attempt at the unconvincing part of Gareth', and implying that he would have excelled whether he was 'reading The Lord Is My Shepherd in Welsh or playing the tongue-tied lover'. Williams had few problems with Burton's acting but found him unable to look sufficiently innocent in one scene where he watches the unattainable love of his life dance. A boy was employed to sing a Welsh folk song to help with the atmosphere, but instead of looking bemused, Burton looked fierce.

It was the sometimes sickly sentimentality of the film that Burton found difficult at times to endure. A night shoot experienced by the *Film Industry* reporter saw fifty artistes, 'most of them Welsh', wandering the village lot at Isleworth humming snatches of the folk song they were about to sing in the peace of the quiet moonlit night, dispelling the usual hustle and bustle of a film unit preparing for a take.

> Somehow the presence of an old horse, placidly standing at a wall and a small flock of sheep, slowly wending their way through the crowd, added to the illusion of peaceful harmony made complete when Nancy Richards, one of the sole survivors of a line of Welsh harpists, sat down at her three-stringed instrument and brought silvery music to blend with the singing.

When the film was released the following year (1949) it was reasonably well reviewed, although the *Film Industry* trade paper took the view that its makers appeared to believe that all 'educated people' should speak Welsh.

> We were severely handicapped, therefore, by knowing approximately three words of that language and a considerable amount of dialogue was totally unintelligible. A dubbed version in English would, we are sure, prove more acceptable.

Despite its poor performance at the box office, Korda spotted something in the young Burton and put him under contract for five years at £500 a year. He then promptly loaned him out to Twentieth Century Fox for three pictures at

£150,000. Burton attracted the odd review referring to 'impeccable acting' and a 'very promising performance', the *News of the World* describing 'the fire of great acting allied to good looks, a manly bearing ... and an innate tenderness that renders his love scenes so movingly real'. Years later Burton disowned his contribution to the production, as he did almost every film role he played. Shown an extract from *The Last Days of Dolwyn* during a television interview in 1967, he condemned his performance as 'febrile' and 'a lamentable thing. Thank God I never have to live through that again, to live through those terrible years of puerility, of idiocy.'

Next, the Worton Hall backlot traded the land of song in favour of the Emerald Isle for *Saints and Sinners*, a warm-hearted Gallic story of a village that believes Doomsday is imminent. Kieron Moore made a return to Isleworth after his appearance in *Mine Own Executioner*, joined by Christine Norden hot off the back of *Night Beat* for this more light-hearted jaunt in Leslie Arliss's much-neglected comedy drama. By October 1948 the unit was settled in on the floor at Worton Hall after their Ireland location. Why there was a huge poster on the wall of one of the buildings bemoaning the fact that critics had savaged *Anna Karenina* isn't entirely clear, although from what the visiting *Film Industry* reviewer surmised it was a reminder of 'the firm need to not consistently turn out turkeys'.

Indeed, the cast and crew were working 'at top pressure' when the reporter arrived, with two units continuing their tasks simultaneously as they did in Ireland. The first unit was preparing to capture the destruction of a hotel built on the backlot that looked much too splendid to burn down. In the film the village bank manager (played by Eddie Byrne) gets drunk and is trapped in one of its top-storey rooms. He leans through the window, completely surrounded by flames and yelling for help, and is then rescued by his fiancée's ex-boyfriend played by Kieron Moore. Truly earning their money, the rescue was staged on the studio floor where two flights of stairs were completely ablaze. Moore was required to dash through the flames, dodging the falling embers to reappear with the fourteen-stone Eddie Byrne on his shoulder carrying him back down the still blazing stairs. Calling for a second take, an overenthusiastic prop man dropped a burning beam in front of Moore as he staggered down the stairs, instead of to the side. This startled Moore so much that he jumped the remaining steps but managed to keep his footing and in so doing deliver director Leslie Arliss a perfect take.

Leslie Arliss had previously directed the most commercially successful of all the Gainsborough melodramas, and arguably the best known, *The Wicked Lady*, starring Margaret Lockwood and James Mason. *The Man in*

Grey, another Arliss classic, made the top ten most successful films of 1943. Sadly, his time with London Films was no match for his Gainsborough days. Film editor Ron de Mattos was just starting out on his long career and was employed as an assistant on *Saints and Sinners*, which he considers a lost opportunity. When he read the script he believed that the film had the makings of one of the best British films ever but was ruined as a result of so many changes and needless alterations. He remembers being called upon to take the finished film to Korda's Piccadilly offices for a screening. En route the editor, Dave Newhouse, told him and the others in the group to make sure they laughed at the appropriate moments, something they all found very difficult to do. At the end of the screening Korda announced, 'Yes, very nice. But I think it needs to be speeded up. Cut a frame from each scene.' This reduced the film's running time by one minute. It enjoyed a muted response in England but went down better in America, albeit in several art-houses.

Ron de Mattos was in the canteen having lunch when Cary Grant and Ann Sheridan sat at his table, taking a break from work on *I Was a Male War Bride*, a comedy based on the true story of one Henri Rochard, a Belgian Soldier who married an American nurse and who managed to enter the United States by qualifying as a war bride; there being no provision for war grooms at that time. The film's director was Howard Hawks, who had entered the film industry in the early 1920s, making his debut as a director with *The Road to Glory* in 1926. His first talking picture was *The Dawn Patrol*, a Second World War drama starring Douglas Fairbanks Jr. Later demonstrating his versatility across all genres, his screen successes included the gangster saga *Scarface* with tough guy George Raft and the acclaimed war drama *Sergeant York*, which netted eleven Academy Award nominations. As well as the *film noir* classics *To Have and Have Not* and *The Big Sleep*, starring Humphrey Bogart and Lauren Bacall, his most famous John Wayne western was *Red River*, shot a year before travelling to Europe to follow up his two previous comedy successes with Cary Grant, *Bringing Up Baby* and *His Girl Friday*.

Born Archie Leach in Bristol, Cary Grant left school aged fourteen to join a troupe of knockabout comedians. Chosen to go to perform in the United States in 1920 he stayed there, impressing Mae West with his combination of virility, sexuality and the 'aura of a gentleman' that suited his brand of 'high comedy with polished words'. His first hit film was *The Awful Truth* (1937), which forged the union with Howard Hawks that led to greater success with Alfred Hitchcock later in his career.

Ann Sheridan was a versatile and charismatic actress with an aptitude for comedy who began her acting career after winning a beauty contest that carried a screen test and a bit part as a prize. Following a less than fruitful career at Paramount she signed with Warner Brothers, where she eventually landed her first substantial role in Howard Hawks' *Angels with Dirty Faces*. Known as the 'Oomph Girl', Sheridan became one of the most glamorous women in Hollywood.

The external locations for *I Was a Male War Bride* were shot in Germany where cast and crew were brought down by an assortment of illnesses. Shooting was suspended for two weeks after Sheridan contracted pleurisy, which developed into pneumonia. Hawks suffered a debilitating itch and Grant contracted a serious case of hepatitis which became complicated by jaundice. Production was halted for three months while he convalesced and arrangements were made to shoot the interiors in England. What scenes were being shot at Worton Hall Ron de Mattos couldn't say. He was busy eating his lunch and quite properly left his distinguished company in peace to have theirs.

The Winslow Boy was a screen adaptation of Terrence Rattigan's successful stage play. Set against the strict codes of conduct and manners of the Edwardian age, the story concerns a father's fight to clear his son who has been expelled from Naval College without trial for allegedly stealing a five-shilling postal order. The father (played by Cedric Hardwicke) and his sister Catherine (Marie Lohr) lead a long-running legal battle that takes them as far as the House of Commons, a faithful representation of which was built at Worton Hall. The former prime minister's son Anthony Asquith arrived at Isleworth on 21 January 1949 to begin direction of the film produced by Anatole de Grunwald. Robert Donat as Sir Robert Morton, the finest barrister in England at the time in support of the family, made his first appearance in the film the following day. Before the close of the first morning's work Asquith had six shots in the can thanks to the 'silent turnover system', which allowed for a few frames of film with an audio tone sent to a recorder for synchronisation without the need for a clapperboard. A crystal-controlled motor was later incorporated in the camera to do away with a sync lead, thus allowing the sound recordists to roam free and be in the right place to collect the tracks without the need for a connecting cord. Production then shifted to Shepperton, along with the credit.

Isleworth never enjoyed a discernible house style. It was a jobbing studio inhabited by jobbing producers, artists and technicians on a job-by-job basis. Its contribution to British film history has by chance and circumstance been fragmented and overtaken by a string of events that have diverted attention towards its more celebrated sibling. Yet Worton Hall is the quintessential story of British film, a manufactory of moving pictures as interesting or as dull, as fascinating or wearisome as the people assembled to produce whatever was deemed likely an audience might or might not pay good money to go and see. G. B. Samuelson oversaw Worton Hall as one of the most successful fantasy factories of the silent era and lived to see his creation attract the likes of Alexander Korda, a man whose ambition airbrushed it out of British film history twice. The growing success of British Lion saw the shadow of Shepperton cast an even wider shadow over its Cinderella sibling, eventually sealing its fate as though it had never existed.

10
The Big Stage

The late 1940s is often cited as the British film industry's bleakest hour. The thirteenth Annual General Meeting of British Lion, held in London on 8 August 1947, however, recognised little of those hard times. The chairman, Hugh Quennell, reflected on the past short year when the company came about, partly from cash raised against Worton Hall Studios and partly against the issue of ordinary shares at a substantial premium. The sum of £1 million was required to repay two outstanding mortgages and for the modernisation, extension and re-equipment of both Worton Hall and Shepperton. The name of the company had been changed to the British Lion Studio Company Limited and those of the individual studios thereafter to be known as the London Film Studios, Shepperton, and the London Film Studios, Isleworth. To the matter of profit and loss, the company carried forward to the next year's account the princely sum of £7,197. As to the future, there was no telling what implications the proposed tax on American films would have. What was clear was the shortage of studio space in Britain against an increasing demand for good British films. British Lion was booked full for 1947–48 at both studios, with all productions guaranteed American distribution through Twentieth Century Fox.

On the asset side, the Shepperton figures were separated from those relating to Isleworth where the freehold land, buildings, fixed plant and machinery were taken in at cost. Of the remaining fixed assets, Quennell mentioned only one, the special effects department, going on to declare that when we took over in April 1946, there was no special effects department able to deal with the many trick shots which appear in any modern film. We have had to supply our own and the figure of £18,931 represents the cost of building it, including overheads, during the period to March 31.

Ned Mann, the head of the company's 'trick department' would doubtless have raised an eyebrow at this point. He had been brought over from America by Korda back in 1934 to head up his special effects department at Worton Hall, overseeing *Things to Come*, *The Man Who Could Work Miracles* and *The Ghost Goes West* before the shift to Denham where his work continued for as short a time as Korda's occupancy.

The fifty-four-year-old former professional car-racing and roller-skating expert, stage actor and director started in the movie industry with the Keystone Cops in 1917 and was later responsible for the special effects in the original Douglas Fairbanks version of *The Thief of Bagdad*. Associated with every major studio in Hollywood except Charles Chaplin's, Mann had returned to Worton Hall as the organising genius of British Lion's special effects department. Quennell's curious pronouncement was not mentioned in *Film Industry* magazine four months after British Lion's AGM when John Huntley travelled 'way out west, far beyond the borders of Kensington and Hammersmith, arriving below the Manor House of Worton Hall to visit Ned Mann's Gulch' and reveal the secrets of the 'lone stage at Isleworth'.

Huntley's first sight of the studio would have been across the red-tiled rooftops of west Middlesex after turning off the Great West Road towards Isleworth. Here the largest man-made structure on the landscape stood out as a grey-clad oversized barn bearing the fading words, painted in huge white letters on its western flank, 'London Films'. This was Worton Hall's piece de resistance, described by Michael Balcon in his autobiography as 'a white elephant in the giant shrubberies of Worton Hall'. The 30,000-square-foot prime asset that made it unique among all British film studios was rarely visited and seldom photographed. As well as special effects, this self-contained outpost also made its own gear, cameras, printers, sets and even processed its own material, screening the results privately in its own theatre. As a result of post-war austerity the unit was called upon to produce items of equipment that would once otherwise have been purchased from outside suppliers. Everything was built there; camera mechanisms, fog machines, spools, tripod heads, cob-web machines, and even the studio's electrically driven camera crane was constructed on-site at Worton Hall.

This specialist team was headed by Cliff Richardson and his team of assistants overseeing the engineering, pattern and plaster shop, the back-projection department and continuity. The laboratory boasted a state-of-the-art combined optical printer and full-size Monopack processing plant for the new multilayer film stock, replacing the three colour-separated strips. As well as the chief electrician and the librarian, there were in all about 150 people employed in Korda's special effects department at Isleworth. Such was the magnitude of the monumental structure so central to their activities that when used for a street scene, both sides could be lined with shops and houses with room for horse-drawn vehicles to pass each other. Its primary role was for the laying out of miniature sections of countryside, villages or dock-sides, anything that could not be obtained more realistically or economically by sending out a location unit. These miniature sets took anything up to a month to lay out on the floor and shooting could take up to three days depending on the complexity of the scene, the most complex being anything that involved the animation of trains, buses and miniature people built up in plaster, fretwork cut-outs, wooden models and painted back-cloths. Cast-metal mouldings were manufactured from the adjoining pattern and engineering shops, which included the forge, set up when Korda first took control of Worton Hall in 1935.

Interviewed by David Blake in 2004, former electrician Joe Gillnet confirms that the giant stage was never lagged for sound simply because it was only ever used for special effect photography, the general idea being the ability to have someone close in the foreground and somebody at the furthest extent of the stage 'with a lot of light poured in'. This offered a depth of focus that miniaturised the people in the background by foreshortening the distance, which was a prerequisite for *Things to Come*. Joe was living in nearby Whitton at the time and travelling each day to work at Denham, a gruelling journey. His father, who was chief accountant at British & Dominion studios, had a word with the chief engineer at Worton Hall, where Joe was taken on as an apprentice electrician in 1933 for one shilling an hour, thus becoming 'a millionaire overnight'!

Lighting such a vast area as the silent stage was a noisy affair. Mobile generators came on open trucks and there were only the studio lamps to call upon. A company called Morrison's was the first to develop lamps with an even field of light. These were stored in the electrical shop by Jennings Foundry where the lamps were cast in two halves from moulds. When cool, the electricians assembled both halves. They were then packed ready for when shooting commenced in the silent stage. For the entrance to the underground city in *Things to Come* the whole width of the huge stage was filled right to the end. Because there were so many generators, 'all of unknown ability and likely to be overloaded', a small army of electricians walked around with blow lamps looking out for solder dropping from the red-hot connections. The unwieldy electrical cables came from America and arrived bare, so it was another job for the electricians to visit nearby fire stations to collect old hoses, which were taken back to Worton Hall and threaded over the cable as a covering. 'They were virtually impossible to bend – you needed about four of you to stand on them – they were bloody big cables. It really was hard – people don't know how lucky they are today.' No one knew the capacities of these cables so it was a highly risky matter of rushing around with big stand-up blow lamps complete with a solder pot on the top. Joe would come home with the front of his trousers splattered with solder. The danger and the pain didn't enter into the equation. 'Stand still, steady yourself,' he was told as the solder fused two lengths of cable into a lug designed to make the ends tight. Unbelievably, Joe's job was to hold the bare ends of the cable over his shoulder as the solder was dripped into the lug.

Film Industry's John Huntley confirmed on his visit to this mysterious world that much had evolved since the 1930s when the stage was built. Lighting remained the all-important factor in the filming of miniature sets, using high camera speeds to 'iron out the bumps' and to scale up the perspective of the action. Recalling the sixteen years before Hugh Quennell's call for the establishment of a special effects department at Worton Hall, Ned Mann recounted one animation sequence for *The Man Who Could Work Miracles* that lasted non-stop for thirty-six hours. 'Once started on this kind of stop-motion set-up, there's no let-up until it's in the can.' The scene in question was the draper's shop in which everything puts itself away; gloves fold up and jump into their boxes, suits pack themselves away, a tailor's dummy adjusts its clothing and parcels tie themselves up. Using stop-motion photography, Mann explained that often the best tricks they did were the simplest. Isleworth didn't go in for some of the more 'fancy new developments' used elsewhere; the clue to Quennell's enigmatic pronouncement. The real trick, Mann maintained, was learning by experience and applying well-established principles. But clearly he'd had his day, telling Huntley that he wasn't exactly in charge at Worton Hall any more, but that his job was now to set up the department, train the staff and then hand over to Cliff Richardson. 'Then I guess I'll be going back to the States.'

A month before Huntley arrived at Worton Hall, Julien Duvivier had shifted his production of *Anna Karenina* to Isleworth for additional scenes set in the Moscow Opera House. The model embracing the 'great scenes of Moscow' occupied the entire big stage area where a continuous lake was filmed by an automatic camera travelling 400 feet on a trolley in the centre of the roadways built among the miniature sets, giving the effect of a ride on the back of a sledge through the snow-covered streets. Cars and pedestrians were included, as were street lamps shining along a great panorama of buildings 'giving a most realistic shot when viewed in the studio theatre'. Away from the snows and storms of the Russian scenes, Vivien Leigh and Kieron Moore moved to the Venetian palace sequence, said to be one of the loveliest in the film. From a typical Italian entrance hall, with alcoves leading up stone stairs to the rooms above and through the windows in the upper room, was a vista of Venice in the distance complete with a gondola plying the canal at night, achieved by a camera mounted on a wooden raft travelling behind the miniature vessel in the giant studio's water tank. At one point the camera follows it under a bridge, involving some accurate timing for the model bridge to be pulled away as soon as it is out of shot to allow the camera passage on its raft. 'Timing is vital with us,' Ned Mann told the *Film Industry* reporter, remembering the occasion when a solid metal model train hit a camera head-on during a tricky shot, leaving only a mass of cogwheels and celluloid to mark the spot where the camera had been. A similar catastrophe overtook the unit when the camera had to fall from a tree to obtain a special effect but hit a limb on the way down.

The weather was also in Ned Mann's gift. During his tour, Huntley watched a snow scene being prepared requiring 126 tons of salt and 3 tons of Perspex chips. The salt provided the static snow while the Perspex rained down from 30-foot rotating drums as snowflakes. Electricians were warned that all copper connectors had to be kept well clear of any salt to avoid acute corrosion troubles. Even though this method of obtaining snow was now technically frowned upon, 'these days you have to take what you can get' was Mann's response. Alternatives included marble dust, 'which gives a lovely glistening effect with a little naphtha sprinkled over it', although the naphtha gave off a violent smell when under the hot lights. Pyrene foam was used to make icicles. Dipped in paraffin wax, they were nailed up where required. Wind machines were an important component in the special effects arsenal and lengths of perforated metal tubing were used for storm and rain sequences. Fog was produced by a set of gadgets in which a jet of oil was vaporised through an electric heater element and then blown out of a nozzle. By passing this vapour through a dry ice chamber, it cooled to lay more thickly on the ground.

Back-projection effects were handled by the special effects department at Worton Hall, as well as at Shepperton, which possessed a giant 24-foot back-projection screen of its own in addition to a number of smaller ones. This process was closely allied to the work of the optical printing department, planned to become the largest and most up to date in the country. Explosions, hurricanes, special props, hanging miniatures, train wrecks, tank work, 'in fact everything in the book that calls for set economy, spectacle and out-of-the-ordinary technique' was all part of the job for the team at Isleworth. Poppa Day, the foremost exponent of the art in Britain, was still in charge of glass shots, but the fact that neither he nor Mann enjoyed a film credit wasn't an issue. 'Maybe I'm old fashioned about these things,' Mann explained, 'but I still think that for the normal film we should hold on to our tricks and not publicise them in advance.' There were exceptions. In *Things to Come*, for example, the rocket ship was obviously a product of 'intentional trickery', but for the regular film depicting a street or a train crossing the countryside then it was matter of striving for reality in order not to detract from the film. As in any discipline of stage management, if the endeavour is obvious to the audience then it is a failure. And so it was agreed that even for an esteemed trade paper like *Film Industry*, Ned Mann's Gulch and the Lone Stage of Worton Hall should be allowed to retain some of their secrets. But three months after Huntley's visit, in March 1948, the process of dismantling the mighty structure for its transfer to Shepperton began.

A short paragraph published in *Cinema Studio* in June records the moment that the first entire film stage in England was removed by contractors from one studio to another. Destined to be used for films of a more 'spectacular nature', it survives second only in magnitude to the 007 Stage at Pinewood, which comes in at 59,000 square feet. Its removal was first mooted in 1935 when Alexander Korda ordered it to be transferred to Denham. But the magnificent folly he had created in Buckinghamshire was already too large for the British production market to fill and so the plan to extend it even further with this giant refugee was scrapped. How, fourteen years later, the massive 250-foot by 120-foot structure was so quietly spirited away from Isleworth to overshadow Shepperton without any apparent comment or observation at either end is something of a mystery. Neither local authority has any record of the removal or arrival of the largest film stage in Europe, and the biggest story to capture the interest of the local papers was a Christmas party thrown by British Lion for its employees at Isleworth and a large scout hut shifted from one end of Shepperton to the other.

Just walking the inner perimeter of this great shed today is to appreciate what an undertaking this removal and resurrection was. Joe Gillnet recalls that it was an Irish firm who moved the stage 'in record time'. Rather than try and dig out the massive stanchions they cut them off, leaving the structure 5 feet lower than it used to be. These stanchions are massive steel girders sunk vertically into hefty concrete parapets of nuclear bunker proportions. The limitless sheets of drab asbestos cladding the structure are attached to the mighty steel skeleton by hundreds of thousands of nuts and bolts. Once disassembled, a modern-day low-loader would have difficulty in attempting the move in under a dozen trips. The mind boggles to consider so much steel and asbestos trundling down the narrow lanes of West Middlesex. The final ignominy when the structure was reassembled saw the faded legend 'LONDON FILMS', originally painted in large white letters on the west end of the structure rearranged as 'DONLON LMSFI'. It's still possible to make out some of them to this day, as they remain barely visible from the direction of Studios Road.

H Stage at Shepperton remains virtually as it was built, albeit a little shorter. It's still a 'silent stage' and was never soundproofed as some accounts have it, for to do so would cost more than to demolish and rebuild it. What makes this stage even more unique is that as well as an interior water tank, the entire floor area can be flooded to a depth of 5½ feet. On the face of it, the ideal piece of kit for filming *The African Queen*, where placing valuable Hollywood actors in toxic, crocodile-strewn waters was not an option. This vast, confined and controllable environment was custom-made for the many water-based scenes shot out of Africa involving the hauling of the queen through the undergrowth and fighting the rapids; except that by the time filming had begun at Isleworth, the stage had been shifted to Shepperton. Lilian Haynes, whose father was a props man on *The African Queen*, remembers 'the Big Stage' *in situ* at Worton Hall for the film, but an aerial photograph taken two months before the UK filming began shows it most definitely gone.

11

The Good, the Poor and the Indifferent

The second Nigel Balchin novel to be filmed at Worton Hall after the relative success of *Mine Own Executioner* was *The Small Back Room*, an adaptation of his wartime best-seller about the love affair of a neurotic back-room scientist working on a devilish German booby-trapped bomb device that killed his colleague as he attempted to take it apart. Nigel Balchin served during the war as a brigadier in the psychological warfare department and thus had first-hand experience of military service and the human mind. The story revolves around Sammy Rice (played by David Farrar), whose life is warped by his physical disability but finds redemption in solving the problem of the new German bomb, a not atypical scenario worked by the Powell and Pressburger partnership, whose arrival at London Films followed a successful but strained period at Rank.

Emeric (Imre) Pressburger worked as a journalist, translator and short-story writer in Berlin before turning to screenwriting. Like many of his Hungarian compatriots, he left Germany for England in the 1930s and settled into the film industry, scripting Alexander Korda's *The Challenge* (1938). And it was Korda who assigned him to rewrite *The Spy in Black* (1939), where he first met Michael Powell who was directing the film. Pressburger became Powell's preferred screenwriter and secured his first producer credit on *One of Our Aircraft Is Missing* (1942), the first of fourteen major feature films made between 1943 and 1955 bearing the now famous Powell and Pressburger joint-credit.

Like Guy Hamilton, Michael Powell began his long and distinguished film career at the Victorine studios in Nice in the 1920s where he worked for the

Hollywood director Rex Ingram as a bit-player and general assistant. From there he entered the emerging British film industry as a story analyst and stills photographer. Later he formed a partnership with American producer Jerry Jackson to make quota quickies, honing his directing skills on twenty-three films between 1931 and 1936 before moving on towards his trademark approach with films such as *The Edge of the World* (1937) and *The Spy in Black* (1939), which mark his transition in style. The first real Powell-Pressburger project was *Contraband* (1940), which takes full advantage of the atmospheric opportunities offered by a blacked-out London.

Powell worked on Korda's patriotic flag-waver, *The Lion Has Wings* (1939) and directed parts of *The Thief of Bagdad* the following year before Korda transferred the production to Hollywood. It was then that Powell and Pressburger created the Archers banner and arguably the most fruitful partnership in British film history. In his autobiography Powell wrote that in the days before the war, 'we were little men and Alex was a big one. We did not aspire to be great. It was not our scene. We were ingenious, resourceful, inventive and courageous, but we were not great. Alex was great.' Although it looked as though it might be difficult to make good pictures with him and his associates, the atmosphere he engendered was one of huge enthusiasm that was 'a million miles from the bourgeois tantrums of John Davis, whose tall shadow was falling across his master, Arthur Rank'. Although Powell and Pressburger were happier at London Films, their previous good fortune didn't follow them. The public at this time was fed up with reminders of the war and Korda's yearning for international success hampered The Archers' projects, which suffered from his customary interference. An exception was *The Small Back Room*.

Powell cast Kathleen Byron as Susan, a role wholly contrary to Sister Ruth, the nun who goes mad with lust in the Himalayas in *Black Narcissus*. Jack Hawkins returned to Worton Hall, as did Leslie Banks and Robert Morley in supporting roles. Cyril Cusack, the celebrated Irish stage actor, made one of his most memorable screen appearances as the stammering corporal, and Sam Kydd, potentially the *Guinness Book of Records*' prime contender for the most screen appearances in British films, plays a sentry. Sid James, best remembered for the incurably lascivious persona honed to such comic effect in the *Carry On* series, plays one of his signature American barmen, Knucksie Moran, and Patrick Macnee, the debonair John Steed in TV's cult series *The Avengers*, makes an uncredited appearance. Remarkably, given his small-screen persona, Macnee was to enjoy only minor roles in less than a dozen films across his thirty-year career, most notably in the

Bond movie *A View to a Kill*. Playing an army officer is Michael Gough, the British character actor who has appeared in over 100 British films, achieving cult status among horror fans due to his frequent appearances in the genre throughout the 1960s. But just as the great Shakespearan actor Sir John Gielgud is remembered as the butler in the *Arthur* films, so Gough has earned similar immortality in his recurring role as Alfred Pennyworth in the first four *Batman* revivals.

Making his debut screen appearance as 'the dying gunner' was another milestone name in British cinema history, Bryan Forbes. Fresh out of uniform, he landed the tiny role in Michael Powell's new film for the princely sum of £25. Asking when he would receive the script, Forbes' agent delivered the news that there were no lines but that it was a very important part nevertheless. 'I believed him and duly presented myself at Worton Hall Studios,' recalls Forbes, where he was led onto a set comprising a sea of imitation grass where he lay ignored by the cast and crew for the entire morning. 'Filming in those days was an unhurried affair,' he recalls in his autobiography, *Notes for a Life*.

After lunch Forbes was directed to lie down again and after twenty minutes' observation from a variety of angles, Powell declared him too clean and so his face was smeared with a gritty mixture of black pan-stick ground gramophone record and then bandaged, leaving only the eyes and mouth visible. Then the lighting process began and Powell felt that the leaves strewn about the scene were too messy and ordered them to be cleared, which caused hours of discussion and debate, ending with Powell advising the shop steward to go and 'get a bloody gardener'. Lines of demarcation finally observed, a wrap was called and filming held over for the following day. Although Michael Powell was not a man given to praising actors lightly, having eventually pronounced the scene acceptable he sent the young Forbes home in his own Rolls Royce, fifty pounds richer.

Bryan Forbes appeared in a number of notable films until he turned to screenwriting and then to directing, beginning in 1961 with *Whistle Down the Wind*. *The L-Shaped Room* earned Leslie Caron an Oscar nomination, as did *Séance on a Wet Afternoon* for Kim Stanley, who played the psychic. In 1969 Forbes was appointed chief of production and managing director of Associated British (EMI). It was a step too far. Apart from Joseph Losey's *The Go-Between*, which won the Golden Palm at Cannes in 1971 and proved a substantial critical and commercial success, Forbes' film career never recovered. The dead leaves story from his earliest days was not even faintly apocryphal. The British film industry was on its self-inflicted slide towards near-ruin, faithfully aping all the excesses of Hollywood without any of its ruthless discipline. Britain boasted major talents; a wealth of actors and directors, cameramen and technicians, all given artistic freedom and generous budgets, only to be squandered. Forbes contends that every section of the industry contributed to its decline and fall and that any attempt to impose a manufacturing pattern on a shared creative process was ultimately doomed to failure.

The Red Shoes represents the pinnacle of Powell/Pressburger partnership and its inevitable descent. It was a big-budget movie that went on to become one of the fifty biggest money-earners in film history, whereas *The Small Back Room* had a comparatively modest budget and was reasonably successful. *Film Industry* trade paper for January 1949 reflects that Powell and Pressburger had long been accused of producing brilliant pictures with no warmth or human appeal. In *The Small Back Room* the paper's critic observed that they had given the lie to that theory by making a film not only technically brilliant, but at the same time an absorbing and a tender if unconventional love story, gathering around them an equally brilliant crew of technicians and particularly good casting. 'By what magic The Archers persuaded famous actors to accept tiny parts, they do not disclose.'

The Third Man marked very much the highpoint of Korda's other celebrated ex-Rank refugee, Carol Reed, before his career went into an abrupt decline. The story of an American writer, Holly Martins, who goes to Vienna just after the Second World War to track down people who knew his friend, Harry Lime, a racketeer who has supposedly been killed in a street accident, it is the quintessential *film noir*, epitomised by its low-key lighting, bleak urban setting and corrupt, cynical and desperate characters. *The Third Man* is now considered one the greatest British films ever made. The rich story behind the film is well documented elsewhere with people who were around at the time adamant that all the UK filming was done at Shepperton, which is by no means the case.

Cinema Studio for 5 January 1949 reported that shooting for the film in Vienna began on 22 October 1948, the British crew returning to England on 15 December to recommence filming by the main unit at Worton Hall where it maintained an average of two and a half minutes footage per day. *Film Industry* magazine watched Carol Reed get through three set-ups on Thursday 6 January and had the entire unit packed up and ready to shift production to Shepperton by three o'clock that afternoon. How such an unforgiving schedule came about was explained in part during in an evening with Guy Hamilton hosted by BAFTA in July 2010. Then working as first assistant director to Carol Reed on the film, Hamilton explained that being 'an American actor', Orson Welles couldn't be expected to work down the sewers of Vienna. On the former boy wonder's eventual arrival to work on the film he looked about him in disgust, declaring the conditions were not what he was used to and refused to join the Brits in the filthy underworld where they even ate sandwiches devoid of cellophane. The thought of waste water pouring onto his body was too much for the star to bear and so other arrangements had to be made.

'We've got so many other things to do,' announced Reed. 'We will just have to build a sewer in Shepperton.' As Hamilton recalls, there were numerous occasions where he would step in above and beyond the call of first assistant, which did much to engender Reed's respect and appreciation. By liaising closely with the production managers, Hamilton saw the schedule revised to help overcome the many difficulties confronting completion of the production, mostly generated by Welles. Studio space was getting tight at Shepperton and Worton Hall was booked for *The Glass Mountain*, the Michael Dennison and Dulcie Gray wartime romance. The celebrated Italian baritone Tito Gobbi was booked to join the cast at the end of his tour and return with them to complete the interiors at Isleworth. With a two-week period offering some spare capacity, Hamilton provided a logistical solution in terms of booked studio time across Vincent's Korda's seventy-five sets. As Vienna was being constructed 5 miles west at Shepperton, so the Kartnerstrasse beer cellar was built at Worton Hall for the scene featuring Major Calloway (Trevor Howard) treating Martins (Joseph Cotten) to a drink, a set that could also be changed to a pub if need be. Harry Lime's apartment, featuring Martins' painful interrogation of the porter (Paul Hoerbiger) about Lime's accident was also created at Worton Hall.

Joseph Cotten was introduced to film acting by Orson Welles, appearing first in his pivotal *Citizen Kane* (1941) followed by *The Magnificent Ambersons*. Trevor Howard was already a major face of British cinema, entering the annals of British cinema history as Dr Alec Harvey in a tale of unconsummated middle-class adultery with Laura, played by Celia Johnson in David Lean's *Brief Encounter*. It was this steady, courteous and reassuring type symptomatic of his style that Howard lent to the part of Major Calloway so flawlessly in *The Third Man*. Bernard Lee was another redoubtable sort who played innumerable police inspectors, superintendents, brigadiers and colonels. But it is as the dogged and loyal Sergeant Paine in *The Third Man*, shot by Harry Lime to no purpose, that remains an abiding image of the character actor who would end his career playing 'M' in the first eleven Bond movies.

The Third Man opened to huge critical acclaim both sides of the Atlantic, winning Robert Krasker the Academy Award for Best Cinematography, Black and White. Carol Reed was nominated Best Director and Oswald Hafenrichter for Best Film Editing. It won the BAFTA Award for the Best British Film and was nominated BAFTA Best Film from any Source. It took the Grand Prize at the Cannes Film Festival and the Directors Guild of America Outstanding Directorial Achievement in Motion Pictures, awarded to Carol Reed. The film has now become one of the few British films regarded as a great classic of international cinema, but when later asked why he had originally agreed to terms that were obviously to his disadvantage, Korda confessed that he didn't believe the film would be the success it turned out to be.

In 1949 the Supreme Court in the United States forced the big studios there to surrender control of their chains of cinemas, thus breaking their monopoly on distribution and allowing exhibitors to screen whatever they liked, a move that would ultimately benefit British cinema. In looking towards a National Film Policy, the president of the Board of Trade, Harold Wilson, started with the proposition that all film finance, whether private or funded though the National Film Finance Corporation (NFFC) depended ultimately not only on production and distribution guarantees, but also on a circuit release. In Britain that came down to Gaumont-Odeon and the ABC circuit. Wilson argued that no matter how much work the NFFC did to aid the financing of a film, the whole business was dependent on their judgement. Widely regarded as undesirable, it was referred twice to the Monopolies and Mergers Commission, but to no avail.

The Board of Trade insisted that the production and distribution of films should be strictly separated wherever state aid was involved. As a consequence Sir David Cunynghame and Harold Boxall resigned from the board of British Lion so as to make this separation legal. Nevertheless the company found itself under attack from all quarters over its NFFC loan, especially when it was increased to £3 million. But, as Harold Wilson explained, outside of the Rank Organisation, the greater number of independent producers was associated directly or indirectly with the British Lion Corporation, which seemed to the government to provide the quickest and surest way of preventing the complete breakdown of the industry. Although the money was used to make a large number of films that Korda had little or nothing to do with, he was perceived as the guiding force. He had made it plain in

October 1948 that his London Films Productions would cease flying the 'Sir Alexander Korda presents' banner, making him effectively not so much a producer as an administrator.

Overall the years 1944 to 1949 saw a run of high-quality, memorable and commercially successful films never before or since produced in Britain; a period in which Worton Hall played its part as either host or ancillary, gradually giving ground to Shepperton as the focus of investment drifted in that direction. When G. B. Samuelson first opened for business at Worton Hall it was a prime spot, close to London, with acres of ground to extend the business and for exterior shooting. It came complete with the requisite administration block in the form of a comfortable roomy old mansion, the same as at Ealing, Pinewood and Shepperton. When Samuelson's former director Dave Aylott returned to Worton Hall for a short time in 1928, extensive building work had started, and more so in 1935 when London Films had taken over the studios and the orchards had started to disappear. On his last visit in 1949 he hardly recognised the place, surrounded as it was by housing. The Hall had changed very little, with only part of the flower gardens, the lawns and cedar trees remaining. The old glass studio had been converted into stars' dressing rooms and there were three sound stages, with carpenters', plasterers' and electricians' shops, together with administration offices where the orchard and kitchen gardens used to be.

Ealing was by now similarly surrounded by housing, but had established itself as a 'brand' long before the war, launching in 1949 its trademark productions with the consecutive releases of its now-famous comedies. Pinewood would eventually become home to the hugely successful *Carry On* series, as well as high-octane action productions such as the *Bond* movies. Even Down Place, further west from the capital on the banks of the Thames, was due a makeover when Hammer Film Productions renewed its lease to create Bray Studios, from thereon home to the most famous horror film brand. Worton Hall continued much as it had always done, turning out an eclectic array of pictures from a diverse mix of talent. *Circle of Danger* (1950), for example, marked 'atmospheric' director Jacques Tourneur's foray into the world of independent production.

After directing features in France in the early 1930s, Tourneur shifted to Hollywood where he found success with MGM, directing second units and two-reel productions until he found his niche at RKO for producer Val Lewton. With cult classics such as *Cat People* and *I Walked with a Zombie* (both 1943) he adapted the *film noir* genre using light and shadow to send shivers down the spine. *Circle of Danger* was a David E. Rose Coronado production under a distribution deal set up with Eagle-Lion. Joan Harrison, formerly an assistant to Alfred Hitchcock, was the producer. Mystery writer Philip McDonald wrote the screenplay from his novel, *White Heather*, the title under which the film went into production. The story revolves around American Second World War veteran Clay Douglas who comes to Scotland to investigate the death of his brother on a special mission in France during the war. Inquiring from former war buddies as to the circumstances surrounding his brother's death, Douglas hits a wall of silence. Although not a *film noir* as such, parallels are drawn between it and what is described as the 'Tourneur universe', one pundit opining that the film at least looked a lot better than the average British film of the period; the lighting, the camera movements, décor, and compositions all showing great care.

Playing the part of Clay Douglas was Ray Milland, the Welsh-born actor discovered by an American talent scout. The pinnacle of his career came in 1946 when he won the Best Actor Academy Award for his portrayal of an alcoholic in Billy Wilder's *The Lost Weekend*. Milland was the first Welsh actor ever to win an Oscar and one who still holds the record for the shortest acceptance speech of any Oscar winner, simply bowing and leaving the stage. He would go on to give strong performances in *Close to My Heart* and opposite Grace Kelly in Alfred Hitchcock's *Dial M for Murder*. Somewhere in between he found himself at Isleworth opposite Patricia Roc, an actress who made her name in costume dramas, co-starring with the likes of John Mills and Michael Redgrave in films such as *Millions Like Us* and *The Wicked Lady*. Noel Coward described her as a 'phenomenon, an unspoiled movie star who can act'. For ten consecutive years from 1943 she was voted one of Britain's top ten box-office stars.

Other cast members include Marius Goring, who had built a formidable reputation on the stage, especially for Shakespeare. There is little hint of this with regard to his screen career, invariably cast as a villainous Nazi or homicidal maniac. He made his first professional stage appearance in 1927, appearing in Korda's *Rembrandt* (1936) and other films until making his screen reputation in *The Case of the Frightened Lady* (1940), which had been a hit for him on stage. But even after the international acclaim he received for his work on *The Red Shoes* (1948) he continued to consider himself essentially a stage actor. And Dora Bryan, the petite blonde adept at wide-eyed innocents whose naiveté was played for laughs, was another up-and-coming character actress cutting her teeth on celluloid at Isleworth. It was after spending eight years honing her craft at the Oldham Rep that she made for London and was cast in a production of Noel Coward's *Private*

Lives, where the man himself suggested her stage name. She broke into films playing a small role in Rank's *Odd Man Out* (1946) before going on to play a number of eccentrics and low-class floozies brimming with middle-class aspirations, of which Bubbles Fitzgerald in *Circle of Danger* was but one. Her finest screen performance is undoubtedly Rita Tushingham's gin-soaked mother in Tony Richardson's *A Taste of Honey* (1961).

No sooner had Bryan finished with Bubbles Fitzgerald than she was back at Worton Hall, typecast as Janey Jenkins, brazen floozy and sexual predator in *The Cure for Love*. And joining her in what is possibly the earliest confirmed on-screen sighting as the archetypal strong-willed, no-nonsense, sharp but fair Northerner not afraid to speak her mind when it suited, was Thora Hird. She made her stage debut in 1911 at the age of two months and became a household name on television from the 1960s onwards. Directed by Robert Donat, *The Cure for Love* was for him a labour of love. His only film as director, producer and co-adapter, it was based on a play written by his close friend, the Salford-born writer Walter Greenwood, best known for his novel *Love on the Dole*. Donat directed the stage version at the Westminster Theatre in 1945 and had spent several unsuccessful years trying to get the film version made. Heroically investing the £20,000 he had earned for *The Winslow Boy*, *The Cure for Love* was one of three low-budget films costing £50,000 each that Korda (as executive producer) decided could be done well and enjoy considerable box-office success. Together with a distribution guarantee through British Lion, Donat first set about restructuring the script, which centred on Jack Hardacre, who is on leave in his small Yorkshire town after three years in the army and finds himself attracted to his mother's lodger, Milly (played by Renne Asherson), much to the chagrin of his old sweetheart, Janey Jenkins.

As Donat awaited news of which Korda studio his film would be booked into, so *Film Industry* announced on 7 April that *The Angel with the Trumpet* had taken to the floor at Isleworth. Carrying forward Korda's spring offensive, the cavalcade-type story about the fortunes of an Austrian family since 1888 was an elaborate, romantic costume piece rushed through a nine-week schedule, including two weeks shooting at Isleworth before moving to Shepperton to make room for Robert Donat's film on 2 May. Anthony Bushell, also directing for the first time, gave most credit for the rapid progress of *The Angel with the Trumpet* to his lighting cameraman, the by-now renowned Bob Krasker. In the first three days' shooting, twenty-one set-ups were in the can despite the huge problems with lighting, costume and make-up arising from the difficulty in matching the scenes taken from an Austrian version of the same subject completed shortly after the war. This recycling of previously shot scenic and general background material was the main factor in bringing the schedule down from an average four months to two, although it was a matter of false economy.

After the massive lighting proposition of *Bonnie Prince Charlie* and the disjointed shooting frenzy on *The Third Man*, Krasker took this latest set of challenges in his stride. The four changes in period comprising the film were not shot in continuity, which placed huge demands on costume and make-up and the pace of construction on Worton Hall's two stages. Weeks of research had gone into the design and building of a composite interior set of a Viennese house constructed to change in appearance from period to period. The French set dresser Dario Simoni had given the Viennese settings the perfect Continental flavour, and scenic artist Ferdi Bellan had in forty-eight hours completed reproductions in delicate colour of two mural panels in an Austrian royal hunting lodge. The special emphasis placed on costume, especially the profusion of ancient military uniforms requiring the right decorative details such as medals and uniform trappings of the time, harked back to the Samuelson days and the resourceful Jack Clair scouring London for similar artefacts to make the picture appear completely authentic.

With *The Angel with the Trumpet* eventually shifted to Shepperton, so the Donat picture moved into Worton Hall. And having got what he wished for, Donat found the task not without its challenges. Throughout the pre-production process he had complained constantly to Greenwood that all of his best ideas were going to characters other than his. 'Remember,' he chided the writer, 'your poor bloody star is the one who sells the film, and you might at least acknowledge the fact by giving him something worth doing occasionally.' By the time the film was about to go into production, Donat was taken ill. According to his biographer he was told that if he could not meet the start date then Worton Hall Studios would have to close. This explains the beseeching letter Donat sent to the president of the Board of Trade in which he sets out his own personal ambition as the making of a quality film at low cost, and not a star vehicle. He looked to shave off a considerable amount of the film's £175,000 budget by full rehearsals and proper planning, but in the same breath was having to sacrifice among other things rehearsals, due to his ill health that had given out twice during the film and had added as much as £45,000 to the costs. Nevertheless he was endeavouring to come in under budget.

Donat hoped that the minister would find the time to see the film, explaining that he honestly believed it got nearer to a slice of truly British life and character than any British comedy produced thus far. 'I cannot speak for my own performance,' he concludes, 'but there is no doubt whatever that the other performances are of the highest possible order.' Even more extraordinary was Donat's play on his shared Lancastrian roots with the minister 'that they both knew so well'. Harold Wilson's reaction to this bizarre epistle is not recorded by the actor's biographer.

Donat's first and last excursion into film production went to the floor at Worton Hall in the first week of May with an immediate cessation of his declared policy of frugality. Considering her bust too small for the part, Dora Bryan was sent to a sculptor who set about an amplification process using the same plaster cast system to that used to cast cobblestones, street ornaments, paving stones and decorative brickwork peculiar to the film's setting. It would have been much cheaper to have gone on location or have allowed the production designer to recreate the look himself, but Donat had already decided on a stylisation that required Oscar-winning art director (for *Great Expectations*) Wilfred Shingleton and stills cameraman Harold Hanscombe spending five days taking numerous photographs of rustic Lancashire villages and small factory towns. With further research using prints and paintings by Charles de la Tour, Shingleton was equipped to build Donat's 'completely authentic portrait of small-town life in the North' with touches of antiquity applied to all of the woodwork on the set cottages by means of acetylene burners and wire brushes.

Master plasterer Bert Brown was responsible for manufacturing the pavements and streets by taking the casts made on location and then converting them into semi-circular rubber plates bolted onto rollers that were driven across wet concrete on the floor of the set. The result was a perfect reproduction of cobbled streets and antique stone paving. In addition the cement street produced authentic footstep and traffic noises and was impervious to both natural and studio rain. 'After seventeen years in the business I have never seen a more useful device,' Brown admitted. The new moulding plastic called Vino-mould had a greater tensile strength and elasticity than the standard gelatine. Rarely splitting, it made plaster casting simpler and more efficient and speeded up the complete process. Presumably Dora Bryan's augmentation fared as well as the cobbles and pavements.

The Cure for Love allowed production manager W. J. Kirby a fifty-five-day studio shooting schedule with one week's location work. Set building lasted a month, with erection and striking speeded up with the use of rollers under the flats. As many of the sets as possible were pre-fabricated in the studio shops to cut down construction time on the stage floors, although more could have been achieved if there was the space. The unit spent seven days on the exterior set of the Lancashire village with its freshly cast winding cobbled streets and low, mean cottages that acted as a reminder to Donat of his own upbringing, especially with the torrential rain the set seemed to attract. But none of this innovation and ingenuity did anything to assist Donat in his ambition to make his film within budget and on time. An especially hot summer aggravated his fragile constitution, causing him to retreat for hours to his dressing room, which resembled a small hospital. When fit enough to work he found himself at times unable because of Dora Bryan and Gladys Henson who played her mother. So funny were they that it took as many as twenty-five takes before they could control their giggles. The film therefore took much longer than planned. Dora Bryan's contract, for example, was for twenty days. Every day she would go in and have her hair and make-up done but often wouldn't see the camera. It was six months by the time she was released.

The film proved a huge hit in the north of England, but in London its reception was muted. The *Monthly Film Bulletin*'s review consisted of three words: 'Antediluvian regional farce.' Other reviewers were kinder. The *Sunday Dispatch* felt it bubbled with humour, while Margaret Hinxman of *Time and Tide* wanted to know when would comedy directors 'forego the affectation of those fatal extra twenty minutes?' It was all too theatrical, she bemoaned, with its stagey entrances and exits and scene changes 'only lacking in the final nicety of a curtain fall'. The leading roles she considered to be 'grossly overwritten, almost to the point of caricature' with the humour meandering between straight comedy, raucous farce and the ultimate absurdity of burlesque. And yet, for all its faults, she loved the film.

Film reviewer Caroline Lejeune, writing for *Daily Sketch*, also thought the film was 'prime fun'. Born a few streets away from Donat where she used to see him as a boy riding his tricycle, she had been 'deeply touched, and just a fraction amused' by the friendly efforts of her southern colleagues to protect her as a northerner against *The Cure for Love*. When she came out of the press screening, 'full of rich and secret enjoyment', they clustered around her with well-meant apologies, realising that the film was fictitious, that real Lancashire people were quite different, not the burlesques portrayals they had witnessed playing against artificial and unrealistic sets. But then, as Lejeune confided to her readers, the secret of *The Cure for Love* was a joke for northerners by northerners. It wasn't meant to be realistic or documentary, but a fiction in the native idiom, 'done with the Lancashire tongue firmly fixed in the Lancashire cheek'.

Michael Wilding, for Wilcox-Neagle Productions, intended to mark a high point in the quality of production at Worton Hall with a comedy, *Into the Blue* (or *Man in the Dinghy*). Sadly it served only to baffle *The New York Times*, firstly with regard to the choice of producer. In its view, Herbert Wilcox was not a man 'renowned for qualities of wit and humour in his eminently proper British films'. Like his man in the dingy, the film had 'become beached at the Sixtieth Street Trans-Lux cinema' and did nothing to enhance his reputation.

> It is a dismally unfunny fable about the pains to which a man and wife are put by a repulsively debonair fellow who stows away on their vacation yacht. And for something like eighty-three minutes it wheezes and bumps along with some of the stuffiest attempts at British humour since Bertie dunked a frog in Nanny's tea.

The film marked a return to Worton Hall for Jack Hulbert; perhaps one too many, for he was likewise lampooned among 'the considerable dead-weights that appear in this lustreless film … as a lantern-jawed British Babbitt … in the style of the third-rate music halls'. Odile Versois, a former child ballerina with the Paris Opera Corps de Ballet who turned to acting, making numerous films as a leading lady and specialising in fragile, often tragic heroines in romantic dramas, was similarly ridiculed. 'This cocoon-to-butterfly creature … whom Mr Wilcox must have discovered in a church theatrical' is summarily dismissed as 'a dreary French girl who mouses around in a knitted cap and a state of fearful expectation until she suddenly emerges a sensation in one of Madame's evening gowns'.

But most depressing was 'the archetypal urbane leading man who never quite reached the highest level', Michael Wilding, recently returned from Hollywood where he featured in two of Alfred Hitchcock's films, *Under Capricorn* (1949) and *Stage Fright* (1950). In *Into the Blue* he played the stowaway 'in a manner that he and Mr Wilcox probably calculated to be arch', his character portrayal involving

> considerable cocking of his handsome head … causing his eyes to sparkle gaily and crinkling his face in chummy smiles. The fact that he and his whole venture turn out to be virtual frauds sends one forth wishing grimly that the people aboard that yacht had tossed him briskly, the moment he was discovered, to the sharks. Then they might have had a nice vacation and everyone might have been spared a boring show.

Anna Neagle appears wisely to have taken a rain check on her husband's latest venture.

After jumping ship from Rank where he had forged a strong track record in light comedy with Frank Lauder, Sidney Gilliat joined Korda to make *The Happiest Days of Your Life*, some scenes of which may have been shot at Worton Hall. Gilliat as producer/director next set himself a difficult and fascinating problem, according to *Film Industry*'s Pat Bowman, who paid a visit to Isleworth in November 1949. Jack Hawkins headed a strong support cast for Douglas Fairbanks Jr and Glynis Johns in *State Secret*, an escape-from-tyranny story, although the rest of the cast included so many foreign actors that the credibility of the film was threatened by them all speaking broken English with different accents. Making his British screen debut as part of this diverse assembly was Anton Diffring, who had fled Nazi Germany in 1939 and spent the duration of the war interned as an enemy alien in Canada, where he began his acting career. Moving to the United States, he eventually came to Britain where found work continuously in film and television ironically as the archetypal Nazi; his part in *State Secret*, naturally enough, that of a severe state policeman in the tale of an eminent surgeon who is contacted by the authorities of an Eastern European country to save the life of its president, but the operation fails and the president is replaced by a lookalike, which places the surgeon in a difficult and dangerous situation.

State Secret was applauded by the acclaimed journalist, historian, biographer and novelist Leonard Mosley as 'one of the best thrillers a British, or any studio for that matter has made for years'. To form an effective and convincing background to the story, Gilliat had to create an entirely fictitious Central European country called Vosnia. It had to be completely credible and that included the language. Korda suggested Esperanto but no one could be found to teach it, and so Miss Shields of the London School of Languages was employed to invent an entirely new language, Vosnian, which she achieved across a staggering vocabulary of over a thousand words and phrases.

In the wake of *The Third Man*, Korda wanted the film to be shot in Austria, which Gilliat considered absurd; the whole proposition of moving between the various occupied zones was a nightmare only too familiar to Bob Krasker and Guy Hamilton, both happy to avoid the darkness and especially sewers. Italy was Gilliat's preferred location, and at a third of the budget for Austria won the day. In his American star, too, there was an odd parody of the problems experienced by Carol Reed. As Leslie Gilliat explains in Gareth Owen's *The Shepperton Story*, he found Douglas Fairbanks Jr an 'odd character', eating up valuable shooting time in his largely self-appointed role as America's unofficial ambassador. Since Fairbanks' contracted time represented serious money, anything extra was out of the question and so ingenious use was made of a previously recorded commentary piece which was used to cover Fairbanks' point of view walking down a long corridor.

Bob Krasker particularly enjoyed himself on the set of the operating theatre created at Worton Hall, which provided fascinating photographic material under the brilliant, hard lighting where he was getting the most out of the contrast of the white-clad figures with the slightly darker cream of the walls. Art director Wilfred Shingleton had got the idea for the ultramodern set while cracking a boiled egg one morning, which gave him the inspiration for the futuristic domed-roof design constructed and equipped with the latest apparatus, including an anaesthesia outfit that excited the envy of the chief surgeon from the Middlesex Hospital, called in to advise on correct procedure. Shingleton's share in the creation of Vosnia also included the design of its buildings, a confection of architecture from northern Italy variously influenced by Austria and Hungary; not so much things to come, but a compilation of that which had come about.

A more cheap and not-so-cheerful project churned out of Worton Hall at the close of the 1940s was *The Late Edwina Black*, which saw British cinema's most prolific film director Maurice Elvey weave the story of a sickly Victorian woman who dies suddenly and a post-mortem that reveals her body contains a fatal dose of arsenic. Playing the husband is David Farrar who, riding high on the critical acclaim of *The Small Back Room*, went to Hollywood where his career nosedived spectacularly. Inspector Martin of Scotland Yard, who solves the mystery over a cup of tea, is played by Roland Culver, steadfast support in over ninety films between 1931 and 1983 as the impeccable English gentleman not given to displays of emotion; corrupt if required, blinkered and blustery as necessary across a plethora of authority figures. His role as the tenacious police inspector was reported to have been an exception.

Ralph Smart's production of *Curtain Up* boasts a fine cast headed by Robert Morley, Margaret Rutherford and Kay Kendall, with the up-and-coming Michael Medwin and Joan Hickson given a line or two. Michael Pertwee's screenplay concerns a small-town repertory company meeting one Monday morning to start rehearsing the following week's play, a dreadful offering written by the aunt of one of the theatre's directors. The British Film Institute describes this film as typical of the escapist comedy common in the early 1950s. A well-observed ensemble piece aimed at the widest possible audience, the arrival of television would soon become the natural home for this kind of popular entertainment, forcing independent film producers to find new ideas capable of wooing audiences out of their armchairs. In this, *The Wonder Kid* (or *Entführung ins Glück*) held the promise of such edge. Directed by Karl Hartl and then re-dubbed into German, Bobby Henrey, the juvenile star of *The Fallen Idol*, is cast as the seven-year-old musical genius who escapes his avaricious manager to a remote Alpine village where he falls into the hands of a gang of kidnappers led by a fundamentally decent chap (played by Robert Shackleton) who, with his girlfriend (Christa Winter), protects the lad from the other less savoury felons, notably a young Oskar Werner, ten years away from international recognition.

Across these dubious treats, the studio facility at Worton Hall was doing what it did best and doing it on a continual basis. It was a small studio where small films were made for small amounts of money. Production costs overall in the industry had been reduced by an average of 45 per cent, with films shot in a much shorter period and on a much less spectacular basis than Korda's earlier ambitions. In the greater commercial scheme of things Worton Hall was keeping its head above water, which was more than could be said for its parent interests. By the end of 1949 London Films owed £1,350,374 to British Lion and both showed substantial losses. Around half a million pounds extra revenue was expected within the next three years from the Eady Plan, a scheme created by Treasury official Sir Wilfred Eady that put an extra penny onto the price of a cinema seat, granting producers a proportion of box-office receipts.

Meant as a makeshift measure, the Eady Plan became increasingly important as time went on; benefiting those producers whose films enjoyed a screening around 13 per cent of the box-office receipts. Alexander Korda throughout continued to hover above it all, fundamentally smelling of roses. In less than five years his old and new films had earned £1,760,000 in Europe, proving the experts wrong. Contrary to predictions, Korda also proved that films had an infinitely longer shelf-life than was generally expected, with even original financial failures such as *Things to Come* gradually recovering costs over time. The London Films/British Lion relationship with Worton Hall was meanwhile growing evermore tenuous, although the ageing studio was not quite finished yet. There was one last chapter to come that should have cemented its place in British film history, but yet again was relegated to the footnotes in favour of its feistier sibling.

'Curse of the African Queen Strikes Windmill' was the *Croydon Guardian*'s lead story in October 2008 in relation to the plight of the Shirley Windmill that had survived the Blitz, several lightning strikes and threats of demolition, but now was under threat from a new enemy. Rose-ringed parakeets were sharpening their beaks on the 150-year-old windmill's sails, causing thousands of pounds' worth of damage. The same newspaper reported that the noisy green invaders had also caused £10,000 worth of damage to the spire of the local church by pecking at the shingle. These exotic birds, which come from Africa and Asia, are thought to have started breeding west of London in the 1950s, the abiding theory being that a pair, or even a whole flock, escaped from Shepperton Studios during the making of *The African Queen*. So ingrained has this urban myth become that in 2004 *The Times* reported on the floatation of Pinewood/Shepperton Studios under the headline '*African Queen Studios to Float*'. However, not a single frame of the film was shot at Shepperton.

12

The African Queen

Writing for *Moviemail Online* in 2001, film director Desmond Davis recalls the first time he met John Huston was on the set of *The African Queen* at Worton Hall studios. The unit had just returned from Africa and needed a clapper boy. This was 1951 and Davis had been an assistant cameraman (focus puller) for some years, but the chance to work on a Huston picture with Humphrey Bogart sent him scurrying out to the studio in spite of the loss of seniority. As he explains, 'If actors talk about the magic of theatre before curtain up then I must confess to the same feeling as I opened the film stage door.'

Despite the final credit of the *African Queen* announcing quite clearly and categorically 'Isleworth Studios', film historians and other reporters over the past half-century have doggedly persisted that filming out of Africa was completed at Shepperton. Although much has and continues to be documented about the primitive conditions endured by cast and crew in the seething jungles of the Congo, little concerted attention has been paid to the British adventure west of Claridge's. The stoic mentality of cast and crew in the making of *The African Queen* is now the stuff of legend. But the film's enduring appeal, due in no small part to the spirit of these professionals, also persisted in the decaying facility at Isleworth, which was in harmony with the parsimonious production process from start to finish. Sam Spiegel, the film's American producer, was all too familiar with the facility, having suffered the consequences there of his Buster Keaton debacle *The Invader* some years earlier. But in Spiegel terms it was ideal. It was easy on the pocket and therefore hugely attractive.

As already stated, the background to *The African Queen* is well documented elsewhere and is précised here only to provide a little context. It was a project that originally came about through the often tempestuous partnership Spiegel had forged with John Huston. Horizon Pictures was their independent film company so named in the fond hope that one day they might see the horizon. The film rights to C. F. Forester's novel *The African Queen* had already made the rounds. One version has it that John Collier bought the rights from Warner Brothers in 1949 and wrote a screenplay based on the book with a view to producing the film himself. Instead, he sold the property to Horizon. John Huston, however, recalls having bought the script directly from Warner Brothers for $50,000, which he and Spiegel didn't have. Horizon was heavily in debt so Spiegel secured a verbal option, providing operating capital via a mortgage on his home and 5 per cent of the film's possible profits to the mortgage holder. He then approached Sound Services Inc., a company that supplied sound equipment to studios for use of their equipment on location in return for a credit in the titles. With this agreement in place Horizon was then able to purchase the screen rights to *The African Queen*.

Spiegel also secured a deal with the Woolf brothers to shoot *The African Queen* in England with Romulus putting up all the production costs below the line for technicians and equipment and laboratories. John and James Woolf formed Romulus Films as a holding company for a new distribution company called Independent Film Distributors (IFD), which distributed its films through British Lion and Lion International overseas. IFD financed all of the films it distributed through British Lion and paid all of the distribution costs, including prints and advertising, which enabled British Lion to distribute films at a low cost. Seventy per cent of these films were financed by guarantees from IFD, 20 per cent from the National Film Finance Corporation and 10 per cent from Romulus Films. But the sheer lack of good films saw IFD lose most of its capital and force Woolf to go into film production where, under the umbrella of British Lion, Romulus Films would go on to produce a string of high-quality successful, self-financing productions.

United Artists had just been taken over by Arthur Krim and Robert Benjamin on a loan provided by the Chicago financier Walter E. Heller and was looking for a product to distribute. Heller secured an agreement that he would fund all of the costs for *The African Queen* above the line for the writers, the director, the producers and the stars in return for the American distribution rights. Through Horizon Enterprises Spiegel would provide a completion guarantee bond. Humphrey Bogart would receive $35,000 in cash with $125,000 as a deferred payment, plus 25 per cent of the film's profits, and Katharine Hepburn was in for $130,000 plus 10 per cent of the profits, while Huston was to take $87,000 and half the share of the profits of Horizon Pictures, the parent company of the new Horizon Enterprises. Spiegel's own producer's fee was deferred, but his expenses were not, and would be huge.

Set against the start of the First World War, the story of *The African Queen* follows prim missionary Rose Sayer and gin-soaked Canadian riverboat captain Charlie Allnut as fate throws them together after the Germans burn down the village where Rose and her brother, the Reverend Samuel Sayer, had set up a mission station. The shock kills Samuel, which determines Rose to exact revenge on the Hun, eventually convincing Charlie that they must sink the German gunboat. This they manage to do against all odds, falling in love along the way and getting the German gunboat captain to marry them seconds before the couple's home-made torpedoes sink the vessel, leaving the newly-weds to drift to safety on the nameplate of the *African Queen*.

'It was 1950, almost 1951,' Katharine Hepburn recalls in her memoirs. She immediately warmed to the idea of playing the part of Rose once she knew that Humphrey Bogart would be playing the cockney Charlie Allnut as a Canadian. She set off on an eight-day voyage to Liverpool as a means of avoiding the press, and it was early April when she arrived at Claridge's in London before joining the cast and crew making for Africa via Rome. The deal Sam Spiegel made with Romulus Films provided the sterling required, which got them the eastern distribution rights. Inevitably, given Spiegel's track record, Horizon's side of the deal fell through when he was unable to provide the completion guarantee. The Woolf brothers were likewise experiencing difficulty raising their half of the £1 million budget. The National Film Finance Corporation, which was putting up a fifth of the British production costs, was advised by Michael Balcon that *The African Queen* did not qualify as a British picture, even though it was to be made with British technicians and in a British studio, as it had two American stars and an American director and co-producer.

With the production deal breaking down, when Spiegel failed to produce the necessary cover for the risks of filming with Hollywood stars in darkest Africa, Heller refused to pay Hepburn and Bogart their fees despite the fact the latter was already bound for London with his wife Lauren Bacall and their small son, Stevie. Spiegel installed the family at Claridge's along with Katharine Hepburn while he began renegotiating their contracts. Bogart was now to get no money up front, his cash fee deferred until the picture began to make money and his share of the profits increased to 30 per cent. Hepburn agreed to defer half of her fee but refused any notion of finding the money to pay her substantial hotel bill. She didn't mind doing the film for nothing so much as having to pay for the privilege. Spiegel managed to persuade the hotel manager to give him credit in the knowledge that both he and the Woolf Brothers were too deeply committed not to arrive at a solution. If the film was to be called off both parties would each lose at least half a million dollars.

John Huston was of little help to Spiegel in London. In some respects he appeared to enjoy creating problems, nearly killing the deal five times according to Spiegel. Huston appears to have taken an almost sadistic pleasure in aggravating the situation at every turn. It's not clear if he enjoyed embarrassing his business partner, or if he was against Spiegel's support of the film being made in England in order to comply with the law, but at the first production dinner for the Anglo-American production he was particularly spiteful. He knew that the Woolf brothers were unaware of Spiegel's misadventures on the shooting of *The Invader*, where his financial shenanigans had led him to be jailed for three months and then deported from Britain. He shouted across a dinner table to his partner 'let's drink to the Old Bailey', much to the amusement of everyone except Spiegel. Still deeply humiliated by the experience, he feared that the Woolf brothers would start asking questions and the deal would be dead. 'Hungry,' sneered Huston across the table to his partner, 'but he can't eat.'

Eventually the British contingent saved the day and produced the completion bond. Hepburn was assured that the lawyers would have everything settled by the time she and Bogart arrived in Africa, a situation that persisted along with all the other discomforts encountered in the Belgian Congo and Uganda, except for Huston, who thrived as a latter-day Hemingway. Although the film was ahead of its time in taking an entire cast and crew on location to the 'Dark Continent', it was a curious nod to history to when Alexander Korda had sanctioned an expedition to Africa a decade earlier when making *Sanders of the River*, also shot at Worton Hall. While John Huston has much to say in his memoirs about his time in Africa making the film he has nothing to say about the time he spent in Isleworth finishing it. There is some debate about what percentage was shot in Africa and in the United Kingdom, whereas it is clear from watching the film that the greater part was shot in Isleworth. Dysentery and malaria and other sicknesses cut short the filming in Africa, with nine members of the crew sent back to England. Huston wanted to continue but was faced with a mass revolt.

As well as flying in and out of Africa, Sam Spiegel occasionally ventured west of his plush Grosvenor Square apartment to the Isleworth Studios where the film was to be finished with the secondary characters. Exterior sets were built at Worton Hall to match those in Africa, such as the First Methodist Church at Kungdu, where a stand-in double for Robert Morley was used for later cross-cutting at Isleworth. Hepburn recalls one stage set for the minister's house, 'a charming, rather large ground-floor tropical house' and another for Rosie's house. The first scene shot on arrival was with Morley, as the broken brother – sick and delirious after the German raid on the village – dies, leaving Rosie alone.

Desmond Davis remembers a 'pool of light in the dark cavern of the stage' where Hepburn, Morley and Bogart sit around the table in a typically English parlour scene played out against the stifling heat of Africa. Davis was surprised by Bogart's diminutive stature, especially against the lofty elevation of John Huston parked by the huge three-strip Technicolor camera wrapped in a blue soundproof blimp. Dressed in a safari jacket with a scarf knotted round his neck, Huston addressed everyone as 'kid' or 'honey', according to their sex. As Charlie demurely munches on his bread and butter and the rumbling of his stomach serves to horrify his decorous missionary host, so Ron De Mattos was later paid the princely sum of twenty-six guineas to record the sound of his own empty belly dubbed onto the scene.

The African Queen was shot in Technicolor when the majority of films at this time were shot in black and white. Making a return to Worton Hall as a skilled practitioner of this new art was the distinguished cinematographer Jack Cardiff. The three rolls of film running through the Technicolor camera at one time required a lot of light, the searing arc lights known as 'brutes' adding more than a touch of jungle humidity to the scene. Desmond Davis explains how through the dazzling wall of light it was hard to detect any of the skilful modelling or subtle translucent shadow that would appear later on the screen. The scene was filmed in one long-running three-shot and then covered in three close-ups, one for each of the principals. Huston kept takes to a minimum, often just the one without even the conventional 'safety take'. Davis asked about this, to which Huston replied, 'Listen kid, when you've got it, you've got it.' Cardiff, commenting later, initially felt that Huston's laid-back approach was ruining the film until he realised that his casualness disguised a complete grasp of the project.

Having completed the whimsical tea party, Huston moved on immediately to the next scene. He appears never to have done any 'prepping'. Not for him storyboards, a script covered with copious notes or pin figures and diagrams. Instead he would light a long thin cigarette and wander about the empty set before getting the actors to run the scene. Then, using one hand to frame his shots, he would create the scene with Jack Cardiff and camera operator Ted Moore following his footsteps. The line-up complete, he would then leave the set, returning when everyone was ready, his direction to the actors minimal, famously believing the act of casting was in itself the major statement of character.

In her account *The Making of The African Queen*, Katharine Hepburn recalls the water tank constructed in one of the stages at the 'tiny' Worton Hall studio for all of the underwater sequences and those passages where she and Bogart drag the *Queen* through the reeds. The tank was about four feet deep with the reeds and Bogart's hatred of swimming in it. 'He froze,' she recalls. 'I swam all winter in Long Island Sound; 10 degrees above zero and with a north wind blowing is my record.' Before shooting one scene she remembers the 'African backwater' having to be cleared of old buns, which had been thrown in after a tea break. But the most enduring passage was where Bogart emerges plastered in blood-sucking leeches. He famously insisted that rubber leeches be used, but Huston refused to use fakes and called in an expert who arrived at the studio with a tank full of the creatures. 'What's the matter, Bogie?' Hepburn chided, 'you scared of a leech? Try one,' she said. 'You try it first, kid,' he retorted. She couldn't and so in the end, the torso used for the close-up was that of the breeder, while the rest of the day was spent trying to invent a material that would stick rubber leeches to Bogart's frame. 'Dear Bogie,' recalls his co-star, 'I'll never forget that close-up of him after he kisses Rosie, then goes round the back of the tank and considers what has happened.'

Ron de Mattos, who was working at Worton Hall at the time, remembers a large area of backlot flooded to recreate an African lake suitably planted on one bank with jungle vegetation and with a canal dug where some of the water sequences were shot. Thanks to a number of production stills recently unearthed, this 'lake' (all 9 inches deep of it) was created on a small piece of open ground between the site of the Big Stage site and the back gardens of houses lining Worton Road. No larger than a football pitch, a 30-foot-high hill was created upon which sat a pint-sized Fort Shona, the German military post guarding the river. A real tribute to the film-makers, with this diorama as the backdrop and a front section of the *African Queen* ahead of the camera with a few tropical shrubs, the studio footage seamlessly matches the footage shot in Africa.

The *Köningen Luise*, the German gunboat patrolling the lake where the Ulanga River empties, was constructed on a high platform close to the 'lake'.

Desmond Davis explains that it was built 15 feet high to clear the trees and leave the deck against the sky. Theodore Bikel, who played the German first officer aboard the *Louisa*, remembers the scenes including the aft section of the gunboat and the deck where the couple are about to be hanged. The vessel, constructed as it was on its high scaffolding with only a sky view was in Hepburn's opinion 'a very weak scene', and that of the little steamer finally blowing the gunboat to smithereens 'slightly silly', and the finish too abrupt.

The sequence of the *Queen* in Africa shooting the rapids was created with the use of model boats made by monks from the local monastery at Ponthierville. The nuns were responsible for creating Bogart and Hepburn figurines. At Isleworth various mock-ups of the boat were made, both stern and aft. As with the German gunboat, these sections were fixed to an open-air scaffold construction on rockers and surrounded on three sides by mighty water dumps. Sufficient to scare the pants off a modern health and safety inspector, great wooden chutes delivered many hundreds of gallons of water onto the Hollywood stars. Even in the studio they endured a constant soaking from banks of rain heads and water hoses as the blue screen behind them threw up even more violent encounters shot on location.

Members of the crew were also prone to the odd mishap that would today make headline news or create a frenzied feeding ground for compensation lawyers. Percy Haines was a props man who was in the wrong place at the wrong time while rigging the sequence where Bogie braves a hail of German rifle fire to fix the shattered steam pipe. A series of charges were laid to give the impression of bullets peppering or ricocheting off the pipework. Percy was for some reason up close and personal when the rig accidentally ignited. His daughter, Lilian, heard of the accident hours later when she and her mother were told that Percy had been taken to hospital. 'When we got there his face was black and singed and his eyebrows gone,' she recalls, 'but otherwise he was fine, just a bit shaken.' Mercifully, Percy went on to enjoy another twenty years in the business.

Everyone went over to the tank after work on Saturday afternoon to watch it being filled. 'We worked a six-day week,' recalls Hepburn. The first scene was due to be shot there on the Monday, but then on the Sunday it burst and with such force that the crane next to it was torn and twisted like it was a hairpin, the huge stage door smashed down. Luckily it had been filled in a day early. Ted Skate, a cameraman on the film, told Joe Gillnet that it was the first time ever they had seen a whole tank explode. Desmond Davis puts the catastrophe down to the water chutes plunging far too much water into what was no more than a timber construction lined with a bitumen skin. Hepburn states that another tank was quickly commandeered at 'EMI', although that company ran no studio of its own. Ron De Mattos believes that the underwater filming was transferred temporarily to Elstree, probably for the scene showing Bogart underwater repairing the propeller. But then Theodore Bikel, Angela Allen (continuity on the picture) nor Desmond Davis recall any shift of filming out of Isleworth. Indeed the tank had done its job by the time of the disaster and what remained was achieved on the lot.

The film was completed mid-August 1951 and the next battle was for distribution. United Artists didn't believe that the public wanted to see Bogart looking unshaven and unkempt, and Hepburn was no longer the draw she had once been. Loew's cinema chain, the biggest in the United States, didn't feel they could place the film, which had to have a public release before the end of the year in order to qualify for the 1951 Oscars. Rising to the challenge, Spiegel rented New York's 3,000-seater Capitol Theatre, which was about to be torn down, and screened the film there, making $90,000 in the first week. This immediately changed the tune of the distributors and duly attracted a raft of Academy Award nominations for Katharine Hepburn (Best Actress), John Huston (Best Director) and James Agee (Best Screenplay). Humphrey Bogart won Best Actor. *The African Queen* had cost Horizon almost $730,000 to make and cost Romulus $248,000. On first release United Artists predicted a gross of $3 million, realised at $4.3 million.

John Huston considered the first ten reviews of the film in England to have been the best he had ever read. He believed that *The African Queen* was the greatest film ever made. It certainly caused a sensation, smashing every previous Warner record by a large margin. It remains a testament to Sam Spiegel's relentless tenacity and is probably his greatest achievement. Receiving the distribution rights for the eastern hemisphere created an opportunity for the Woolf brothers to go on to produce some of the most important films in British cinema history, such as *Room at the Top*, *Alfie* and *Day of the Jackal*. *The African Queen* continued to make money, eventually becoming Spiegel's biggest-earning picture. The negative reverted to him in 1960, earning $250,000 for its television network première in 1970 and $750,000 after three showings. 'And those were supposedly the lean years,' he recalls.

13
The Final Analysis

British Lion had incurred high production losses, which worsened when the Republic Pictures Corporation of America ended the business relationship. British Lion benefited directly from the government loan, not Alexander Korda's London Film Productions, as was generally supposed. Although, as the largest single unit, it did consume most of the loan and so was bound to take the lion's share (no pun intended) of the blame when things started to go wrong. When the time came for the loan to be repaid in October 1951, it was announced that 'no repayment could be made without curtailment of production' and part of that 'curtailment' meant the sale of assets, which meant Worton Hall.

Douglas Fairbanks Jr then made a return to his old British base with his newly formed Dougfair Corporation and brought with it the kiss of death for the film industry in the form of television. *The Foreign Legion* was originally planned as a pilot but the series went unsold and so was incorporated into *Douglas Fairbanks, Jr., Presents*, a quality long-running anthology series usually with lesser-known actors, hosted, narrated, produced and frequently starring Fairbanks himself. Shot on location in the Sahara desert and the interiors at Worton Hall, *The Foreign Legion* concerns a patrol that is attacked by a local Arab tribe that captures one of the legionnaires. The hero, Sgt Flint, is played by Charles McGraw, the gravelly voiced and rugged cop or gunman of many a *film noir* classic of the 1940s and 50s, who would find true screen immortality as the gladiator trainer in the 1960 epic *Spartacus*. Typecast as the villainous Amir Dhow was Martin Benson, who would graduate to top-notch baddie in 1964 as the arch villain Solo in the James Bond movie *Goldfinger* and a year later shift gear with his biggest break, playing Kralahome the Vizier in the film version of *The King and I.*

Sonny Tufts, the obligatory fading American movie star brought in to assist US sales, originally pursued a career in opera, arriving in Hollywood via Broadway in the 1940s to appear as a supporting artist in light comedies. Disqualified from military duty, the field was open for him to evolve into something approaching a star, but by the time he passed through the gates of Worton Hall he was well on the road to becoming a figure of fun, his career immersed in scandal and drink. It speaks volumes that it was his name used to generate publicity for *The Gift Horse* over British stars lacking the magical allure of Hollywood. Elizabeth Allan got a mention in the *Middlesex Chronicle* as having latterly appeared in *Twice Upon a Time*, also made at Worton Hall, which was still awaiting release. Allen was an English actress, but one closely associated with Hollywood, having made her first production there in 1933 under contract to MGM. Of the fifty or so films she had made in England and Hollywood her most memorable appearances were as David Copperfield's tragic young mother in George Cukor's film of the same name, and as Lucie Manette in Frank Lloyd's *A Tale of Two Cities.*

A comedy, *Twice Upon a Time* shares the same plot as the later *Parent Trap* where a pair of twin sisters who are separated when their parents divorce meet again by accident when they are both sent to the same summer camp and then conspire to put things right. Elizabeth Allan was joined by Worton Hall returnees Jack Hawkins and Michael Gough, and camera operator Freddie Francis. An otherwise undistinguished piece, *Twice Upon a Time* has particular significance in so far as it was the only film ever directed by Emeric Pressburger and it was the last release (in 1953) of a film made at Worton Hall studios.

The Gift Horse was one of the better British war films around at this time. It starred the inimitable Trevor Howard as Lieutenant Commander Hugh Fraser, a disgraced former naval officer who re-enlists in the Royal Navy during the Second World War and who transforms the languid crew of his run-down destroyer into an efficient fighting force. The story was based on the daring raid undertaken in 1942 by HMS *Campbeltown*, which destroyed the French port of St Nazaire, the only dry dock outside of Germany able to accept and repair the German pocket battleships *Tirpiz* and *Bismarck.* Enjoying second billing was Richard Attenborough, a long way off from becoming Britain's pre-eminent actor, director, producer and winner of two Academy Awards, four BAFTAs and three Golden Globes. He had begun his acting career in 1942 playing a deserting sailor in Noel Coward and David Lean's *In Which We Serve*, going on to specialise in playing spivs and other lowlifes until landing the breakthrough role of Pinkie Brown, the psychopathic young gangster in *Brighton Rock* (1947).

This was the first time that the up-and-coming Attenborough had worked with Howard, declaring him to possess a 'fundamental truth beyond what we normally describe as acting'. Howard played the skipper of the ship and Attenborough saluted him always, on and off the set. Moreover he was one of those actors that delighted in being paid handsomely to do something he loved doing. Another face that would eventually become a household name was James Donald, as the ubiquitous 'No. 1', best known as Major Clifton, the stoic British Army doctor in the 1957 blockbuster *Bridge on the River Kwai*, which won him huge critical praise at home and in the United States.

The Lost Hours is a memory-loss thriller starring Mark Stevens and Jean Kent with quality support from the likes of John Bentley and Garry Marsh as well as a generous sprinkling of the usual suspects, such as Sam Kydd playing a motor mechanic, Thora Hird as a hotel maid and Ballard Berkley in 'a minor role'. Set in London, a former American pilot gets into a fight during a reunion of former wartime buddies and RAF pilots. He wakes up the next day in a strange hotel room with blood on his suit and unable to remember how he got there. He then discovers that the old pal he fought with the previous night has been murdered, and he is a prime suspect. Directed by David MacDonald, the film was produced by Robert Baker and Monty Berman who later went on to make a series of B-pictures for Eros Films, invariably striking a deal with American actors to tempt US distribution. *The Lost Hours* (otherwise *The Big Frame*) was the only film in this series made at Worton Hall.

The fading Neagle/Wilding partnership followed the fortunes of the studio with a last-hurrah ensemble piece called *Derby Day*, a blend of drama, romance and comedy across a diverse bunch of race-goers on Derby Day. From a woman who has murdered her husband to a working-class couple excited about going to the races but who end up listening to it on the radio in the car-park, it was directed by Herbert Wilcox with Anna Neagle and Michael Wilding supported by fellow Worton Hall veterans Googie Withers, Nigel Stock, Sam Kydd, Michael Ripper and Richard Wattis, as well as Ralph Reader, the actor, theatrical producer and songwriter who would find fame and fortune staging the Gang Show variety entertainment for members of the Scouting Movement. Playing the part of Tiger Wilkes was Alfie Bass, who had begun his film career appearing in wartime documentaries and in a number of post-war features before television made him a household name in the late 1950s, starring in *The Army Game* and its sequel, *Bootsie and Snudge*.

And just as the new medium had drawn Douglas Fairbanks Jr back to Worton Hall, so was it reflecting a rapidly changing Britain in the 1950s, a watershed period for British culture that began with Labour's defeat by the Conservatives at the 1951 General Election, marking a shift from state control to increased individual freedom. The Conservative election slogan promised to 'Set the People Free'. Rationing would at long last come to an end and Britain would enter a period of increased affluence and freedom, with many of the old social and cultural structures beginning to be challenged, particularly by the young. Deregulation coincided with a steady increase in affluence due to post-war regeneration schemes, many of them originating in America. Massive increases in the production and availability of consumer goods stimulated mass consumption where people would come to expect to have luxury goods such as refrigerators, cars and 'the biggest time-waster ever invented', according to the *Daily Mirror* – television. 'People will sit watching for hours even when they don't care much for the programmes they're viewing,' it uncannily predicted. 'It's so easy to sink into an armchair and switch on entertainment until bedtime.'

A Royal Commission was called for to investigate this threat to the cinema and theatre, but was demonstrably undermined with the televising of the Queen's Coronation in June 1953, watched live by around 27 million viewers in the UK and in Germany, the Netherlands, France, and Belgium. It proved the catalyst for the mass purchase of television sets despite the fact that it would be another two years before an alternative service would be available to the single channel operated by the British Broadcasting Corporation for around seven hours a day. The detractors of Independent Television claimed that commercial television would be too American, that the British public would balk at their programmes being interrupted by adverts, and it would never achieve the high standards of the BBC. This passage in British entertainment history appears unbelievably archaic to those of us now taking for granted this multi-channel world and all of its offshoots. The rise of home entertainment made British film-making less profitable, ultimately putting an end to the many a London film studio.

The sale of the Worton Hall Studios in May 1952 made front-page news, albeit in the local paper. The estate was sold to the National Coal Board to meet its pressing need for increased research in the mining industry. As a new central research establishment, Worton Hall could be used immediately for some of the work in hand, with the rest coming about once the post-war building restraints eased. British Lion didn't anticipate any large-scale unemployment, the intention being to transfer all of its equipment and facilities to Shepperton. But the Film Industry Employment Council issued a statement regarding the loss of Worton Hall as 'a crippling blow' to British film production, following on from the losses of other studio space. Unless this trend was reversed, the council warned, it would make it almost impossible for the film industry to increase output above its already low level and to assist the government by maintaining the British quota to save valuable US dollars.

In the House of Commons on Tuesday 20 May 1952, Mr S. Swingier (Labour MP for Newcastle-under-Lyme) asked the president of the Board of Trade what was his policy with regard to these concerns, and if he would take the necessary action to prevent the sale or lease of film studios to non-film-producing companies. Worton Hall Studios in Isleworth was a case in question. In view of the recent sale to the National Coal Board, would the government take steps to requisition these studios, he asked. Mr J. Parker (Labour MP for Dagenham) also demanded to know what steps were being taken to prevent unused film studios passing into the hands of other industries to the detriment of future film production in Britain.

In reply, Mr H. Strauss, parliamentary secretary to the Board of Trade, stated that as far as the board was aware, no film producer in Britain was at present prevented from making films by the lack of studio space. Indeed, the remaining studios were not continuously occupied to their full capacity and if the studios at Isleworth and Denham remained available, the output of British films would not be increased, nor would any dollars be saved. In these circumstances intervention by the Board of Trade was regarded as neither necessary nor desirable. Undaunted, the honourable member for Newcastle-under-Lyme alleged that the film quota was being flagrantly violated, and demanded to know if the minister was to stand idly by while the capacity of the film industry was being whittled away, and his bargaining power with Hollywood steadily diminished. Mr Strauss concluded that there were no members of the House that would wish to see British film production hampered by lack of studio space. The only question arising was whether there was any reason to think the film industry was being hampered in the way suggested. He was firmly of the opinion that there was not. The question of quotas is a distinct question, he added. The quota had been fixed for the coming year on the assumption that there would be ample studio space available.

There is a local legend that suggests the demise of Worton Hall came about by the building of London (now Heathrow) Airport, the sheer size and scale of which was already impacting on large areas west of London. Aircraft noise had been a factor for decades, with polite notices to pilots painted on the studio roofs at Isleworth since before the Second World War. By 1950 the nation's major airport was expanding so fast that increased noise would have been a factor, but no more than that experienced at Twickenham or indeed Shepperton at times. More of a discomfort factor would have been the malodorous Mogden Sewage Works, now literally in the studio's former backyard. Disquiet over the stench of the water purification process had risen consistently together with the mosquito population. In 1948 over 7,000 local residents signed a petition for something to be done to eradicate these nuisances. Fifty years on and local residents are still waiting.

Both these factors would have assisted in British Lion's quest to reduce the size of the organisation by shipping out to Shepperton, but timing was the major factor. For it was exactly when British Lion were looking to sell that the National Coal Board had come to realise that their existing resources at the Central Research Establishment (CRE) near Cheltenham were insufficient for future requirements. Worton Hall was one of several properties inspected for a second establishment. Negotiations for its acquisition commenced in March 1952 and the contract was signed in May. British Lion vacated the premises on 30 June and the following day the acting director of the Central Research Establishment moved into an office in the old mansion.

Ted Higgins was the personnel manager at Worton Hall from 1948 responsible for the welfare of the whole 256 staff, '210 males and 46 women. It was the happiest studio of all the British studios. We were more like a family there than an industrial concern,' he told David Blake in 2004. In the final days, staff and crew constantly asked when they would start the next picture. Promises were made but it was clear that the future of British Lion lay with Shepperton. 'We were the little brother or the little sister and we were having the bits that fell off the table,' Higgins recalls, placing the beginning of the end for Worton Hall in 1948 when Korda decided to shift the big stage to Shepperton.

> Once they took that stage away from Isleworth that was the finish … It was like a great big empty shell as a rule until they came along and did one or two shots of Bonnie Prince Charlie … But we could always go in there for anything out of the ordinary that couldn't be got on the smaller stages. Directly they took it down … that was good-bye Worton Hall … The writing was on the wall!

It has been said that Korda's greatest mistake was to go on making films after 1947 when he could have retired comfortably off the income of his old films, but he chose not to. The final break between Korda and British Lion came with the withdrawal of government support in 1952, when the British Lion deficit had increased by more than £400,000. In October that year Korda had to lend £50,000 to his own company to finance reissues of earlier pictures. In November the debate on the Cinematograph Bill in the House of Commons contained a sharp attack on Korda by MP William Shepherd, who concluded that it might be to the advantage of the British Lion Film Corporation if they employed an executive producer other than Sir Alexander Korda. Korda, he reminded the House, was associated with 'the lush days of the film industry' and was not 'attuned to making films at a cost of £120,000 a time'. Labour and Tory members, the film technicians union and staff roundly defended Korda, who announced that whenever he made 'safe' films he failed and whenever he made 'crazy ones', he made a lot of money and so did his backers. But the right honourable member for Cheadle had a point, for the total loss now stood at £2,217,035; more than two-thirds of the original government loan.

When taken over in July 1952 there were only six people employed at Worton Hall. That figure soon increased to 200, with a target of 150 more in the coming years. During the first eighteen months of occupancy by the Central Research Establishment, extensive conversion work had taken place across the 70,000 square feet of floorspace within the five-acre estate. A number of former film company employees stayed on, including carpenters, electricians and labourers. The work may not have been as exciting or glamorous, but the service they provided to the country's most important industry was considered indispensable. The *Middlesex Chronicle* returned in February 1954 to see how the newcomers were settling in. On 'the great indoor stages' where Humphrey Bogart, Anna Neagle and Paul Robeson once trod, mining apparatus was now being tested, instruments assembled and new developments perfected to prevent the risk of explosions of methane gas. In one section of what was formerly the stars' dressing rooms, a number of young engineers were putting the final touches to the assembly of dust samplers.

Mrs Eva McGill, the canteen manageress, had worked at Worton Hall for six years and so had experience of both camps.

When it was a film studio there was quite a lot of variety and excitement, and quite a few people might have thought they were living in the stars. But

I am much happier now and I feel that my work is much more valuable and worthwhile. Besides, regularity in the eating of meals by everybody working here makes the task of canteen workers much easier.

The mansion itself was only superficially altered and remained much as it was when erected in 1790. Then it had been built to meet the requirements of an individual. It was adapted at the turn of the twentieth century to meet the needs of the film industry. 'It's now serving an industry of even more vital importance,' observed the *Middlesex Chronicle*. 'Perhaps it may be entering upon its most useful, if not its finest, phase.'

The estate at Worton Hall went up for sale in 1969 for a reported £7 million, a sum that caused the local council to break off negotiations with the National Coal Board to buy the land for housing. The property had become surplus to requirements to the NCB, leaving local councillors to wrangle over the economic viability of the site as it gradually developed into the trading estate it remains to this day. By 1980 anxious local residents feared their 'peaceful backwater' would be overtaken with heavy traffic and noise, and complained about the destruction of 400-year-old trees as the estate was transformed into a centre of light industry. At the time of writing the mansion is being converted into eight luxury flats to complement the five houses built on the rear lawn. The cutting rooms and preview theatre have gone. The giant footprint of the big stage has long since been covered with industrial units. The three sound stages and associated buildings survive, while other legacies lie in less corporeal quarters assembled within these pages as witness to Worton Hall's contribution to the British film history.

Alexander Korda's last years were lonely ones, calling upon old friends and colleagues for company in an ever-reducing lifestyle compared to the vim and vigour of his heyday. In June 1954 the government called in its loan, terminating the support it had given to British Lion. Sir Wilfred Eady condemned British Lion as 'the baby born of the unholy wedlock between public funds and private enterprise'. Korda himself had lost £500,000 in the debacle. Characteristically, when asked by the receiver if he could suggest anybody to succeed him as chief of production, Korda replied, 'It isn't easy … you see, I don't grow on trees.' He and British Lion went their separate ways and for the last time Korda set about rebuilding a shattered empire.

The President of France decorated him personally with the Legion of Honour, marking his devotion to French culture and the art of cinematography. He was the first winner of the Golden Laurel Award, founded by David Selznick, for a contribution to international goodwill and understanding through films. He was made a Commander of the Italian Order of Merit and in June 1955 received the Freedom of the City of Berlin. Still busy plotting and planning new ventures, the last film to bear his name was *Smiley*, based on Moore Raymond's book about an Australian boy's life in the outback. It was finished a few days before Christmas 1955 and a week or so before he died, in January 1956. He would have made a wonderful Prime Minister of Hungary, Winston Churchill said of him, 'if he had Rockefeller for his Chancellor of the Exchequer'.

As for Bertie Samuelson, there is a plaque dedicated to him in Neville Street, Southport, the site of his first film hire company, now an amusement arcade. He was made bankrupt in 1929 and thereafter remained on the fringes of the film industry, directing a few quota quickies during the 1930s and launching a number of business ventures, such as a circulating library. During the war he supervised two nitrate film depots in the Birmingham area, by which time he was suffering from diabetes. Ironically he ended up working as a clerk in the offices of British Lion Films. He died on 17 April 1947 at his home in Crook House at Great Barr in Staffordshire. His four sons followed him into the film industry, setting up the Samuelson Film Service, which later became the Samuelson Group, at one time the world's largest supplier of audio-visual equipment before becoming a corporate presentations company. David, the eldest son, was awarded the Academy Award for Merit in 2003 for the development of the Louma camera crane and remote-control head, which changed the way films are made. Sydney was appointed Britain's first Film Commissioner in 1991 and knighted four years later. His grandsons, Marc and Peter, continued Samuelson Productions Ltd, with *Tom & Viv*, an adaptation of the Michael Hastings period play about the troubled relationship between the writer T. S. Eliot and his first wife, Vivienne Haigh-Wood. Of its many awards the most ironic, as it is poignant, was the BAFTA nomination for the Alexander Korda Award for the Best British Film, which went to Bertie's great-grandsons.

Filmography

Mostly the year given is UK distribution, but these can vary; WH/- denotes where Worton Hall shared production with other studios. GO attaches those films identified by Gareth Owen, and DB those identified by David Blake.

SAMUELSON FILM MANUFACTURING COMPANY

A Study in Scarlet (1914)
The Great European War (1914)
Incidents of the Great European War (1914)
Christmas Day in the Workhouse (1914)
A Son of France (1914)
The Life of Lord Roberts, V.C. (1914/15)
The Face at the Telephone (1914/15)
A Cinema Girl's Romance (1915)
Buttons (1915)
John Halifax, Gentleman (1915)
The True Story of the Lyons Mail (1915)
Buttons (1915)
The Angels of Mons (1915)
The Adventures of Deadwood Dick (1915):
How Richard Harris Became Known as Deadwood Dick
Deadwood Dick's Vengeance
Deadwood Dick and the Mormons
Deadwood Dick's Red Ally
Deadwood Dick Spoils Brigham Young
Deadwood Dick's Detective Pard
The Dop Doctor (1915)
Infelice (1915)
The Great Adventure (1915) DB

TURNER/IDEAL
Caste (1915) DB

TURNER/BUTCHER
A Place in the Sun (1916) DB

SAMUELSON FILM MANUFACTURING COMPANY
Milestones (1916)
A Fair Imposter (1916)
The Girl Who Loves a Soldier (1916)
Just a Girl (1916)
A Pair of Spectacles (1916)
The Valley of Fear (1916)
Nursie! Nursie! (1916)
Dr Wake's Patient (1916)

DREADNOUGHT PRODUCTIONS/SAMUELSON FILM MANUFACTURING COMPANY
The Sorrows of Satan (1916)

IDEAL FILM COMPANY
Whoso Is Without Sin (1916)
The Second Mrs Tanqueray (1916)
The Fallen Star (1916)
Lady Windermere's Fan (1916)
The Vicar of Wakefield (1916)

SAMUELSON FILM MANUFACTURING COMPANY
The New Clown (1916) GO
Her Greatest Performance (1916) GO
My Lady's Dress (1917)
Little Women (1917)
In Another Girl's Shoes (1917)
Tinker, Tailor, Soldier, Sailor (1918)
God Bless Our Red, White and Blue (1918)

DIAMOND SUPER/SAMUELSON FILM MANUFACTURING COMPANY (?)
Hindle Wakes (1918)

IDEAL FILM COMPANY/IDEAL FILMS/SAMUELSON
Onward Christian Soldiers (1918)
The Way of the Eagle (1918)
The Admirable Crichton (1918)
The Elder Miss Blossom (1918)
The Man Who Won (1918)

Damaged Goods (1919)
The Right Element (1919)
A Member of Tattersall's (1919)
Quinney's (1919)
Faith (1919)
Hope (1919)
Charity (1919)
Some Artist (1919)
Gamblers All (1919)
The Bridal Chair (1919)
Convict 99 (1919)
The Edge o' Beyond (1919)
Her Own People (1919)
The Right Element (1919)
Linked by Fate (1919)
Mrs Thompson (1919)

H. B. PARKINSON
The Secrets of Nature (1919)

SAMUELSON FILM MANUFACTURING COMPANY & OTHERS
The Husband Hunter (1920)
A Temporary Gentleman (1920)
Aunt Rachel (1920)
The Honeypot (1920)
The Last Rose of Summer (1920)
All the Winners (1920)
Her Story (1920)
Nance (1920)
The Pride of the Fancy (1920)
The Winning Goal (1920)
For Her Father's Sake (1921)
Love Maggie (1921)
The Magistrate (1921)
Mr Pim Passes By (1921)
Tilley of Bloomsbury (1921)
The Game of Life (1922)

HARDY
Bluff (1921)
The Scourge (Fortune's Fool) (1921)
The Recoil (1921)
The Reaping (1921) DB

BRITISH-SUPER FILMS
Stable Companions (1922)
Brown Sugar (1922)
If Four Walls Told (1922)
The Faithful Heart (1922)

Castle in the Air (1922)
The Right to Strike (1922)

NAPOLEON FILM COMPANY

A Royal Divorce (1923)
Should a Doctor Tell? (1923)
I Pagliacci (1923)
Maisie's Marriage (1923)
Afterglow (1923)
This England (1923)
The Knockout (1923) DB
A Couple of Down and Outs (1923) DB

SAMUELSON FILM MANUFACTURING COMPANY (SPONSOR)

The Knockout (1923)
The Devil's Isle (1923) DB

BRITISH-SUPER FILMS

The Hotel Mouse (1923)

NAPOLEON FILM COMPANY

The Cost of Beauty (1924)
The Unwanted (1924)
Who Is the Man? (1924)

G. B. SAMUELSON/LISLE PRODUCTIONS

She (1925)

G. B. SAMUELSON FILMS

Milestone Melodies (1925):
Auld Langs Syne
Little Dolly Daydream
I Do Like To Be Beside The Seaside
Her Golden Hair Was Hanging Down Her Back
They Wouldn't Believe Me
Twisted Tales (1925):
How It Happened
The Motorist
The Choice
The Eternal Triangle
Should A Mother Tell
4th October
A Great Mistake
Home Without Evidence
Skeleton Keys
Driven From Home
The Mercy of His Wife
Death of Agnes

Last Turn Melodies (1925) DB
Best Tails (1925) DB

RECIPROCITY FILMS
Proverbs (1925):
You're Never Too Late To Mend
Out of Sight Out of Mind
Absence Makes the Heart Grow Fonder
All that Glistens Is Not Gold
Man Proposes God Disposes
Do Unto Others
There's Many a Slip
Those Who Live in Glass Houses
A Stitch in Time
Never Put Off Until Tomorrow What You Can Do Today
Laugh and the World Laughs With You

G. B. SAMUELSON FILMS
Twisted Tales (second series) (1926):
Gentleman Burglar
The Only Way Out
Oil on Troubled Waters
Out Of Scent
Paternal Instinct
Betrayed
Dear Heart
The Last Shot
A Protector Intervenes
Without The Options
If Youth But Knew (1926)

GRAHAM WILCOX
White Heat (1926) DB

MALINS
Romance of The Price Ring (1926) DB:
For My Lady's Happiness
When Giants Are Fought
For A Woman's Eyes
Gypsy Coverage
The Phantom Foe
Find The Woman
The Fighting Gladiator

H. B. PARKINSON
The Chicken Game (1926)

BRITISH SCREEN PRODUCTIONS
Twenty Years Ago (1926)

GLORY FILMS
Land of Hope and Glory (1927)

G. B. SAMUELSON FILMS
Motherland (1927)

BRITISH SCREEN PRODUCTIONS
Bad Sir Brian Botany (1927) DB
Frozen Fate (1927)

W & F
Victory (1927) DB

NEW ERA NATIONAL PICTURES LTD
Q Ships (1928)
The Somme (1928) DB

G. B. SAMUELSON FILMS
For Valour (1928) DB
Little Drummer Boy (1928) DB

BRITISH SCREEN PRODUCTIONS
Hoop-La/The Lion Tamer (1928) DB
Master and Man (1928) DB

G. B. SAMUELSON FILMS/VICTORIA FILMS
Yesterday Today (1928) DB

G. B. SAMUELSON FILMS
The Bells of St Mary's (1928) DB

H. B. PARKINSON
Night Patrol (1928) DB
Not Quite A Lady (1928) DB
The Second Mate (1928) DB
The Streets of London (1928)

BRITISH-SUPER FILMS
Twenty Years Ago (1928) DB

H. B. PARKINSON
The Broken Romance (1929) DB
A Broken Silence (1929) DB

EDWARD G. WHITING
The Dizzy Limit (1929) DB

CARLTON FILMS
Downstream (1929) DB

H. B. PARKINSON/PIONEER
Human Cargo (1929) DB
Lure Of The Atlantic (1929) DB

ENCORE FILMS
Life's A Stage (1929) DB

BRITISH SCREEN PRODUCTIONS
Three Men in a Cart (1929)
The Big Show (1929)
Spirits (1929)
Jackie's Nightmare (1929)
Jackie and the Beanstalk (1929)
House Warmers (1929)
Cupid in Clover (1929)
A Runaway Holiday (1929)

BRITISH SOUND FILMS
Dark Red Roses (1929)

BRITISH SCREEN PRODUCTIONS
London Melody (1930)

PATRICK K. NEAL
In A Lotus Garden (1930) DB
Morita (1930) DB
Romany Love (1930) DB

EDWARD G. WHITING
The Woman From China (1930) DB

MACNAMARA PRODUCTIONS
Birds of a Feather (1931)

MAJESTIC/NEW ERA FILMS
The Other Woman (1931)
Jealousy (1931)
The Wickham Mystery (1931)
Inquest (1931)
Collision (1931)

GEOFFREY BENSTEAD
Stepping Stones (1931) DB

REGINALD FOGWELL PRODUCTIONS
The Written Law (1931)
Guilt (1931)
Madame Guillotine (1931)
Betrayal (1932)
The Temperance Fate (1932)

ENGLISH FILMS
The Television Follies (1932) DB

NEW ERA NATIONAL PICTURES
Spotting (1933):
Touching Stories
The End of the Act
Lipsky's Christmas Dinner
The Ace of Trouble
The Jade
The Greatest of These
Husbands Are So Jealous
Of Scent
An Affair of the Heart
The Delusion
The Green Leather Wallet
Spoils

BUTCHER'S FILM SERVICE
Broken Rosary (1934)

CITY FILM CORPORATION
Money Mad (1934)

NEW ERA PRODUCTIONS
The Crucifix (1934)
Face (1934) DB

BRITISH & CONTINENTAL PRODUCTIONS
The Invader (1934)

LONDON FILM PRODUCTIONS
The Man Who Could Work Miracles (1934)
Things to Come (1935) WH/Denham
The Ghost Goes West (1935)
Sanders of the River (1935) WH/Shepperton
Moscow Nights (1935) WH/Denham
Forget Me Not (1936)
Wharves & Strays (documentary short) (1935)
The Fox Hunt (animated short) (1935)
Miss Bracegirdle Does Her Duty (1936)

CAPITOL FILM PRODUCTIONS
Love in Exile (1936) WH/Elstree

CRITERION FILM PRODUCTIONS
Accused (1936)
Crime Over London (1936)
Jump For Glory (1937)

TRAFALGAR FILM PRODUCTIONS LTD
Under Secret Orders (1937)

GRAFTON/TRAFALGAR
Mademoiselle Doctor (1937) DB

LIBERTY FILMS
Captain's Orders (1937)
Too Many Husbands (1938)

REDD DAVIS PRODUCTIONS
Special Edition (1938)

NEW GEORGIAN
You're the Doctor (1938)

GEORGE SMITH (GS) ENTERPRISES
His Lordship Regrets (1938)
Shadowed Eyes (1939)
Miracles Do Happen (1939)

VENTURE FILMS
The Body Vanished (1939)
Mistaken Identity (1939)
Trouble for Two (1939) DB
Two Days to Live (1939) DB

SAVOY FILM PRODUCTIONS
Shadow Eyes (1939) DB

GRAND NATIONAL/JACK RAYMOND PRODUCTIONS
You Will Remember (1940)

GRAND NATIONAL/JACK HULBERT PRODUCTIONS
Under Your Hat (1940)

PYRAMID AMALGAMATED PRODUCTIONS
Spellbound (1940) (Re-released in 1943 and again in 1946, taking alternative names.)

PENNANT PICTURE PRODUCTIONS
The Shop at Sly Corner (1946)

ASSOCIATED BRITISH PICTURE CORPORATION
Piccadilly Incident (1946)

JOHN BAXTER
Grand Escapades (1946) DB

ASSOCIATED BRITISH PICTURE CORPORATION
While the Sun Shines (1946) DB

BRITISH LION FILM CORPORATION/HAROLD HUTH PRODUCTIONS
Night Beat (1947)

PEAK FILMS
White Cradle Inn (1947)

PENDENNIS
Call of the Blood (1947)

LONDON FILM PRODUCTIONS
Anna Karenina (1947) WH/Shepperton
Bonnie Prince Charlie (1947) WH/Shepperton
Mine Own Executioner (1947)
The Small Back Room (1948)
The Fallen Idol (1948) WH/Shepperton
The Last Days of Dolwyn (1948)
Saints and Sinners (1949)
The Winslow Boy (1949) WH/Shepperton
The Third Man (1949) WH/Shepperton
The Angel with the Trumpet (1949) WH/Shepperton

RENOWN
The Glass Mountain (1949) WH/Other?

HOWARD HAWKS PRODUCTIONS
I Was a Male War Bride (1949) WH/Other(s)?

BRITISH FILM CORPORATION/INDIVIDUAL PICTURES
The Happiest Days of Your Life (1950) WH/Riverside/Shepperton

BRITISH LION FILM CORPORATION/IMPERADIO PICTURES LTD
Into The Blue (1950)

BRITISH LION FILM CORPORATION/ELVEY GARTSIDE PRODUCTIONS
The Late Edwina Black (1950)

BRITISH LION FILM CORPORATION/ISLAND FILMS
Cure for Love (1950)

BRITISH LION FILM CORPORATION/LONDON FILM PRODUCTIONS
State Secret (1950)
The Wonder Kid (Entführung ins Glück) (1950) WH/Shepperton

CONSTELLATION FILMS
Curtain Up (1950)

HORIZON PICTURES
The African Queen (1951)

BRITISH LION FILM CORPORATION/THE DOUGFAIR CORPORATION
The Foreign Legion (1952)

MOLTON FILMS PRODUCTIONS
The Gift Horse (1952)

HERBERT WILCOX PRODUCTIONS
Derby Day (1952)

TEMPEON
The Lost Hours (1952)

BRITISH LION FILM CORPORATION/LONDON FILM PRODUCTIONS
Twice Upon a Time (1952)

Sources

ARCHIVAL
British Film Institute
Aylott, D., *From Flicker Alley to Wardour Street* (1949).
Frayling, C., *Things to Come* (London: BFI Publishing, 1995).

London Borough of Hounslow Local Studies Collection
Heston & Isleworth UDC Minutes, 14 January 1914 & 2 April 1914.
Hilton, J. S., *Worton and Worton Hall: A Short History* (London: National Coal Board, 1954).
Maxwell, G. S., *Highwayman's Heath* (Thomasons Ltd, 1935).

Samuelson Archive
Dunham, H. and D. W. Samuelson, *Bertie: The Life and Times of G. B. Samuelson* (unpublished).

NEWSPAPERS AND PERIODICALS
In addition to the voluminous researches of Harold Dunham and David Blake:

Cinema Studio 16 June 1948, 5 January 1949.
Daily Mail 2 July 1996.
Daily News 7 April 1935.
Daily Sketch 18 January 1950, 16 January 1952.
Daily Telegraph 18 December 1935.
Film Industry October 1946, March 1947, April 1947, August 1947, December 1947, February 1948, 2 April 1948, 15 July 1948, 26 August 1948, 21 October 1948, 4 November 1948, 30 December 1948, 13 January 1949, 27 January 1949, 24 March 1949, 7 April 1949, 21 April 1949, 19 May 1949.
Illustrated London News 12 January 1952.
Kinematograph and Lantern Weekly 13 August 1914.
Kinematograph Monthly Film Record November 1914, 21 March 1935, 19 March 1936.

Kinematograph Weekly 16 May 1940, 9 August 1934, 21 March 1935, 16 January 1936, 29 January 1949.

Middlesex Chronicle 4 July 1914, 2 June 1928, 18 August 1934, 6 October 1934, 20 October 1934, 13 April 1935, 12 December 1935, 23 January 1936, 26 December 1936, 21 March 1947, 20 June 1947, 16 May 1952, 3 April 1970.

New York Times 1 November 1951.

New York Times 26 March 1946.

Sunday Dispatch 1 January 1950.

The Bioscope 15 October 1914.

The Cinema 9 July 1914, 15 October 1914, 25 May 1916, October 1925, 13 August 1947, 24 September 1947.

The Daily Film Renter 31 January 1946.

The Motion Picture Studio 14 January 1922.

The Star 3 December 1935.

The Sunday Times 7 April 1935.

The Times 3 April 1935.

To-day's Cinema 2 November 1938, 27 August 1940, 21 May 1946, 2 November 1945.

WEBSITES AND OTHER MEDIA

BFI Online.

BFI Screenonline.

Internet Movie Database (IMDb).

Moviemail-online.co.uk.

Redfern-gallery.com.

TCM.

The African Queen: Embracing Chaos: Making the African Queen (2010).

Walterpercyday.org.

PHOTOGRAPHS AND ILLUSTRATIONS

Academy of Motion Picture Arts and Sciences.

David Blake Archive.

David Samuelson Archive.

Derek Hunt.

John Doran.

Les McCallum.

Tony Hillman Archive.

Wisconsin Center for Film & Theater Research.

Bibliography

Armes, Roy, *A Critical History of British Cinema* (Oxford University Press, 1978).

Barrow, Kenneth, *Mr. Chips: The Life of Robert Donat* (Methuen, 1985).

Betts, Ernest, *The Film Business: A History of the British Cinema 1896–1972* (Allen & Unwin, 1973).

Bouchier, Dorothy, *Shooting Star* (1996).

Cardiff, Jack, *Magic Hour: The Life of a Cameraman* (Faber & Faber, 1996).

Ceram, C. W., *The Archaeology of the Cinema* (Thames & Hudson, 1965).

Christie, Ian, *Arrows of Desire: The Films of Michael Powell and Emeric Pressburger* (London: Waterstone, 1985).

Drazin, Charles, *In Search of the Third Man* (Methuen, 2000).

Drazin, Charles, *Korda: Britain's Only Movie Mogul* (Sidgwick & Jackson, 2002).

Fairbanks Jr, Douglas, *The Salad Days* (William Collins Sons & Co., 1988).

Forbes, Bryan, *Notes for a Life* (Collins, 1974).

Fraser-Cavassoni, Natasha, *Sam Spiegel* (Simon & Schuster, 2003).

Fujiwara, Chris, *The Cinema of Nightfall: Jacques Tourneur* (John Hopkins University Press, 2000).

Hepburn, Katharine, *The Making of The African Queen, or How I Went to Africa with Bogart, Bacall and Huston and Almost Lost My Mind* (Century Hutchinson Ltd, 1987).

Huston, John, *An Open Book* (Alfred A. Knopf, 1980).

Knight, Vivienne, *Trevor Howard: A Gentleman and a Player* (Muller, Bond and White, 1986).

Korda, Michael, *Charmed Lives* (Allen Lane, 1980).

Kulik, Karol, *Alexander Korda: The Man Who Could Work Miracles* (W. H. Allen, 1975).

Lobjoit Collins, Jessie, *Key of the Fields: The Lobjoits and Covent Garden* (The Britannia Press, 1990).

Low, Rachel, *The History of the British Film* (Allen & Unwin, 1948–71).

Lukins, Jocelyn, *The Fantasy Factory. Lime Grove Studios, London: 1915–1991* (Venta Books, 1996).

Meade, Marion, *Buster Keaton: Cut to the Chase* (Bloomsbury Publishing Ltd, 1996).

Miller, Ruby, *Champagne From My Slipper* (1962).

Owen, Gareth, *The Shepperton Story* (The History Press, 2009).

Pearson, George, *Flashback: An Autobiography of a British Film-Maker* (Allen & Unwin, 1957).

Powell, Michael, *A Life in Movies: An Autobiography* (William Heinemann Ltd, 1986).

Ross, Robert, *The Complete Terry-Thomas* (Reynolds & Hearn, 2002).

Sinclair, Andrew, *Spiegel: The Man Behind the Pictures* (Weidenfeld & Nicolson, 1987).

Tabori, Paul, *Alexander Korda* (Oldbourne, 1959).

Threadgall, Derek, *Shepperton: An Independent View* (British Film Institute, 1994).

Warren, Patricia, *British Film Studios: An Illustrated History* (B. T. Batsford Ltd, 1995).

White, Rob, *The Third Man* (Routledge, 2002).

Wise, Damon, *Come By Sunday* (Sidgwick & Jackson, 1998).

Wood, Linda, *The Commercial Imperative in the British Industry: Maurice Elvey, A Case Study* (British Film Institute, 1987).

Index